TARGUMIC APPROACHES TO THE GOSPELS

Essays in the Mutual Definition of Judaism and Christianity

Studies in Judaism

TARGUMIC APPROACHES TO THE GOSPELS

Essays in the Mutual Definition of
Judaism and Christianity

Bruce Chilton

Lillian Claus Associate Professor of New Testament
The Divinity School
Yale University

UNIVERSITY
PRESS OF
AMERICA

LANHAM • NEW YORK • LONDON

Copyright © 1986 by

University Press of America,® Inc.

4720 Boston Way
Lanham, MD 20706

3 Henrietta Street
London WC2E 8LU England

ISBN (Perfect): 0-8191-5732-5
ISBN   (Cloth): 0-8191-5731-7

All University Press of America books are produced on acid-free
paper which exceeds the minimum standards set by the National
Historical Publications and Records Commission.

For the Revd Prof. Barnabas Lindars, S. S. F.

AKNOWLEDGMENTS

Prof. Neusner's invitation to contribute a volume of my essays to "Studies in Judiaism" came as a delight and privilege, and I am happy to accept. The programme of the volume, together with my particular understanding of the nexus of issues involved, are discussed in the Introduction. Much of the material presented here is previously unpublished; where a previously published piece has been incorporated, the details of the original publication are noted. Even in the latter case, however, considerable additions have been introduced. The scheme of abbreviations used will be familiar to those for whom the volume is intended.

Barnabas Lindars has shown many of us how it is possible to retain what is best in traditional methods of scholarship, while remaining open to new possibilities of inquiry. His willingness to accept my dedication of this volume to him honours me. In a field long blighted by the parochialism of biblical scholars, some of whom deliberately ignore Rabbinica, and by the hostility of some experts in Jewish literature to critical methods, Prof. Lindars stands unashamedly for an appreciation of the New Testament in the context of the Judaism of the period. Through him, I might also be permitted to thank my many colleagues in Britain, whose dedication to critical research is no less effective (and supportive) for its evident calm. As this volume goes to press, a review of my earlier work, A Galilean Rabbi and His Bible, has been appeared in CBQ 48 (1986) 329-331. The moment might be appropriate to thank the author, Prof. Martin McNamara, both for his encouraging appreciation, and for his pioneering contribution to the field of Targumic study.

Lastly, a few words of thanks are in order. The A. Whitney Griswold Research Fund of Yale University has supported the production of the ms in the Yale Computer Center. Arthur Shippee, a graduate student of the Department of Religious Studies, has kindly prepared the index, and checked the proofs of the volume. His timely help, and that of Michele Sebti, my operator, have been invaluable.

B.D.C.
New Haven

CONTENTS

to the Targum. Their consistent understanding is widely enough represented
as to provide an exegetical framework
of readings, which is focused on the
messianic vindication of Israel.

ESSAY 5--
Shebna, Eliakim, and the Promise to Peter

The promise to Eliakim in Targum Isaiah
22:22 is not an historical cipher, but
represents a social perspective on the
Temple in the period prior to A.D. 70.
The usage of similar language in the
Matthean promise to Peter (16:19) may
possibly be understood best within a
cultic context.

ESSAY 6--
John XII 34 and Targum Isaiah LII 13

An argument has been made in favour
of reading John 12:34 as an allusion
to Targum Isaiah 52:13. Neither the
presentation in John, nor the meaning
of the Targumic passage, supports
the contention.

ESSAY 7--
Gottesherrschaft als Gotteserfahrung.
Erkenntnisse der Targumforschung für
den neutestamentlichen Begriff
"Königsherrschaft Gottes"

There is a persistent tendency among
interpreters to understand "the
kingdom of God" in Jesus' teaching as
a Christological cipher. The sense of
the phrase in the Targums, however,
demands a more exclusively theological
exegesis.

ESSAY 8--
Regnum Dei Deus Est

Within the Targum of the Latter Prophets,
"the kingdom of God" consistently refers
to divine intervention, sometimes on

behalf of all people, sometimes on
behalf of Israel in particular. The
imagery and languge employed is to some
extent consistent with Jesus' teaching.

ESSAY 9--
Jesus, the King and His Kingdom

From time to time, scholars offer
portraits of Jesus as a political
revolutionary. Such attempts must do
justice to the understanding of God's
kingdom in Judaism, without importing
modern notions of what kingship
might imply.

ESSAY 10--
Targumic Transmission and Dominical Tradition

The "Poem of the Four Nights" is presented
in related, but distinct versions of
Exodus 12:42 in Palestinian Targumim.
Their relationship is compared to the
stories of Jesus' temptation in the
Synoptic Gospels. The interest is not in
in any question of dependence, but in how
material was transmitted within the world
of early Judaism.

ESSAY 11--
A Comparative Study of Synoptic Development:
The Dispute between Cain and Abel
in the Palestinian Targums and the Beelzebul
Controversy in the Gospels

A "Synoptic Problem" of greater complexity is provided by the Palestinian
Targumim at Genesis 4:8. The dispute
between Cain and Abel may be compared
to Jesus' reply to critics in Matthew
12:24-30/Mark 3:22-27/Luke 11:15-23.
In the cases of both the Targums and
the Gospels, to establish genetic
influence is problematic, but to
describe the distinctive profile of each
document becomes more straightforward
under a comparative approach.

APPENDICES

INTRODUCTION: The Practice and Prospect
of Targumic Approaches to the Gospels

The term "approaches" appears in the title of the present volume
in order to acknowledge that our project is indebted to the contribution of Matthew Black in his classic study, An Aramaic
Approach to the Gospels and Acts.[1] But the word "Targumic" is
designed to distinguish the present perspective from what has gone
on before, much as the plural, "approaches," intimates that current practice requires more flexibility than once seemed
necessary. Black's thesis was that Aramaic traditions were sometimes misconstrued in the Greek of the New Testament, so that
retroversion into Aramaic was necessary to establish their meaning. His claim was convincingly argued, with diligent recourse to
the evidence then available, and to the theories of the development of the Aramaic language which were in fashion at the time.

Black's book was first published in 1946 (on the basis of lec-
tures given previously, in 1940), and was partially responsible
for renewed interest in Aramaic sources among English-speaking
scholars. (Other factors in that renascence are considered in my
earlier work, The Glory of Israel, which is discussed below.) His
lucidity and assurance commended itself to readers who could per-
ceive the underlying philological issues Black concerned himself
with, whether or not they were trained Aramaists. The mystique of
An Aramaic Approach enabled it to survive telling criticisms, even
those of Joseph Fitzmyer.[2] Black committed himself to the antiquity of Aramaic sources which have subsequently been shown to be
late, and was too eager to date the Palestinian Targums in particular to a period earlier than the evidence warrants.[3] Moreover, he
was probably too confident of his own ability to distinguish a
"Semitism," that is, the intrusive influence of a Semitic language
upon a Greek text, from local Greek dialects and deliberate variations in style, both of which demonstrably approximate to Semitism
on occasion. That the book claims with so little qualification
that the transliterated and translated forms of the New Testament
warrant an "Aramaic approach," rather than a "Hebrew approach,"
may also be taken to reflect an optimism which has been overtaken
by events (especially, discoveries at and about Qumran). A more
sober technique of the detection and analysis of Semitisms has
been developed by Max Wilcox.[4] Indeed, Wilcox's most recent article marks a significant departure from the primarily philological identification of Semitisms.

The danger of studies of diction alone, as James Barr has signally demonstrated,[5] is that they lead all too easily to the
fallacious conclusion than one can study a word in one language,
say Hebrew, and import its various meanings into the Greek New
Testament. Barr's book rightly and helpfully contends that meaning derives from the use of words in linguistic and literary

contexts; words do not have meanings apart from continuous utterances, and therefore they should not be studied in an abstract manner. Although such an awareness may seem elementary, treatments of the New Testament continue to convey the impression that there is a holy language, a code, in which every document of the Bible is spoken. That tendency is all the more invidious when such attempts at definition move directly from "the Old Testament" to the New, without giving serious attention to how scripture was understood and spoken of in early Judaism.[6] The result is to promote an _Ersatz_ of fundamentalism: a Bible which is infallible only in a linguistic ghetto of holy meanings.

Wilcox operates on a fuller linguistiuc basis than have some of those who pursue a philological approach, and he attends to the conceptual problems posed by the multi-lingual milieu in which the traditions conveyed in the New Testament achieved written form. That in itself is a notable accomplishment, albeit one which forever puts in some doubt many assertions as to the precise, Aramaic antecedents of the New Testament, including some which have been made with a remarkable lack of caution. Some scholars, for example, continue to warm their hands on Jeremias's old chestnut about "Amen" in Jesus sayings, as if questions had never been raised in respect of its Aramaic provenience. For that reason, the present volume opens with a consideration which accords with Wilcox's shift from philological to linguistic analysis. Indeed, the first essay may be said to move more decisively in that direction than Wilcox does, insofar as Syriac sources, as well as Aramaic, are systematically taken into account. At the same time, the potential importance of the Old Syriac Gospels, for construing traditions about Jesus, is underlined; as compared to the level of interest manifested earlier in the century, those manuscripts have of late not received the attention they merit. Although it may seem odd to begin a volume with "Amen," it might be remembered that the peculiarity at issue in dominical sayings is the _introductory_ and asseverative usage of the term. In any case, it is as well to state from the outset that a serious consideration of the usage "Amen," in respect of the available evidence, undermines any confidence in the once accepted program of isolating the _ipsissima vox Jesu_ by means of linguistic criteria.

In addition to inserting a degree of linguistic sophistication into the study of Semitisms, Wilcox's article marks another important development. The reference to Judas in Acts 1:17, as being "numbered among us" and acquiring a position by lot, is reminiscent--to Wilcox's mind--of Genesis 44:18 in certain of the "Palestinian" Targums (namely Cairo Geniza D and Neophyti).[7] The questions emerge, of course, (1) whether the haggadic expansion in the Targums is necessary to explain the text of Luke, and (2) whether the material presently in the Targums was extant and associated with Genesis 44:18 at the time Acts was composed. Wilcox does not pose these questions _expressis verbis_, but he does

2

implicitly address them. He argues that vv. 17-19 of Acts 1 "look non-Lukan and disturb the flow of thought from v. 16 to v. 20" (p. 990). That those verses represent an earlier tradition concerning Judas, directly or indirectly, indeed seems plausible, but there is scarcely any immediate indication of dependence upon the specifically Targumic tradition. Wilcox may or may not be correct in the speculation that a pun on ḥlq, meaning both "lot" and "field" (perhaps owing to a confusion of radicals) is the matrix of the tradition (p. 991), but that does not support the argument for dependence on the Targums specifically. Similarly, in the absence of any attempt to date the material in the Palestinian Targumim generally, or the documents themselves, Wilcox can merely--but quite correctly--argue that "the so-called Palestinian Targumim may have existed in a rather more fixed form and at a far earlier date than is frequently argued" (p. 992). The word "may" is what makes Wilcox's statement of the case thoroughly apposite; unfortunately, it also gives his conclusion a thoroughly speculative tone.

Wilcox's study of Acts 1.15-26 was first published in New Testament Studies 19 (1972-3) 438-452, and--together with the work of Martin McNamara (which I have discussed elsewhere)[8]--it deeply influenced my own approach to the relationship between the Targums and the New Testament. The requirements of an exegetical treatment of that relationship seemed to me to be twofold: (1) Targumic traditions must, as far as is possible, be shown to be early enough to warrant the suspicion that they have influenced passages of the New Testament, and (2) the New Testament passages concerned must be better explicable on the supposition of such influence than on other bases.

Both of these criteria might appear to be blindingly obvious to any historically minded person, but their application causes resentment in some quarters. There has been, for example, a persistent fashion to see in any possible allusion to Genesis 22 in the New Testament a deliberate evocation of the idea of the Aqedah, according to which Isaac actually died an expiatory death on Mount Moriah.[9] No person of taste can deny the power of the Aqedah as a reflection of human nature, and it may be more to the point than the scriptural version of the story. Particularly, it is a striking image of what we have done to ourselves during the course of this century, as Wilfred Owen's poem, "The Parable of the Old Man and the Young," so eloquently brings out:
When lo! an angel called him out of heaven,
Saying, Lay not thy hand upon the lad,
Neither do anything to him. Behold,
A ram, caught in a thicket by its horns,
Offer the Ram of Pride instead of him.
But the old man would not so, but slew his son,--
and half the seed of Europe, one by one.[10]

3

Has there ever been a civilization as keen as ours to sacrifice its promise of life time and again, regardless of the counsels of religion or wisdom? No matter when the Aqedah is dated, it is perhaps most explicable of the experience of our century, as the culmination of many centuries of the hasty willingness to sacrifice lives, provided they are the lives of others. The question remains, however, whether this image, as expressed in the Targums, is early enough to have influenced the New Testament, and whether (if it is that early) it did in fact exert such influence. As the second and third articles indicate, the evidence of both the Palestinian Targums themselves, and of other Jewish and Christian sources, permits of a positive answer to neither of those two questions at this stage.

Since the original publication of the articles on the Aqedah, in 1978 and 1980, no refutation of their findings has appeared. Indeed, subsequent studies have on the whole taken positive account of the more rigorous dating of traditions, which it was the program of my approach to put into effect. Geza Vermes has nonetheless dismissed the attempt to date and exegete documents which allude to Genesis 22 as "ill-conceived criticism," although he does not burden the reader with a consideration of the evidence, or--for that matter--with an account of what his derisory comment might mean.[11] More blatantly, he has (in writing) referred to the present writer as the "nigger in the woodpile," owing to my understanding of how the Aqedah developed within Rabbinic literature. Dr Vermes has devoted an essay of his most recent volume to the ignorance of Jewish studies among scholars of the New Testament.[12] I share his sorrow at the present situation, but fail to see that he offers any encouragement to those who wish to do something about it. It is a case of damned if you don't, and slurred if you do. My hope is that the present volume will promote a reasoned approach to the issues concerned, so that the language of personal vilification will no longer demean our discourse.

The difficulty of dating the motifs and materials of the Targum is compounded by the lack of a consensus concerning the dates of the documents themselves, and their overall ideological profiles. For that reason, an analysis of the Targum of Isaiah became my preoccupation for several years; the result was a volume entitled The Glory of Israel. The Theology and Provenience of the Isaiah Targum.[13] Readers are referred to that volume for a full explanation of my method, but the fourth and fifth essays in the present volume outline and instance the techniques of analysis which are employed. The enthusiastic response of reviewers came as something of a surprise, since I had expected a qualified reaction, and I should particularly like to acknowledge the great encouragement I derived from reading the assessments of D. Bourget, Richard Coggins, Robert Gordon, Bernard Grossfeld, Otto Kaiser, Peter Nickels, Stefan Reif, Josep Ribera, R. Tournay, and Richard White.[14]

4

The dating which I have suggested for the Isaiah Targum would allow of the theoretical possibility that traditions contained in it were current at the time of Jesus. That possibility led to a consideration of whether what could have been was in fact the case: the result was that dominical sayings were analyzed to determine whether references or allusions to Targumic tradition would provide the best explanation of their meaning. Dominical sayings, it might be explained, are the most likely candidates for analysis, in view of several considerations. Isaian themes are very prominent within them; they manifest Semitism from time to time, which would be consistent with Targumic influence; and (most importantly) a reading of the New Testament with a copy of the Targum to hand will quickly show that the frequency of correspondence is greater in the case of dominical sayings than in the case of any other sort of material within the New Testament. The book which documents this study, A Galilean Rabbi and His Bible (see n. 8), also includes an introduction for general readers, and a theological consideration of Jesus' style of preaching on the basis of Targumic traditions. In view of the intended readership of the book, it seemed wise (1) not to rest the argument on possible, but tenuous allusions to Targumic tradition, and (2) to emphasize repeatedly that the traditions of the Targum, not the document we call the Targum, are at issue.

The reaction to the book has been startling, in that it has occasioned the most enthusiastic, and the most disparaging, assessment of my work to date. Pride of place must be given to the review by Jacob Neusner, both in The Journal of Ecumenical Studies, and in his own volume, Formative Judaism V.[15] Prof. Neusner confirms that the book's thesis "has attained the status of fact," and provides what is to date the most lucid appreciation--and just criticism--of the last, theological third of the book. Although none of them has repeated Prof. Neusner's judgment that the author of A Galilean Rabbi "does everything right," Casimir Bernas, Christopher Bryan, John Court, Anthony Hanson, Daniel Harrington, J. D. Hutchinson, Graham Jenkins, John Koenig, and an anonymous reviewer in the Supplements of the Birmingham Theological Society have all welcomed the book.[16] It was, of course, reassuring to have my argument received positively, especially among more popular reviewers, and experts in Judaica.

What was especially gratifying to find in the reviews mentioned above was that my argument was so clearly understood. In the conclusion, I considered two points which might bear notice here: (1) "Jesus did not depend on the Targum as we know it, but he does seem to have been influenced and informed by traditions which the Targum preserves better than anything else" (A Galilean Rabbi, p. 139), and (2) "one might reasonably observe that the Targum conceivably just happens best to preserve material which in the time of Jesus had nothing to do with the book of Isaiah" (p. 141). The first of these observations is frequently offered in the volume, in order not to give the impression that the Targum as we know it was available to Jesus. In respect of the second point, I came (and come) to the conclusion that the traditions Jesus was familiar with were in his time associated with the book of Isaiah. But I forwarded the latter finding as a matter of probability, not certainty (Rabbi, pp. 141, 142). Because these materials are associated with Isaiah in the Targum, and because Jesus refers to Isaian texts and/or contexts when using the materials, the connection of them to Isaiah in Jesus' time seems more probable than the notion they floated freely, independently of one another and the biblical text.

Inevitably, however, a few readers reviewed the book as if its thesis were that the Targum is related to the Gospels as one text incorporated directly within another. Apparently, some people, even scholars, have trouble imagining that the sayings of Jesus were passed on orally before they reached their translated form in the Gospels as we know them. Our Gospels, in their received forms, were certainly not composed with the Isaiah Targum in mind. Despite frequent repetitions of that disclaimer, three reviewers wrote as if that were my thesis. An anonymous writer in Durrant's British Weekly comments from a conservatively evangelical perspective; for him or her, my address of hermeneutical issues is offensive, since I fail to show that the Targum is cited word for word in the Gospels.[17] Robert Gordon, whether or not he shares the conservative stance of the reviewer just mentioned, reveals an ignorance of how the New Testament developed, in that he also anticipates the verbatim quotation of any source Jesus might have used.[18]

In respect of the last point, special notice should be taken of Michael Goulder's review in Theology.[19] Dr Goulder, in agreement with other reviewers, accepts my analysis of the Targum of Isaiah, and acknowledges "the possibility of links with the Gospels," and the "substance" of that possibility (p. 306). He nonetheless concludes, "I do not think he has carried his point as yet." That conclusion is inevitable, because he mistakes my "central thesis," which is, on his view, "that Jesus accepted the interpretations of Scripture in the Targum" (p. 304). Dr Goulder himself has an exclusively literary model of the antecedents of the Gospels,[20] and it seems he has not permitted my book to speak within the framework of the non-literary model which it posits. He and I appear to be speaking different critical languages, and that situation underscores the need for many of us in the field of research concerning the Synoptic Gospels to engage seriously with the issue of how traditions regarding Jesus were passed down prior to the redaction of the sources we can read today. Although Dr Goulder and I appear to be on different sides of the fence at the moment in respect of that underlying issue, I greatly appreciate his attempt to cope with the evidence he admits my work has uncovered.

6

In several senses, the last place in this brief review of reviews is occupied by the reaction of Philip Alexander.[21] He repeatedly accepts both my analysis of the Targum and my thesis of its relationship to the sayings of Jesus. He feels called upon, however, to defend Geza Vermes against my criticism that he consistently fails to discuss the dates of the Rabbinic material he uses in analyzing the Gospels. Alexander contends that I also use the documents of later Judaism to explicate Jesus' sayings (p. 239): that is true, but the point is that I discuss the date, theology, and provenience of the Targum, and only then its possible relationship to Jesus' teaching. Dr Vermes does not proceed in that manner, which is the simple observation which Dr Alexander misses in his loyalty to his mentor.

What bothers Dr Alexander most is, "It is surprising to find so much space devoted to conveying very elementary information" (p. 239). Had he read the preface of A Galilean Rabbi before undertaking to write the review, he might have been less surprised: the aim of the book, to educate more general readers than I had previously addressed, is there clearly set out. Indeed, it is interesting that he accepted the commission to write the review at all, since his competence in the field of New Testament has never been established, and he obviously is impatient with those who require the explanation which one third of the book is designed to provide. The last third of the book is theological, of course, and Alexander refuses even to discuss it, on the grounds it is not "strictly academic" (p. 238). He would appear to share that opinion with the anonymous writer in Durrant's British Weekly, whether or not on the grounds of religious conservatism. In any case, Dr Alexander has, by some unmentioned chain of thought, concluded that theological reflection is to be excluded from academic discourse. Rarely during the post-War period has such a sectarian point of view been so openly expressed in a scholarly forum.

The bulk of Dr Alexander's review, however, is taken up with the attempt to suggest that I failed in A Galilean Rabbi to understand Rabbinic literature. This attempt can only be sustained by means of the well-known technique of quoting statements out of context. Dr Alexander regularly employs two gambits in order to efface the qualifications of my original statements: 1) the time-dishonoured triple dots before and after phrases, and 2) the concatenation of words and phrases from different sentences. So, for example, he quotes me as stating that Yohanan ben Zakkai was "selfless but determined" in his confrontation of Vespasian (p. 240). He simply omits to mention that, at that point, I am paraphrasing Gittin 56a, b. After I have done so, I caution, "it must be borne in mind that Josephus also claimed to have acclaimed Vespasian prophetically (cf. Jewish Wars III.8:9), and that the story about Johanan has been seen as legendary in recent discussion (cf. Saldarini [1975])." Somehow, Dr Alexander never manages to observe that statement, which is made only one sentence after

7

some of the phrases he cites (and also on p. 20). His concern is to find stray phrases to prove I am an historicist.[22] Such selectivity accounts for many of his criticisms regarding my handling of Talmud. On the other hand, Dr Alexander is quite right to point our that the story about Moses visiting Aqiba's academy in Menaḥoth 29b can be read more satirically than I suggest (p. 240). Had I been writing a book regarding the Talmud, not the Targum of Isaiah, I would have mentioned various possibilities in respect of several Talmudic passages. (As it stands, my treatment is merely intended to illustrate "that the rabbis were fully aware of their own creativity" [p. 22], which is a point of view Dr Alexander claims to share.) As is expressly explained, however, the introductory section of the book is designed merely to give general readers a taste of Rabbinica. Anyone who aspires to read Talmud should surely be able to understand the program of a book intended for general readers.

There are a handful of cases in which Dr Alexander alleges error on my part. He attacks my dating of Midrash Rabbah, since in his view it is "hardly earlier than the thirteenth (sic) century!" (p. 240). That remark is a classic instance of trying to reclaim your cake after you have eaten it, since he earlier defends Dr Vermes for using the same source to explicate the New Testament. Be that as it may, there is substantial agreement among genuine experts in the field that the scriptural exposition of Midrash Rabbah is, on the whole, to be ascribed to the Talmudic period, which is precisely what I said.[23] Dr Alexander can only sustain his remark by introducing his own phrase, "present form" (of the collection, he presumably means), in order to press Midrash Rabbah into a later period. At this point in the review, he also introduces italics into his quotation of my book, without admitting he has done so; the entire episode is an exercise in legerdemain. In most of his published work, Dr Alexander seems dedicated to good, scholarly practice, but in the present review his desire to discredit me has got the better of his habits. The same must be said of his sarcastic remark to the effect "There is no 'probably'" about the ascription to Judah ben Illai in Megillah 3:3 (p. 240); on the same page (in which his misquotation of what I said about Yoḥanan appears), he rebukes me both for giving qualified credit to rabbinic ascriptions, and for questioning them. The simple fact of the matter is that critical editions of the Mishnah refer merely to "R. Judah," so that a judgement of which Judah is concerned must be a matter of inference. Whatever the source of Dr Alexander's supreme assurance is, it is not the text of Megillah 3:3. Under the category of false accusation, mention must finally be made of Dr Alexander's charge that I "did not bother to look up the Talmud" to cite the story about Judah ben Illai's comment in respect of Exodus 24:10 in Kiddushin 49a. As a matter of fact, I called attention to the textual phenomenon which Alexander taxes me for being ignorant of in an article which appeared four years prior to the publication of A Galilean Rabbi

8

(and which is reprinted here, unchanged in regard to the issue in question, as the tenth essay). Dr Alexander's schoolmasterly rebuke ("There is really no excuse for it," p. 241) might be turned back on him: people who set themselves up as experts ought to know what is happening in their fields. The substance of his charge, that a reader of the edition of Talmud cited would not find what I referred to, is simply false.[24]

To Dr Alexander's credit, he does from time to time comment on the Targum in the course of reviewing my book. Unfortunately, all the points he raises are more fully discussed in The Glory of Israel: not a single sentence of his review takes up the actual topic of A Galilean Rabbi, namely, the relationship of the Targum to the Gospels. Even when he discusses Targumic matters, Dr Alexander's normal good sense seems to have deserted him. At one point, he demands, "Are there any (sic) Targum manuscripts that are not (sic) mediaeval?" (p. 241). If he would reflect on this rhetorical question at a more tranquil moment, he might recall that fragments of the Palestinian Targums from the Cairo Geniza are dated prior to the Middle Ages, and that the Codex Neophyti is, without question, considerably later. It is a pity to see expertise so clouded by venom.

Amazingly, after throwing all those brickbats, Dr Alexander concludes that my "literary-analytic approach to the Targum is to be welcomed" (p. 241), and that the "idea behind this book was undoubtedly a good one" (p. 242). And so the questions emerge: why does he fail to cope with the thesis of my book, if he believes the idea is workable, why does he distort my position, and why does he make outlandish statements in the attempt to prove me incompetent?

Two reasons come to mind. In his penultimate paragraph, Alexander complains that my earlier study, The Glory of Israel, is "still sub judice among Targum experts" (p. 242). In the world of criticism, of course, everything is always sub judice, at least in principle. By the time his review appeared, all of the assessments cited in n. 14, and some of those mentioned in nn. 15, 16, had already appeared. On any list of those expert in the field, the names Bourget, Gordon, Grossfeld, Harrington, Kaiser, Neusner, Reif, Ribera, and White would have to figure prominently. Taken together, they represent a consensus in respect of my work among those working in America, Britain, France, Germany, and Spain. So far, no scholar (including Dr Alexander) has challenged the theory of origins I have offered, or the evidential relationship with the Gospels to which I have called attention. Dr Alexander apparently has some other arbiter in mind, a censor who should decide when experts will be allowed to speak to general readers.[25] The mediaeval dating of some Targumic manuscripts is, lamentably, reflected in the mentality of some Targumists. A more immediate reason for Dr Alexander's uncharacteristic and unscholarly behaviour is that the journal in which his review appears is edited by Geza Vermes, whose activities in respect of me are evidently not limited to making racist remarks.

The interesting feature of reviews of A Galilean Rabbi (including Dr Alexander's), from the perspective of the present discussion, is that the book's contention, that there is a relationship of influence between material in the Targum and dominical sayings, has been generally accepted. The fifth essay in the present volume takes up another instance where that may be the case. The example was not presented in A Galilean Rabbi, since it may be questioned whether there is an actual citation of or allusion to Isaiah in Matthew 16:18, 19. There is, for that reason, a less direct relationship arguable than in the case of passages discussed in my monograph. The sixth essay is an early work, in which I argued against the influence of the Isaiah Targum on a passage in the New Testament. Its inclusion here is designed to remind readers of the critical criteria which need to be fulfilled before the argument of Targumic influence becomes plausible.

The next three pieces evince my interest in the theologoumenon of God's kingdom, which was the initial cause of my interest in the Targumim. In them, the thesis is developed that direct influence by the Isaiah Targum on the New Testament is not the only point of interest. At times, the Targum simply happens to be a good resource of the theological language which was used within early Judaism. Similarly, but more radically, the last two articles leave the question of influence completely aside. The argument in them is that, at one stage in their growth, the evolution of the Gospels is comparable to that of Pentateuchal Targumim.

Targumic approaches to the Gospels, then, comprise a range of activities. There is the attempt to use them to understand linguistic features which may help us to understand the language of the New Testament (as in essay 1), as well as the more particular quest for exegetical traditions which may, or may not, or may partially, be perceived in the New Testament (as in essays 2 and 3). Within the latter effort, it becomes unmistakably clear that Christian sources can only be understood in relation to Judaic sources when the latter are appreciated in their own terms. In the case of the Aqedah, the converse of that generalization may also be valid. For precisely that reason, quite aside from specific instances of dependence or reaction, the study of early Christianity and Judaism involves an openness to the possibility of their mutual definition. That becomes more obviously apparent when one attempts to understand the relationship of Christian and Judaic sources in their uses of common theologoumena (essays 7-9), and in their possibly analogous patterns of development (essays 10, 11). That effort, in turn, will perhaps awaken fresh interest in the Targums as literary construals of scripture.

The continuing progress of our discipline, however, requires that certain conditions obtain. The study of Targums, and of Judaism generally, can no longer be regarded by the practitioners of theology and biblical studies as if it were an addenda, to which only a coterie of Semitists need attend. That attitude is, perhaps, best illustrated by the frequently voiced opinion of an editor of a biblical journal that "Targums are not in the mainstream of Old Testament study" (see n. 13). That dim parochialism is as vicious, in its way, as the academic sectarianism which would restrict the study of Targums to a self-selecting guild of "experts." If either parochialism or sectarianism prevail, we shall have lost an opportunity to see how scripture was understood within early Judaism and rabbinic Judaism. And that is of proper and necessary concern to any person anywhere who is interested in "the Old Testament," in Judaism, or in the sources of early Christianity. The day may at last be coming, when we can understand what makes Judaism and Christianity related but distinctive approaches to a single God by means of related scriptures. By becoming more critically aware, we may even find we can be ourselves without heaping abuse on those who happen to come from traditions which differ from our own.

1   M. Black, An Aramaic Approach to the Gospels and Acts
(Oxford: Clarendon, 1967). Günther Schwarz has more recently pursued a similar line of analysis, cf. Biblische Notizen 11 (1980)
43, 44, 45; 12 (1980) 32-34; 13 (1980) 56; 14 (1981) 46-49, 50-53;
15 (1981) 46, 47; 20 (1983) 56, 57, 58; 25 (1984) 27-35, 36-41;
NTS 27 (1981) 270-276; ZNW 70 (1979) 249; 71 (1980) 133-135,
244-247; 72 (1981) 264-271; 272-276, 277-282; 73 (1982) 136, 137;
75 (1984) 136, 137, 138. A difficulty of Schwarz's approach, it
should be noted, is his uncritical acceptance of Black's program
of research, as is reflected in his translation of An Aramaic
Approach into German without revision, cf. Die Muttersprache
Jesu. Das Aramäische der Evangelien und der Apostelgeschichte:
Beiträge zur Wissenschaft von Alten und Neuen Testament 15
(Stuttgart: Kohlhammer, 1982). It may be observed that the German
title of the work is even less cautious than that of its English
original, despite important reservations concerning the project
which have been repeatedly expressed. For that reason, I was
asked by Prof. Karl Heinrich Rengstorf in 1981 (while I was working in the Forschungsstelle Antike und Christentum in Münster) to
prepare a brief bibliography of works which any reader of the
German edition should be aware of, despite the omission of Prof.
Black and Dr Schwarz to cite them. That bibliography is here presented as Appendix 1.

2   In CBQ 30 (1968) 417-428.

3   Cf. B. D. Chilton, The Glory of Israel. The Theology and
Provenience of the Isaiah Targum: JSOTS 23 (Sheffield: JSOT,
1982) 7-12.

4   M. Wilcox, "Semitisms in the New Testament," Aufstieg und
Niedergang der römischen Welt II.25.2 (ed. W. Haase; Berlin:
Töpelmann, 1984) 978-1029.

5   J. Barr, The Semantics of Biblical Language (London: Oxford
University Press, 1961).

6   Cf. D. Hill, Greek Words and Hebrew Meanings. Studies in the
Semantics of Soteriological Terms: SNTSMS 5 (Cambridge: Cambridge
University Press, 1967), and Barr's review, entitled "Common Sense
and Biblical Language," in Biblica 49 (1968) 377-387. As Barr
fully demonstrates, the use of "semantics" in Hill's title is misleading; Barr concludes, "I have never read any book which had a
greater gulf between theory and practice." The same criticism is
offered more recently in Moisés Silva, Biblical Words and Their
Meaning. An Introduction to Lexical Semantics (Grand Rapids:
Zondervan, 1983) 21, 29 n. 48. Silva also cautions against the
use of such faulty methods within conservative circles, pp. 22-28.

7   Wilcox, pp. 990-992.

8   In _A Galilean Rabbi and His Bible. Jesus' Use of the Interpreted Scripture of His Time_ (Wilmington: Glazier, 1984 and, with the subtitle, _Jesus' own interpretation of Isaiah_, London: SPCK, 1984) 42-45.

9   Cf. W. R. Stegner, "The Baptism of Jesus. A Story Modeled on the Binding of Isaac," _Bible Review_ 1 (1985) 36-46.

10   The poem is quoted, with pertinent comment, in Judah Goldin's introduction to Shalom Spiegel's classic work (which Goldin also translated), _The Last Trial. On the Legends and Lore of the Command to Abraham to Offer Isaac as a Sacrifice: the Akedah_ (New York: Random House, 1967) xii, xiii (n. 12).

11   G. Vermes, _Jesus and the World of Judaism_ (London: SCM, 1983) 82.

12   "Jewish Studies and New Testament Interpretation," in the work cited above, pp. 58-73.

13   Cf. n. 3. The volume's appearance was delayed somewhat, owing in part to the publishers' indecision, whether Targumic research was in "the mainstream of Old Testament study." Their curious resolution of the dilemma was that they would publish my book, rather than release it to competing bids from Brill and Mohr, but refuse to countenance the publication of books on Targumic subjects in future. I hope my colleagues in the field will take note of this policy (unsatisfactory though it is), in order to obviate disappointment and delay in the communication of their research.

14   D. Bourget, _ETR_ 59 (1984) 255; R. Coggins, _JTS_ 36 (1985) 275; R. P. Gordon, _SOTS Book List_ (1984) 44; B. Grossfeld, _JBL_ 104 (1985) 138, 139; O. Kaiser, _ZAW_ 96 (1984) 300; P. Nickels, _CBQ_ 47 (1985) 514, 515; S. C. Reif, _VT_ 34 (1984) 124; J. Ribera, _Estudios Biblicos_ 42 (1984) 230-234; R. Tournay, _RB_ 91 (1984) 465, 466; R. White, _JJS_ 35 (1984) 106-108.

15   In _JES_ 22 (1985) 359-361, and Brown Judaic Studies 91 (Chico: Scholars Press, 1985) 113-116. The latter is the fuller version, and appears as an article entitled "The Judaic Side of New Testament Studies: Chilton and McNamara."

16   C. Bernas, _Theological Studies_ 49 (1985) 129, 130; C. Bryan, _St Luke's Journal_ 28 (1985) 312, 313; J. M. Court, _JTS_ 36 (1985) 444, 445; A. T. Hanson, _ET_ 96 (1985) 119; D. Harrington, _Int_ 40 (1986) 92; J. D. Hutchinson, _Church of Ireland Register_ (26 April 1985); G. Jenkins, _Common Ground. Journal of the Council of Christians and Jews_ 2, 3 (1985) 18. The review in the publication

13

of the Birmingham Theological Society, a copy of which was sent me by SPCK, is signed by the editor. Inclusion of a review in the present list, of course, implies neither that each reviewer agrees entirely with me, or vice versa. For example, Bernas somehow gets the idea that my description of Jesus as a rabbi was intended in the sense of that term which became current in the period after A.D. 70, which is the option I specifically exclude (p. 34). Minor misunderstandings, however, are taken as beside the present purpose.

17   1 March 1985, 6.

18   In SOTS Booklist (1985) 43.

19   In Theology 88 (1985) 304-306.

20   Cf. The Evangelists' Calendar. A Lectionary Explanation of the Development of Scripture (London: SPCK, 1978).

21   In JJS 36 (1985) 238-242.

22   In his conclusion, however, he can only say, "I detect the ghost of historicism here" (p. 242). I find it fascinating that someone who wishes to banish theology from academic discourse feels free to engage in spectral exorcism.

23   Cf. Jacob Neusner, Midrash in Context. Exegesis in Formative Judaism: The Foundations of Judaism (Philadelphia: Fortress, 1983).

24   Cf. The Babylonian Talmud. Seder Nashim viii (London: Soncino, 1936) p. 246 and nn. 4-6.

25   A similar dogmatism characterizes the review of A. P. Hayman in SJT 38 (1985) 446-448, which is substantially positive in its assessment.

ESSAY 1 --
"Amen": an Approach through Syriac Gospels

In his 1970 study, Klaus Berger challenged the consensus that a non-responsorial use of "Amen" at the beginning of a sentence is distinctively dominical. The single most important piece of evidence he adduced is the phrase ἀμὴν λέγω σοι in the Long Recension of the Testament of Abraham VIII, a usage corresponding to ἦ μήν in LXX Gen 22:17, rather than to כִּי in MT. That is, a Greek-speaking community incorporated the functions of ἦ μήν into the responsorial אָמֵן of the Hebrew Bible and produced a hybrid: introductory, non-responsorial ἀμήν.[1] Berger also observed that introductory ναί functions much as ἦ μήν does, and he argued that ναί usage is another Greek antecedent of the "Amen"-word.[2] These developments presuppose a Hellenistic circle which assimilated (and domesticated) Semitic diction, and Berger was emphatic that "Die Amen-Einleitung selber ist jedenfalls erst auf dem Boden des hellenistischen Judenchristentums gebildet worden."[3]

Having said that, Berger insisted that the "Amen"-word attested "nicht nur die zuverlässige Bezeugung des Sehers, sondern auch die unverfälschte Weitergabe durch die Gemeinde."[4] He agreed with Viktor Hasler that the Evangelists have distinctive habits in the placement of the "Amen" introduction (habits which Hasler explicates with greater precision), but from the tradition-critical point of view Berger made the acute and necessary observation that "Amen" serves as the "Legitimation der Rede des Sehers" and not as a hallmark of charismatic prophecy.[5] This was shown by the simple fact that, in the New Testament, Jesus' "Amen"-words are found "nur im Munde Jesu und nur in den Evangelien," and by the consideration that "die Sprecher der Pneuma-Worte haben prophetisches Selbstverständnis" and therefore had no need of formulaic legitimation.[6] To this one might add that a recent contribution from Fritz Neugebauer questions the persistent notion that charisma obviated paradosis in the early Church.[7] The picture of the "Amen" asseveration, as we may call it, which Berger paints is one which takes account of the evidence, if it is not the only reconstruction which that evidence could be construed to support: Greek Jewish Christians assimilated responsorial Hebrew אָמֵן to asseverative Greek ἦ μήν and used the hybrid ἀμήν in order to claim that the dicta to which it was prefixed were legitimate as revelation and as tradition.[8] In a later article, Berger showed that the first person singular personal pronoun and a verb of speaking often appear in passages which pretend authority,[9] and evidence he cites from Mk, Joh, and Gnostic sources (especially the CE MMAN of the Coptic Epistle of James) convincingly displays a tendency to use "Amen" to claim revelatory and traditional value which grew as the Gospel tradition adjusted to its Hellenistic environment.[10]

15

Berger's reconstruction is clear, consistent and exhaustively argued.[11] Two recent attempts to refute the thesis are quite pertinent, but ultimately unsuccessful.

Joachim Jeremias limited himself to two pages in "Zeitschrift für die neutestamentliche Wissenschaft," 64 (1973), and with magisterial ease found the chink in Berger's literary-critical armour. Jeremias observed that, "auch wenn man das Test Abr für eine jüdische Schrift hält, ist über die Herkunft des die eigene Rede einleitenden 'Amen' bzw. 'Amen, Amen' in Kap. 8 und 20 noch keineswegs entschieden," since Recension A is "wahrscheinlich eine mittelalterliche Komposition."[12] More recent criticism suggests that this recension is linguistically more hellenized than its partner, [13] although the basically Jewish provenience of the work as a whole has not been seriously challenged. Yet even if the "Amen" introduction in Test Abr is taken to represent Christian usage, Berger's case can not be said to be untenable. The fact would remain that Test Abr VIII and XX both present non-dominical uses of "Amen," and the former passage would still attest a possible connection to ἦ μήν in LXX. Of course, this does not prove the derivation of asseverative "Amen" generally from Greek usage. Jeremias has performed an important service in pointing out the weakness in Berger's argument, belatedly spelled out in his article, "dass die Amen-Worte in Test Abr als selbständige traditionsgeschichtliche Parallelen zu den Amen-Worten der Evv zu beurteilen sind."[14] It is true that Test Abr may represent the sort of usage from which that of the Gospels developed, but it may also represent a Hellenizing degeneration of evangelical language. Neither Jeremias nor Berger can conclusively eliminate the possibility which he chooses not to pursue, so that both reconstructions remain plausible, if not fully convincing. The situation could not, however, be fairly described as a stalemate, because Berger's discussion does stand as the most complete to date.

John Strugnell took up a completely different line of attack against Berger. He built on the argument of S. Talmon that "Amen" can be used as an "introductory oath formula" in classical Hebrew, and relied--as Talmon had done--on an allegedly non-responsorial "Amen" usage in a Hebrew ostracon from the seventh century BCE.[15] This position involves a key correction to the pre-Berger consensus on "Amen," because it is inconsistent with the view that non-responsorial "Amen" was a usage unique to Jesus. In a somewhat astringent comment on Jeremias's judgment that the usage in the Yabneh-Yam ostracon is responsorial, Strugnell said, "The ipsissima vox needn't express itself in locutions never heard before."[16] Yet as I read the Cross translation of this text (cited by Strugnell, 178-179), it seems that the "Amen" is introductory in the sense that it opens a sentence, but responsorial in that it replies to a legally formulated charge:

"...all my brethren will testify for me. Truly I am innocent of any guilt."
Further, as Strugnell admits, other editors take the "Amen" responsorially, or emend the text so as to eliminate the "Amen" reading altogether. In any event, one finds it difficult to forget that the ostracon antedates Jesus by more than five hundred years. In a word, Strugnell's suggestion is based on a datum whose testimony is neither unequivocal nor of prima facie relevance to dominical diction. For this reason, his article falls well short of seriously answering Berger's case, although it does serve as a welcome reminder that the present understanding of Semitic languages is not sufficiently comprehensive to reject e silentio the possibility that the "Amen" introduction has a pre-history.

The above few paragraphs are far from a full, critical appraisal of the work reviewed, but I hope they adequately document the following generalization about recent discussion: the crucial linguistic question is whether introductory, non-responsorial "Amen" is indigenously Semitic or Greek. If this generalization is to the point, then certain Syriac versions of the New Testament deserve our special attention, since they constitute the best extant testimony to the attempt to put the Gospels into a tongue related to Aramaic at an early period. Perhaps they have left some indication that "Amen" seemed to them colloquial or, on the other hand, rather foreign. Basically, we want to know if the Syriac evidence is more consistent with a Greek or an Aramaic explanation for the use of "Amen" in the Gospels. We will propose an answer to this question and discuss the implications of that answer for further research after we have considered the evidence. It will perhaps serve to clarify the argument if I say from the outset that I will develop two conclusions: 1. that the Syriac versions with which we will concern ourselves reproduce "Amen" only out of fidelity to the normative Greek text of the New Testament and 2. that the Aramaic asseveration בקושטא ("in truth") is at times reflected in these versions, and may be the locution which Hellenistic ἀμήν renders.

On the strength of Matthew Black's analysis[17] of the Syriac versions, we will look at the Old Syriac Gospel manuscripts (the Sinaitic [S] and the Curetonian [C]) and at the Peshitta (P) as the best witnesses to the earliest attempt at the translation activity with which we are concerned. Although later revisions may also attest primitive readings, by their nature as revisions they do so only sporadically. This is to say that we accept Black's view that the Philoxenian and Harclean versions come late in the day, and we consider that the so-called Palestinian Syriac Lectionary represents a late stage of the New Testament text.[18] First, and obviously, we will see how ἀμήν is rendered in S-C and P. Second, we will consider how they cope with ἀλήθεια, ἀληθῶς, ἀληθής, and ἀληθινός. The inclusion of the second investigation is justified--indeed, it is invited--by Berger's analysis. Again

17

and again, in his book and in his article, he observes that expressions using a form of the term "truth" are used asseveratively in a manner analogous to that of the "Amen" introduction in apocalyptic and Gnostic sources, as well as in the New Testament (e.g., ἀληθῶς λέγω, ἐπ' ἀληθείας λέγω, ἀλήθειαν λέγω).[19] In this essay, such locutions will be called "truth"-stem asseverations. To be sure, he assigns a similar role to other expressions (e.g., πιστὸς ὁ λόγος), but "truth"-stem formulae are (1) the most prevalent and (2) those actually used in the Gospels in place of "Amen"[20] or in a fashion which reminds one of "Amen" usage.[21] For both reasons, "truth"-stem words are to be included in this analysis of the Syriac (S-C, P) handling of the "Amen"-word.

"Truth"-stem introductions are interesting in another connection, as well. "Truly" is quite frequently found in the Peshitta Old Testament (שְׁרִירָאיֹת) as an asseverative locution corresponding to several MT terms (e.g., in Gen, at 3:1 for אַף, at 17:19 for אֲבָל, at 18:13 for הַאַף אֻמְנָם, at 20:12 for אֻמְנָה, at 42:21 for אֲבָל). Two of these renderings explicitly confirm the observation that "Amen" and "truth"-stem usages may be employed analogously, and they suggest that the Peshitta translators took the root אמן to mean "truly." But considered as a whole, such passages lead us to make a second observation, namely that שְׁרִירָאיֹת was more prevalent in Syriac than "Amen" was in Hebrew. Further, in each of the cases cited, Onqelos reads בְּקוּשְׁטָא ("in truth")[22], and this fact, judged against the background of a variety of readings in the LXX equivalents (τί ὅτι, ναί ἰδού, ἄρά γε ἀληθῶς, ἀληθῶς, ναί) invites the suspicion that "truth"-stem locutions are indigenously Aramaic. In this vein, it is striking that the Targum to Isaiah (45:14,15) presents good illustrations of non-responsorial, introductory בְּקוּשְׁטָא derived from neither MT (אַף, אָכֵן) nor LXX (ὅτι, γάρ). The usage also appears at 37:18, and corresponds to אֻמְנָם in the MT (ἐπ' ἀληθείας in the LXX). Reference might also be made to 11:4; 38:2; 42:6; 46:5; 61:8; 64:4. Of course, such data do not prove that this usage was current in the time during which the New Testament tradition was shaped, but the possibility that this was the case must be considered. The Syriac handling of "truth"-stem words is therefore pertinent from the point of view of Aramaic diction as well as from the New Testament perspective developed in the previous paragraph.

Because the Syriac renderings of the terms with which we are concerned are fairly regular, it seems unnecessary to present them in tabular form. It will perhaps be more to the point if I simply note the usual translation, observe deviations from the norm, and comment on the pattern which emerges.

ἀμήν is normally transliterated as אָמִין. There are a few irregularities. The Old Syriac Gospels sometimes repeat the term in Mk, where it stands alone in the Greek (3:28; 14:18, 30), and sometimes fail to repeat it in the fourth Gospel, where it is doubled in the Greek (3:11[S]; 5:19[S]; 6:26[S]; 13:20, 21, 38; 21:18). This interesting phenomenon is to be explained on the basis of the harmonistic tendency which characterizes these manuscripts, probably because they stand under the influence of contemporary fashion.[23] Of course, this tendency is pertinent to the textual pedigree of S and C, not to the linguistic provenience of "Amen." The same might be said of the next group of passages, although it is arguable that these are also linguistically significant. In a number of cases, "Amen" is omitted by C (Mt 6:5; Mk 16:20) and P (Mt 18:19; Mk 16:20) although the remainder of the verse is rendered. It is true that three of these four might have been omitted in the Greek Vorlage(n), as extant Greek manuscripts show (that is, to Mt 18:19 and Mk 16:20). That still leaves Mt 6:5 in C, which is presumably to be explained as a simple error, as indeed the other omissions may be. Except for the apparent influence of C on P at Mk 16:20, the omissions are not consistent between S, C and P, so that they either were inadvertent or (as seems improbable to me) each scribe happened to follow his own Vorlage at these points. On the first explanation, the Syriac scribes tended to overlook "Amen;" on the second, they preferred Greek manuscripts which did so. In either case, we are lead to conclude that "Amen" was very far from a Syriacism by the time these translations were made. A last example of the tendency to omit "Amen," this time from S, confirms this conclusion. At Mk 12:43, S departs from all of the witnesses known to Nestle-Aland and writes אין for "Amen." Whether this should be taken as the lone attestation of a non-extant Greek source, or as an error of seeing, this reading again shows that "Amen" was not quite seen as indispensable, even though the attempt was made to transliterate it as part of the normative Greek text. Of course, this tendency to omit "Amen" in Syriac versions is consistent with the Berger thesis, since it suggests that introductory "Amen" was less meaningful to a Syriac speaker than it was to a Greek speaker. When this is given its due weight, a last--and very slight--irregularity in the Syriac rendering of "Amen" becomes comprehensible. Quite frequently, S-C (Mt 5:26; 10:15, 23) and P (Mt 5:26; 6:2, 5, 16; 10:15; 18:18) add ו before אמיר. At Mt 10:23 in S-C this is particularly striking, because גיר (γάρ) is also present (cf. the addition of גיר at Mk 11:23 in P, but without ו). While P repeats two of the S-C ו additions, it adds several of its own (although it omits the S-C addition of 10:23). While this evidence is too slight to be conclusive, it does at least suggest that there was a certain reluctance to use "Amen" by itself, as it appears in the Greek New Testament; such reluctance is quite understandable on the supposition that the term was not current in spoken Syriac.

Our translators became more adventurous when they came to "truth"-stem words. ἀλήθεια is normally translated by שׁררא, yet at Joh 3:21, S reads שׁפירתא instead. While this is a maverick variant we will see that the Syriac versions at times move away from the rather abstract quality of ἀλήθεια/שׁררא, and the present pas-

sage may be taken as an instance of this tendency. The adverb
שרירא֗ית (which is the equivalent of ἀληθῶς) represents ἀλήθεια in
S-C (Lk 22:59; Joh 8:40) and P (Lk 22:59; cf. Joh 8:40). In these
instances, the Syriac translators saw ἀλήθεια as having asseverative force, and have accordingly rendered it with the adverb. At
Lk 22:59 (ἐπ' ἀληθείας in the speech of a bystander) this freedom
is not as surprising as it is at Joh 8:40 (prepositionless τὴν
ἀλήθειαν in the speech of Jesus),[24] but in both cases it is striking that the noun "truth" was taken as an (adverbial) asseverative
by the Syriac translators while in Greek it was a substantive. At
this stage, the possibility might be entertained that, on the
analogy to the usage of Onqelos and the Peshitta Old Testament,
the predilection of S-C and P for שרירא֗ית corresponds to a use of
בקושטא in the Aramaic Gospel tradition. In fact, at Joh 3:21,
where S reads שפירתא, C has קושתא, i.e., the phonological equivalent of the Aramaic term (cf. Joh 1:14 in P). Far more important,
the parallel "truth" asseverations Mt 22:16 and Lk 20:21 (ἐν
ἀληθείᾳ and ἐπ' ἀληθείας respectively) stand as בקושתא in S-C and
P. This, of course, is morphologically, phonologically and substantively the Syriac equivalent of the Aramaic "truth"
asseveration attested in the Targums. But why should the expression have surfaced at Mt 22:16/Lk 20:21? The answer may be that
the fact that this logion is not ascribed to Jesus made the trans-
lator feel free to indulge his knowledge of an Aramaic locution.
(Such usage may be an archaism, or בקושתא might have been an
expression in spoken Syriac which carried on the Aramaic usage.)
It is notable in this context that Lk 22:59 is also a non-dominical utterance.

So far, we have shown that there is an Aramaic usage which is
reflected in our Syriac versions as a translation of "truth"
asseverations. How is this to be explained? Three possibilities
might be considered: 1) the Syriac locution arose purely as a
translation of the Greek New Testament text, which also influenced
the Onqelos and Jonathan Targums, 2) the Aramaic and Syriac usage
is pre-Christian in origin, but it just happens to be a decent
translation of ἐν ἀληθείᾳ, ἐπ' ἀληθείας and ἀλήθεια,[25] 3) בקושטא
in the Aramaic Gospel tradition was variously translated into
Greek, and its proper form is preserved in S-C and P (בקושתא).
The first possibility is to be rejected, because the normative
status assigned to the Onqelos and Jonathan Targums in Talmud
makes it unlikely that they were extensively influenced by
Christian diction.[26] The second possibility can not be excluded,
but we must bear in mind that our Syriac translators actually
chose to use קושתא for ἀλήθεια on occasion instead of the obvious
and normal rendering (שררא): this suggests that קושתא was not
just a convenient translation. The third possibility is clearly
the most probable, because it is consistent with the very facts
which cast doubt on the other two.

20

It has already been indicated that שׁרירא׳ת is the normal rendering of ἀληθῶς, and such exceptions as there are tend to confirm the pattern already discerned. P twice has שׁררא (Lk 9:27; 21:3), which shows that the Syriac noun could be used asseveratively, and the latter passage actually appears as בקושׁתא in S (C omits the ב). Similarly, ἀληθής, which ordinarily appears as שׁרירׁ, can be represented by שׁרירא׳ת (S-C, P Joh 6:55, although many sound Greek witnesses read ἀληθῶς here), שׁרירחא (S-C, P Joh 4:18) and שׁררׁ (P Joh 19:35). Lastly, the Syriac preference for nouns, rather than adjectives, in "truth"-steam diction is betrayed by the translation of ἀληθινός in our versions. In a majority of cases, שׁררׁ with ר, where one would expect שׁרירׁ, appears, and קושׁתא surfaces at Joh 6:32 in C and P.

Our survey of the Old Syriac Gospel and Peshitta New Testament renderings of "Amen" and "truth"-stem diction has brought us to two clear findings. First, it would appear that "Amen" was preserved out of fidelity to the normative Greek text, not because it was a recognizable idiom. Second, Aramaic בקושׁטא was remembered by the translators as the idiom which Greek "truth"-stem locutions were designed to convey.

The present contribution is concerned with the linguistic provenience and background of "Amen;" the substantive question is, is it a Kennzeichen für die ipsissima vox Jesu? Hasler's work would suggest on the contrary that it is, as a hallmark of charismatic prophecy, a Kennzeichen dagegen. Berger's position is more nuanced in that he sees in the use of "Amen" an attempt by Hellenistic Jewish Christians to ensure continuity of tradition. Strugnell insists that "Amen" has a Semitic background, but in so doing contradicts the assumption that the locution was unique to Jesus. Taken together, the contributions of Berger and Strugnell have definitively upset the facile generalization that "Aramaic" is synonymous with "dominical" and "Greek" with "secondary." Obviously, there were Aramaic-speaking communities with theological concerns, and Greek-speaking communities with a care for the preservation of traditions, so that one may not suppose that a purely linguistic investigation directly settles a historical controversy. If I am correct, "Amen" may be taken (as Berger argues) to indicate the Greek provenience of a saying in its final form, but the same term, as a plausible rendering of בקושׁטא, may be taken to point to the Aramaic matrix of an earlier form of the saying. On this understanding, "Amen" is only a meaningful linguistic criterion when it is read in the context of the other linguistic features in a particular saying. Similarly, it may be a "Kennzeichen der ipsissima vox Jesu",[27] but only when the language and substance of the saying in which it appears lead one to make this historical assertion.

NOTES

Essay 1 first appeared in ZNW 69 (1978) 203-211.

1   Berger, Die Amen-Worte Jesu, BZNW 39, 1970, 15.

2   Berger, 28; see also the citation of Mt 23:36 and Lk 11:51 on 72.

3   Berger, 28; cf. 93, 147.

4   Berger, 32; cf. 162-163.

5   Berger, 150, 160; cf. Viktor Hasler, Amen: Redaktionsgeschichtliche Untersuchungen zur Einführungsformel der Herrenworte "Wahrlich ich sage euch," Zürich 1969.

6   Berger, 159, 129.

7   Neugebauer, "Geistsprüche und Jesuslogien," ZNW 53, 1962, 218-228.

8   Berger, 151.

9   "Zur Geschichte der Einleitungsformel 'Amen ich sage euch'," ZNW 63, 1972, 45-75. One might, however, complain about a rather loose us of the term "apocalyptic" to describe statements which merely pretend authority.

10 Berger, Amen-Worte, 131-146, 93.

11 See the reviews by Margaret E. Thrall in JTS 23, 1972, 190-191 and G. Richter in Bibl 53, 1972, 290-293.

12 "Zum nicht-responsorischen Amen," ZNW 64, 1973, 122.

13 R.A. Martin, "Syntax Criticism of the Testament of Abraham," in: G.W.E. Nickelsburg (ed.), Studies on the Testament of Abraham: SBL Septuagint and Cognate Studies 6, Missoula 1976, 95-120.

14 "Zur Geschichte," 47-50.

15 "'Amen, I Say Unto You' in the Sayings of Jesus and in Early Christian Literature," HThR 67, 1974, 177-182. For Talmon's position, see 180, n. 6.

16 Strugnell, 182.

17 Black, "The Syriac Versional Tradition" in: K. Aland (ed.), Die alten Übersetzungen des Neuen Testaments, Berlin 1972,

120-1590. See also B.M. Metzger, The Early Versions of the New Testament, Oxford 1977, 3-98.

18   B.M. Metzger, "A Comparison of the Palestinian Syriac Lectionary and the Greek Gospel Lectionary" in: E.E. Ellis and M. Wilcox (eds.), Neotestamentica et Semitica, Edinburgh 1969, 209-220, and Early Versions, 75-82.

19   Berger, Amen-Worte, 6 n. 8, 84 n. 74, 95 n. 93, 106, 136, 142; "Zur Geschichte," 47 n. 9, 52, 60, 68.

20   Lk 9:27; 12:44; 21:3.

21   Mt 22:16/Mk 12:14/Lk 20:21; Mt 26:73/Mk 14:70; Mt 27:54/Mk 15:39; Mk 12:32; 14:33; Lk 4:25; 22:59; cf. Joh 1:47; 4:42; 6:14; 7:26, 40; 8:31; 17:8 and Act 12:11; 1 Thess 2:13; 1 Joh 2:5. Further: alêthês--Joh 4:18; 5:31, 32; 6:55; 8:13, 14, 17; 10:41; 19:35; 21:24; alêthinos--Joh 4:37; 8:16; 19:35; alêtheia--Joh 5:33; 8:40, 45, 46; 16:7; 17:17; 18:37. 22 Cf. Pseudo-Jonathan and Neophyti. The Sperber editions have been consulted for Onqelos and Jonathan, the normative Targums, and I have used the recent Peshitta Institute edition of Gen (Leiden, 1977). For the discussion below, see Agnes Smith Lewis, The Old Syriac Gospels, London 1910, and the British and Foreign Bible Society edition of the Peshitta New Testament.

23   See G.A. Weir, "Tatian's Diatessaron and the Old Syriac Gospels," Edinburgh, Ph.D. dissertation, 1969. It may well be that only S had the "Amen" harmonism, because C preserves no reading for the first three and the last four verses cited.

24   It may be that P also saw the latter rendering as rather free and accordingly modified it to šryrt', making it both serve as a substantive (alêtheia) and remind us of the asseverative (šryr'yt).

25   See above on Mt 22:16/Lk 20:21; Joh 1:14; 3:21.

26   Cf. b Meg 3a.

27   It should be remembered that Jeremias presented several other Kennzeichen in the article which bears this name in: J. Schmid and A. Vogtle (eds.), Synoptische Studien (München: Zink, 1953) 86-93.

ESSAY 2 --
Isaac and the Second Night: a Consideration

The "Poem of the Four Nights," i.e., the Passover memorial presented in the Palestinian Targumim at Exodus 12:42, has been at the centre of attention in the development of the post-war consensus on the Aqedah. Primarily as a result of the contribution of Roger Le Déaut,[1] the Poem has been taken as evidence that Isaac was seen as an expiatory figure associated with Passover in pre-Christian Jewish religion. In this sense, Isaac provided a paradigm, it is argued, for Christian soteriology. But we should not imagine that the recent renascence of Targum study alone gave contemporary scholarship the Aqedah. Discussion has long been carried out on how it was that rabbis came to refer to the events of Gn 22, where only the verb עקד is used, with the noun עקדה which seens first to have been associated with binding the Tamid lamb.[2] With this linguistic adjustment, the "Binding" of Isaac came to be seen as actually complete; he was killed and raised by God, he shed his blood and/or was reduced to ashes.

Abraham Geiger's article, "Erbsünde und Versöhnungstod: deren Versuch in das Judenthum einzudringen" opened modern discussion of the Aqedah.[3] As the title suggests, Geiger felt that the Aqedah was the vehicle by which ideas alien to Judaism sought liturgical expression. In his view, the Aqedah is a late assimilation from Syrian Christianity promulgated by the Babylonian Amoraim. In a passionate conclusion, he gave vent to an almost puritanical zeal: "Let us finally free ourselves from this Babylonian diversion and entanglement, let us return to the purified teaching of an earlier age...".[4] Geiger's programme was one of theological reform as well as of critical inquiry, and he is an eloquent spokesman for nineteenth century German Judaism.

Writing in 1912, Israel Lévi complained that Geiger had permitted his "reformist preoccupations" to bias his historical reconstruction.[5] By showing that the Palestinian Amoraim were keenly interested in the theology of the Aqedah, Lévi unequivocally demonstrated that its provenience was not exclusively Babylonian.[6] He saw in the rabbinic New Year liturgy the matrix of the Aqedah, and turned to dating the Musaf for that festival which, he said, linked "the messianic hope" with the idea of "the Aqedah merit".[7] In his dating, Lévi developed a position which is the mirror image of Geiger's. The motif in the Musaf is not expressed in either Talmud, so Lévi looked to an earlier period to discover its roots.[8] That he failed to consider the possibility that it is from a later period must be seen as tendentious. As it happens, not even Rabbi Aqiba "remembered" to explicate the feast as the Musaf does. Nothing daunted, Lévi maintained that Aqiba's was a "hopeless explication" in that it failed to articulate the nationalistic dimension of the Aqedah merit.[9] Bearing in mind

Aqiba's involvement in the Bar Kokhba episode, it seems implausible that he would have ignored such a messianic exegesis, had it been available. In any event, we can see that Lévi pushed his reading of the Musaf further and further back in time on the basis of e silentio (not to say e contrario) argument. He went on to suggest that extant New Year prayers are early, on the totally inadequate grounds that the schools of Shammai and Hillel had discussed the number of such prayers.[10] Yet this is the basis of Lévi's assertion that Paul borrowed the idea of the "virtue of the Aqedah" and, mixing it with "well-known myths," synthesized the soteriology of a self-immolating god.[11]

Lévi had succeeded in showing the weaknesses in Geiger's thesis, but his own alternative might have been regarded as an exegetical curiosity except for what happened subsequently. In 1946, H.J. Schoeps published a contribution in which he explained the development of Pauline theology on the assumption that Lévi was correct about the Aqedah. He asserted that Paul "built the doctrine of the expiatory power of the sacrificial death of Christ on the binding of Isaac, as interpreted in the familiar Rosh Hashana liturgy."[12] He restated his position in "Aus frühchristlicher Zeit" (1950) and "Paulus: Die Theologie des Apostels im Lichte der jüdischen Religionsgeschichte" (1959). The influence on New Testament students of the latter book, in German and English editions, would be difficult to overestimate. Schoeps did not add anything to Lévi's historical reconstruction: he was concerned with the theological implications of a pre-Christian Aqedah. Because he merely followed Lévi, it simply will not do to cite Schoeps by way of asserting that this haggadah is early.

A strictly chronological treatment would require us to deal now with the magisterial introduction to the Aqedah written by Shalom Spiegel for a volume which appeared in 1950, but this work was not cited in the literature with which we will concern ourselves until 1961, and not translated from Hebrew into English until 1967. In the meantime, Eduard Lohse had vigorously challenged the Lévi-Schoeps thesis. In "Märtyrer und Gottesknecht" he came to the firm conclusion "that late Jewish statements about Isaac's death are conditioned by controversy with the Christian preaching of atoning death."[13] While Lohse's argument is too succinct to be fully convincing, he does list several instances in which the Jewish Aqedah seems prima facie to have borrowed details from the Passion (e.g., the motif of Isaac's descent into Gehenna). Even at this stage, then, it was clear to at least one scholar that the thesis of the causal precedence of the Aqedah to New Testament soteriology could by stood on its head. Unfortunately, due account has not been taken of Lohse's contribution. In this question, as in others,[14] consensus has been maintained partially by ignoring arguments against it.

26

The discussion might well have continued in a generalized and rather polemical manner had it not been for Spiegel's work, first published in the "Alexander Marx Jubilee Volume" (by the Jewish Theological Seminary of America).[15] Aside from providing what remains the finest assembly of midrashim on Genesis 22, his study was awarded the Louis La-Med prize for its contribution to Hebrew letters. Spiegel supplemented it with two articles, and Judah Goldin translated it and wrote an introduction which is itself an important contribution. Remarkably, Spiegel's encyclopedic and lucid essay is but the preface to a poem he presents, whose subject is the Aqedah, written by Rabbi Ephraim bar Joseph of Bonn. With great learning and sensitivity, Spiegel traces developments in the understanding of Gn 22 from Jubilees to Wilfred Owen's poem, "The Parable of the Old Man and the Young," and what he definitely shows is that such development must be reckoned with in any account of the Aqedah. The Aqedah is a plastic doctrine in Jewish exegesis which was shaped to meet changing conditions, not a monolithic block of tradition which came into use and remained the same forever. Because he is primarily interested in demonstrating how various strands of the motif were taken up into the poem which he presents, Spiegel is not concerned to construct an exhaustive history of the tradition. Perhaps for this reason, he has none of the mania of other contributors for showing a causal relationship between Judaism and Christianity in the matter of the Aqedah; he simply uses the (mostly Jewish, but also Christian) materials which he has to hand in order to illuminate some of the ways in which Gn 22 was explicated. As a result, he is refreshingly undogmatic: in response to the question whether the Church influenced the Jewish Aqedah doctrine he answers, "Maybe; and again, maybe not."[16] Spiegel is confident enough about the intrinsic value of the medieval poem he interprets that he does not feel constrained to prove the Aqedah is pre-Christian in order to establish its importance. In doing this, he seems to have freed the discussion of two fallacies which were unspoken, but apparently influential: (1) the assumption that a theologoumenon must be early to be valid and (2) the assumption that either Judaism or Christianity must be substantially explicable as a deviation from the other.

Yet Spiegel did not present his essay as an exercise in logic; at every point his assertions are a response to literary evidence. He dismisses Geiger's reconstruction on the basis of the genre of data cited by Lévi, but he also points out that the language of the sources adduced by Lévi is far too late to stand as testimony for a primitive New Year liturgy. His analysis of the sources is punctilious, so that his treatment must be regarded as the definitive refutation of the Lévi-Schoeps consensus.[17] He offers his own admittedly speculative account of the origins of the Aqedah, according to which an initially pagan sacrificial motif has influenced both the Jewish exegesis of the events on Moriah and the Christian view of Golgotha.[18] He allows for the possibility of

27

mutual influence between the Aqedah and the Passion, but explains what he sees as their similarity with reference to this hypothetically common point of origin. Evidence for this opinion is not supplied: it is more an image of Spiegel's perception of the relationship between Judaism and Christianity than a critical explanation. His service to the critic lies in his demonstration of the plasticity of the Aqedah.

Spiegel's survey is a fine basis on which to approach the question of the matrix of the Aqedah and to trace its earliest development. This is the programme of Geza Vermes in "Redemption and Genesis XXII--The Binding of Isaac and the Sacrifice of Jesus," first published in 1961.[19] By this time, Alejandro Díez Macho had discovered and identified the Neophyti Targum and, since this identification came after Paul Kahle's argument that the Palestinian Targum antedates Onqelos, the possibility was entertained that the material contained in this sixteenth century manuscript might stem from the first century, or even before. (A proper account of the impact of this manuscript on Targum studies is provided by Martin McNamara, who himself began work on his thesis one year after the identification of Neophyti.[20]) As a matter of fact, 1961 is a fateful year in the discussion of the Aqedah; just after the completion of Vermes's book, Le Déaut came to very similar conclusions independently in a conference paper.[21] Since that time (cf. n. 1), the antiquity of Targumic readings (most especially "The Poem of the Four Nights" in Neophyti at Ex 12:42) has been the linchpin of a renovated form of Lévi's argument in which the Aqedah is thought to have related not to New Year, but to Passover at the time Paul wrote. Remove that linchpin, and the pre- Christian Aqedah bandwagon runs into serious difficulties.[22]

This necessarily brief résumé of modern discussion of the Aqedah establishes that the mere reference to this motif does not prove or even suggest that the passage in which in appears is early. Le Déaut eloquently maintains that the Aqedah reference in the second of the four night texts in the Poem of the Four Nights is pre-Christian, and his position certainly is not a mere derivative of the old Lévi-Schoeps consensus. Nonetheless, a consideration of the way in which the Aqedah is alluded to in the second night text, and an evaluation of Le Déaut's exegetical comments suggest that this text will not serve as the linchpin in the fashionable argument for a pre-Christian Aqedah.

The relevant texts of the second night, here translated from Le Déaut's reconstruction and available editions, are as follows:

Pseudo-Jonathan

The second night, when he was revealed upon Abraham.

28

Fragmentary Targum (cf. P 110)

The second night, when the LORD's memra was revealed
upon Abraham between the parts. Abraham was a hundred
years old and Sarah was ninety years old, to establish
what scripture says, is Abraham, a hundred years old,
able to beget, and is Sarah, ninety years old, able to
bear? Was not Isaac our father thirty seven years old at
the time he was offered on the altar? The heavens
descended and came down and Isaac saw their perfections
and his eyes were dimmed from the heights, and he called
it the second night.

Neophyti I (cf. P 110)

The second night, when the LORD was revealed, upon
Abraham, a hundred years old, and Sarah his wife, ninety
years old, to establish what scripture says, will
Abraham, a hundred years old, beget, and Sarah his wife,
ninety years old, bear? And Isaac was thirty-seven years
old when he was offered on the altar and the heavens
lowered and came down and Isaac saw their perfections
and his eyes were dimmed from the perfections, and he
called it the second night.

Before evaluating the testimony of these texts on the basis of Le
Déaut's investigation, a brief appreciation of their structure,
context (including length) and substance is called for.

Structurally, the second night is identified with various
moments in salvation history arranged in a sequential pattern.
Primacy of place is given to Abraham's covenant sacrifice, "when
the sun had gone down and it was dark" and "a smoking fire pot and
a flaming torch passed between those pieces" (Gn 15:17). This was
a natural event to associate with la nuit pascale; had not God
promised on this occasion, "Know of a surety that your descendants
will be sojourners in a land that is not theirs, and will be
slaves there, and they will be oppressed for four hundred years;
but I will bring judgement on the nation which they serve and
afterward they shall come out with great possessions" (Gn 15:13,
14; cf. vv. 18-21)? This mention of descendants brings us to
another salvific moment, when an apparent obstacle to the promise
was overcome. After a restatement of the covenant, "Abraham fell
on his face and laughed, 'Shall a child be born to a man who is a
hundred years old? Shall Sarah, who is ninety years old, bear a
child?'" (Gn 17:17). The divine answer, of course, was "yes" (Gn
21:1), and in the understanding of the rabbis from the first century (Le Déaut, La nuit, 151), the birth took place (as did those
of all the patriarchs) on 15 Nisan. Next we come to the third
moment, when God asked for Isaac as a sacrifice (Gn 22:2), and
Abraham's agreement to do so occasioned a confirmation of the pre-

29

vious promise (vv. 16-18). As the age of the principals figured prominently in the Abraham-Sarah section, so now Isaac's age (pace Gn 22:12) is mentioned, and his vision is included (despite the silence of the MT on this point) to explain the blindness to which passing reference is made later in Genesis (27:1). Structurally, then, the second night is understood as the covenantal promise of Gn 15, with the events of Gn 17 and 22 serving as its confirmation.

Within the context of the Poem as a whole, the second night text is disproportionately large. This is plainly intimated by Pseudo-Jonathan, which presents the briefest version, without reference to Gn 17 or 22. In this way, the second night is explicated with a one-sentence reference, as is the case in respect of the other three nights. In the Fragmentary Targum and Neophyti I, the reference to each of the nights is extended midrashically, and in this sense the longer second night text is at home in these versions. Following the reference to the first night (the creation), we find a citation from Gn 1:1-5; allusions to or citations of Ex 4:22; 12:12, 13, 29 (cf. 11:4-9); 15:12, 13 are associated with the third night (Exodus); Jer 30:8 and Ez 30:18 seem to parallel at least some of the language in the messianic fourth night text. In the Neophyti I editio princeps, the first night is referred to in two and one half lines, the second in five lines (and two words of the next), the third in three lines (and two words of the next), the fourth in five lines. The second and fourth night texts in Neophyti (and its companions in presenting the extended Poem) therefore attract special attention in terms of the space devoted to them.

Le Déaut himself is constrained to admit that the provenience of the messiah in the fourth night accords with Amoraic thought, and that "Rome n'est apparue dans notre texte que comme une altération d'un מימרומא primitif (= d'en-haut) sous l'influence de la légende racontée dans Sanh 98a" (La nuit, 369). It is a reasonable inference that the extent of the treatment of the fourth night attests such secondary activity, and the length of the second night reference might be taken as an indication to the same effect. Nonetheless, this argument is in no way conclusive because the fourth night text is sui generis within the Poem, in that it is not so specifically midrashic as the other three. To posit expansion in the second night reference, comparison with the first and third night references is necessary.

Such comparison does in fact suggest the expansion of which the observation of length provoked a suspicion. The mentions of Gn 15 and 17 in the second night text are as explicit as the biblical citations in the first and third night texts. But the reference to Isaac's age and vision are, of course, unbiblical, and to this extent the Isaac-oriented material here is more akin to the expanded messianic material in the fourth night text. Moreover,

30

comparison with the third night text shows the second night Isaac references to be structurally suspect. "To establish what scripture says" is used to introduce the last citation (Ex 4:22) in the third night text; in the second night text it introduces the citation of Gn 17.[23] Remove the Isaac-oriented material, as an ungainly appendage, from the second night text, and it is three lines long, viz., it is of comparable length with the first and third night texts. In a word, these basic observations suggest that, in respect of form and function, this Isaac-oriented material is secondary.

Le Déaut recognizes this, although the present contribution advances more considerations in virtue of which such a recognition is appropriate. He goes so far as to say that the allusion to the Aqedah "dans notre texte paraît être une glose" (La nuit, 153). This is too great an admission, in that "gloss" implies a scribal addition to a literary recension, while our analysis cannot be construed to deny that the second and fourth night texts are organically (if belatedly) targumic. Presumably, he uses the term in a loose way, because he goes on to argue, "cette insertion est aussi sans doute ancienne, puisqu'on la trouve dans toutes les recensions" (La nuit, 153). The latter argument is based on the supposition (expressed on 63, 133, 168) of an early "Palestinian Targum" and on the allegation (cf. 136) of recensional identity in respect of the Aqedah. Both of these are to be examined in turn.

First, Le Déaut is by no means dogmatic on the early provenience of extant Palestinian Targumim. His method is pristine: Targumic exegeses are to be dated with reference to "textes suffisamment datés comme Josèphe, Philon, les Jubilés, le Pseudo-Philon et avec les sources les plus anciennes de la littérature rabbinique" (63, cf. 133). But just this principle makes one doubt the antiquity of the Isaac reference in the second night text. Josephus, the only one of these ancient authorities to discuss the matter, puts Isaac's age at 25; he becomes 37 in Amoraic texts.[24] The vision of Isaac (rather than that of Abraham) is also Amoraic.[25] The texts mentioned by Le Déaut, including the Mekhilta[26] under his last category, simply do not present these details which, it should be stressed, are the very substance of the second night Aqedah allusion.

Le Déaut's second argument for the antiquity of the Isaac insertion is also, taken au pied de la lettre, untenable. It is true enough that Abraham is mentioned in the second night text of Pseudo-Jonathan, the Neophyti margin, Neophyti I, the Fragmentary Targum and, for that matter, Onqelos, but Pseudo-Jonathan, the Neophyti margin and, of course, Onqelos simply do not mention the age or vision of Isaac.[27] Moreover, Le Déaut performed the important service of drawing our attention to biblical and rabbinic passages which indeed present evidence of an ancient association with Passover of some of the themes found in the Poem, but notably not the Aqedah of the second night text.[28]

31

At this stage, it would seem appropriate to propose an amendment to Le Déaut's reconstruction, by suggesting that the reference to the ages of Abraham and Sarah (in respect of Gn 17) in a shorter, more original second night text was completed in the Amoraic period with a reference to the age and vision of Isaac (in respect of Gn 22). A more radical solution would be to posit that the shortest form, that presented in Pseudo-Jonathan, is the earliest, and that the references to Gn 17 and 22 are both secondary.[29] There are three objections to this solution, however: (1) Pseudo-Jonathan has a demonstrably later terminus ad quem than the other Palestinian Targumim,[30] (2) Pseudo-Jonathan is known on occasion, despite its tendency to expatiate, to incline toward a more "literal understanding" and to present "less material which could have been utilized for conveying Christian dogma,"[31] and (3) there is good reason to suspect that Gn 17 was associated with the Poem at an early period (cf. note 28). With Le Déaut and Geza Vermes, I am disposed to infer that Pseudo-Jonathan gives us "le résumé d'un poème primitif plus long, et non un texte primitif bref dont les autres ne seraient que des développements" (La nuit, 136).[32] Our cumulatively substantiated argument is simply that the Isaac-oriented material in the second night text is a post-Christian rather than a pre-Christian "gloss."

The proposed amendment to Le Déaut's reconstruction also explains better than the original scheme does several of his other incisive observations. He sees that the reference to a tradition related to Gn 22 is added "pour compléter le cycle d'Isaac" (La nuit, 137). Insofar as the first two references (i.e., to Gn 15 and 17) in the second night text are to the Abraham cycle, it would seem more accurate to speak of an installation of the Isaac cycle. The point of departure for the addendum is the mention of Abraham's (and Sarah's) age, which invites a comment on Isaac's age at the time of his vision. The relevance of the Aqedah allusion to what precedes is therefore formal, not substantial. In any case, since the allusion does not even mention the binding, it would seem to presuppose that the Aqedah is widely enough known that the mention of a few details would bring the haggadah as a whole to mind.[33] Le Déaut also notes that, since "between the pieces" does not appear in Neophyti I, "la nuit primitive, celle de Gen 15, en liaison étroite avec l'Exode, a donc disparu de ce texte" (La nuit, 139, cf. 147). To speak of the disappearance of the inaugural convenant sacrifice is putting the case too strongly: even when "between the pieces" is excluded, Gn 15 is what is confirmed in Gn 17, and what makes it possible to understand the events described as occurring at night.[34] We may, however, speak of a de-emphasis of Gn 15 in Neophyti I, corresponding to the emphasis on Gn 22. But that is to say that the Aqedah addendum occasioned an alteration in the substance of the second night text. This indicates both that the Isaac-oriented material is secondary and that it is something more than a gloss. Lastly, while Le Déaut insists repeatedly that there was an ancient connection between Passover and Gn 22 (La nuit, 70, 112, 113, 114, 131, 139, 147), he also observes that, as an עולה, the more primitive connection of Gn 22 is with a Tamid-type offering (La nuit, 111, on 1 Chr 21: 113). This is not the place to develop the implications of this fact in detail: it suffices to say that the amended reconstruction better accounts for it than the supposition that the paschal association of Gn 22 and the Aqedah was ancient and unchanging.

This brings us to the end of our consideration, which we might summarize propositionally: the Isaac-oriented material in the second night text is an addendum and, in substance, the addendum is Amoraic. The Poem of the Four Nights can, therefore, no longer be used to substantiate the supposition of a pre-Christian Aqedah.

NOTES

Essay 2 first appeared in Biblica 61 (1980) 78-88.

1   See, above all, "Abraham et le sacrifice d'Isaac" (Chapter III) in La nuit pascale, Essai sur la signification de la Pâque juive à partir du Targum d'Exode XII 42 (AnBib 22; Rome 1963; 1975) 131-212. Cf. his earlier contribution, "La présentation targumique du sacrifice d'Isaac et la sotériologie paulinienne" in Studiorum paulinorum congressus internationalis catholicus 1961. II (AnBib 18; Rome 1963) 563-574. Among those indebted to Le Déaut, the following might be mentioned: R. A. Rosenberg, "Jesus, Isaac and the 'Sufering Servant,'" JBL 84 (1965) 381-388 (who, however, is obviously influenced by Spiegel, whose contribution is discussed below); L. Sabourin, "Aqeda Isaaci et sacrificium paschale in Mysterium paschale et nox messianica," VD 44 (1966) 65-73; J. E. Wood, "Isaac Typology in the New Testament," NTS 14 (1968) 583-589; A. Gaboury, "Deux fils uniques: Isaac et Jésus. Connexions vétéro-testamentaires de Mc 1,11 (et parallèles)," in Studia Evangelica IV (TU 102; Berlin 1968) 198-204; N. A. Dahl, "The Atonement--An Adequate Reward for the Akedah? (Ro 8:32)" in E. E. Ellis and M. Wilcox (eds.), Neotestamentica et Semitica (Edinburgh 1969) 15-29; G. Rouiller, "Le Sacrifice d'Isaac (Genèse 22:1-9)" in F. Bovon and G. Rouiller (eds.), Exegesis. Problèmes de méthode et de lecture (Genèse 22 et Luc 15) (Bibliothèque Théologique; Neuchatel--Paris 1975) 16-35; R. J. Daly, "The Soteriological Significance of the Sacrifice of Isaac," CBQ 39 (1977) 45-75. For a clearly written introduction to the Old Testament story, see R. Kilian, Isaacs Opferung: Zur Uberlieferungsgeschichte von Gen 22 (SBS 44; Stuttgart 1970). In CBQ 40 (1978), 514-546, P. R. Davies and I offer "The Aqedah: a Revised Tradition History," wherein other bibliographical data is to be found.

2   So J. Goldin in S. Spiegel, The Last Trial. On the legends and lore of the command to Abraham to offer Isaac as a sacrifice: the Akedah (New York 1967) XIX-XX.

3   In Jüdische Zeitschrift für Wissenschaft und Leben 10 (1872) 166-171.

4   Geiger, 171

5   "Le sacrifice d'Isaac et la mort de Jésus," REJ 64 (1912) 161-184, 171.

6   Lévi, 171-172.

7   Lévi, 174-175.

8   Lévi, 175-176.

9   Lévi, 176.

10   Lévi, 177.

11   Lévi, 183-184.

12   "The Sacrifice of Isaac in Paul's Theology," JBL 65 (1946) 385-392, 391.

13   E. Lohse, Märtyrer und Gottesknecht (FRLANT; Göttingen 1955) 91.

14   See W. R. Farmer, The Synoptic Problem (London 1964) and H. D. Slingerland, The Testaments of the Twelve Patriarchs (SBLMS 21; Missoula 1977).

15   See n. 2; the development of the essay is discussed on VII-VIII.

16   Spiegel, 103.

17   Spiegel, 88-96.

18   Spiegel, 166-168, and Rosenberg (cited in n. 1).

19   In Scripture and Tradition in Judaism (SPB; Leiden 1961) 193-227 (the second edition appeared in 1973).

20   In The New Testament and the Palestinian Targum to the Pentateuch (AnBib 27; Rome 1966) chapter I. He also summarizes the work of Vermes and Le Déaut on 164-168.

21   Cf. n. 1.

22   As the present study is exegetical, we will leave aside a discussion of the linguistic difficulties in dating Neophyti I in a pre-Christian period. One must, however, at least cite J. A. Fitzmyer, "The Languages of Palestine in the First Century A.D.," CBQ 32 (1970) 501-531 and Grelot's review of McNamara in Bib 48 (1967) 302-306. For a discussion of the relevant passages in Jubilees, Philo, Pseudo-Philo, 4 Maccabees and the Mekhilta, see Davies and Chilton (cited in n. 1). These passages were discussed because they are cited in support of a pre-Christian Aqedah by McNamara (165), Vermes (198) and Le Déaut ("La presentation," 568-569). Summarizing radically, we can say that the last-mentioned source has a second century terminus a quo and should not even be mentioned with non-rabbinic documents (pace McNamara), that the Liber Antiquitatum Biblicarum dates from the second half of the first century at the earliest, and that Josephus also is not a voice from pre-Christian antiquity. Mutatis mutandis, the testimony of 4 Maccabees is also irrelevant. The assurance that

Targumic Aqedah readings are primitive therefore rests on their alleged coherence with Jubilees and Philo. Even a cursory reading shows that their expansions are of a different order from the rabbinic Aqedah.

23   The identical introduction caused a scribe who wrote in the margin of Neophyti to cite Ex 4:22 in the second night. As Díez-Macho notes (editio princeps, 22), "Esta cita escrituraria está desplazada. Pertenece al final de la noche tercera." Prima facie, this seems plausible, but why should anyone include an obvious displacement in the margin? Further, recent research suggests that Neophyti's margin contains references to coherent versions (cf. S. Lund and J. Foster, Variant Versions of Targumic Traditions within Codex Neofiti I (SBLAS 2; Missoula 1977). To this extent, the margin may attest a short second night text, without the Isaac-oriented material, which is what we posit as the earliest version of the tradition.

24   See Spiegel, 48, 49; Daly, 50. Le Déaut (La nuit, 198) ignores the discrepancy in age.

25   Spiegel, 31. Le Déaut's observation (La nuit, 161, cf. 140) that "L'explication de la vision d'Isaac ne doit pas être secondaire dans le récit puisqu'elle a pour but de rendre compte de la cécité du patriarche" is true so far as it goes (cf. Gn 27:1). I would only add that, as such midrashic logic could be applied at any period, elle ne doit pas nécessairement être primitive.

26   Le Déaut's assertion that "Les mentions du sang, et, a fortiori, des cendres d'Isaac paraissent toutes postérieures à l'ère chrétienne" (La nuit, 168, n. 97) damages his case, because the former is mentioned at Mekhilta Exodus 12:13, which is apparently the earliest extant rabbinic dictum relating the Aqedah and Passover. Cf. p. 168: "l'assimilation du sacrifice d'Isaac à un sacrifice expiatoire est une aggadah tardive." I agree, but since the very term "Aqedah" reflects this assimilation, the argument for its pre-Christian date is vitiated.

27   Le Déaut's failure adequately to distinguish between a reference to the biblical, Abraham-oriented Gn 22 and the rabbinic, Isaac-oriented Aqedah is manifest early in his monograph. On page 65, he refers to the "geste d'Abraham, avec sacrifice d'Isaac" as a birth story whose burden is the "vocation d'Abraham."

28   Neh 9 (verses 6; 7-8; 9-21; 22-26) (La nuit, 93); Est 13 (La nuit, 93); Mekhilta de R. Simeon ben Jochai, Hoffmann edition, 27 (La nuit, 151 n. 50). Le Déaut cites the last text by way of making the altogether proper assertion that "Une partie de la tradition juive a placé la naissance d'Isaac un 15 Nisan" (sic).

This opinion does seem to have been common by the end of the first century, which may help us to date the use of Genesis 17 in connection with the second night.

29 This is P. R. Davies's preference, cf. "Passover and the Dating of the Aqedah," JJS 30 (1979) 59-67, 65. His suggestion, however, is purely theoretical, in that it is not developed on the basis of any investigation of Pseudo-Jonathan itself. Nonetheless, the fact that the hypothesis was offered requires that it be answered.

30 In itself, this objection carries little weight; a late document obviously might attest primitive readings.

21 E. Levine, "Some Characteristics of Pseudo-Jonathan Targum to Genesis" Augustinianum 11 (1971), 89-103, 100, 94.

32 Cf. Vermes, 217 n. 2.

33 Le Déaut's citation of T. Cant. 2:17 and T. Mic. 7:20 (La nuit, 137 n. 9) neither helps nor hinders his case. It would help to observe that in the Liber Antiquitatum Biblicarum (18,5) Gn 15 and 22 (without a trace of the Aqedah) are associated. This reflects the exegesis of which the Aqedah allusion of the second night text is a later development.

34 Le Déaut would seem to imply this by printing byn plgy' (from Mahzor Vitry, 308-309 in the Hurwitz edition) in parentheses as part of his Neophyti text (La nuit, 133).

Essay 3--
Recent Discussion of the Aqedah

The publication of my articles on the Aqedah, the first of which
was written with Dr P. R. Davies, has elicited a lucid response
from Dr Robert Hayward.[1] My contributions and Dr Hayward's,
together with those of Davies, represent the discussion of major
texts which have been seen to be relevant to an understanding of
the Aqedah. There is little point in merely reviewing that evidence yet again, especially since the agreement among us is so
significant. A comprehensive, exegetical reader of texts which
relate to Genesis 22 throughout the ancient period is now a
greater necessity than yet another appraisal of what they might
mean. The present purpose is threefold: (1) to comment upon the
new consensus which has emerged, (2) to elucidate points of continuing disagreement, and (3) to introduce a new text of the
Aqedah which has not before featured in scholarly discussion.

--1--

Robert Hayward's contribution is of especial interest, because it
bills itself as the quasi-official communication of a seminar at
the Oriental Institute in Oxford, which met under the chairmanship
of Geza Vermes (pp. 127, 150). As is consistent with the position
of Vermes, Dr Hayward argues that what he calls "the basic substratum of the Targumic Aqedah was in existence by the first
century A.D." (p. 149). Dr Hayward explicitly states that the
Pentateuchal Targums of Genesis 22 "strongly emphasise that he
(sc. Isaac) is an archetypal martyr" (p. 148). The notion that
Isaac is so portrayed in the sources of first century Judaism is
the express finding of Dr Davies's and my analysis (1978, 517-529,
544, 545). Indeed, it was our methodological point that datable
references to Genesis 22 must take precedence over the general
vogue for dating Targums early (pp. 515-517). Dr Hayward cites
Philo, Josephus, 4 Maccabees, and the Liber Antiquitatum
Biblicarum to illustrate his point (pp. 135, 136), the same texts
(and passages) which appear in our article of 1978. Those texts
clearly represent an understanding of Genesis 22 in the first century, an understanding which is to some extent shared in the
Targums. So far, there is perfect agreement among the three of
us. If it is accepted that the portrayal of Isaac as a willing
victim is alone sufficient to warrant the name "Aqedah," then
there is no doubt that the "basic substratum" of the tradition was
current in the first century. But that "if," as we shall see
below, is problematic.

Dr Hayward also acknowledges openly that "certain Targumic traditions require a date later than the first century" (p. 149). He
instances the dispute in Pseudo-Jonathan between Ishmael and

Isaac, a probable reflection of polemic in the Islamic period (pp. 129-132), which is also reflected in Talmud and Genesis Rabbah (p. 130 n. 17). That precise point is made in my analysis of 1978 (p. 543); Dr Hayward's agreement with me on this point is obscured by his omission to cite the source of the idea, but the degree of consensus remains.

Dr Hayward's contribution, in its general procedure of analysis, would appear to reflect a willingness in the Oriental Institute to admit that the provenience of Targumic interpretations of Genesis 22 might be as late as the Islamic period. Such a movement away from the portrayal of a monolithic Aqedah as an exclusively first century doctrine[2] is, in view of the discussions of 1978 and 1980, most welcome.

--2--

Obviously, however, points of disagreement, in both matters of detail and fundamentals, remain. The first of these concerns the interpretation of Philo's De Abrahamo.[3] Dr Hayward cites the notice in De Abrahmo 172, that Abraham and Isaac were of one mind, to conclude that, according to Philo, Isaac knew he was about to be sacrificed (p. 135). He comes to that conclusion, because he explicitly reads the passage in terms of Fragmentary Targums to Genesis 22:10, where Isaac does specifically ask to be bound, lest he struggle, and spoil the sacrifice (p. 135 and n. 53). In fact, however, even a superficial familiarity with De Abrahamo will reveal that the passage cited deals only with the journey to Moriah, not with the moment of the offering, which is specifically explicated more than twenty paragraphs later (198, cf. Davies and Chilton, 1978, 519-521). As a matter of fact, Isaac must ask in 173, "Where is the victim?" The difference from the Fragmentary Targums must be obvious to any critical reader. The point may not seem to be of the greatest moment, since Dr Hayward and I are agreed that a martyrological understanding of Genesis 22 was a feature of Judaism in the first century. But to pluck a sentence out of Philo, and explain it in terms of an undated Targumic passage which renders a different part of the story, is poor practice (pp. 135, 136) and must not be accepted as scholarly procedure.

The failure proves not to be merely procedural. Fragmentary Targums, Neophyti I, and Pseudo-Jonathan expressly refer to the possibility that Isaac, in his struggle, might pollute the sacrifice.[4] Dr. Hayward is concerned to establish that the fully sacrificial understanding of Genesis 22 was already current in the first century, and for that reason he distorts the meaning of the passage in Philo. In fact, Philo's clause does not require a Targumic background in order to be understood; Dr Hayward invokes the Targumim here in a vain attempt to prove their interpretations of Genesis 22 are early. Philo is made to say what must be said

40

for the Targumic Aqedah to be primitive. Circularity so obvious is not frequently found. The argument is necessary for Dr Hayward's position, because he wishes to argue that, in the first century, Isaac was portrayed as consciously accepting the role of "the lamb of sacrifice, who, although not killed, is fully and completely offered" (p. 148). The thought might be worthy of Philo, but he does not actually express it. Instead, Philo argues that the sacrifice was "complete and perfect" purely from the perspective of Abraham's intention; he expressly states that the intended action was not followed through, which is where he parts company with rabbinic exposition of the Aqedah (De Abrahamo 177). The position of the Palestinian Targums, in which Isaac's sacrificial intent features prominently, is not that of Philo. Particularly, Philo's Isaac is not told, as is the Isaac of Neophyti and the Fragmentary Targums, "You are the burnt offering, my son."

Why is it that the Targums stress the sacrificial intention of Isaac himself? That there is such an emphasis is recognized on all sides; my difference with Dr Hayward regards how it should be explained. In our article, Davies and I suggested (1978, 514, 515), taking up an observation of Judah Goldin's, that the term `qdh particularly was applied to the "binding" of Isaac, because it alluded to the manner of tying the lamb of the Tamid prior to its slaughter (Tamid 4:1). That connection was made, because in the same period the rabbis came to view the intention of sacrifice on Moriah as actually accomplished. In the Mekhilta (Pisḥa 78, 79), God is said to recall "the blood of Isaac's Aqedah" when he remarks the blood on the lintels of Israelite houses.[5] Once the Aqedah--now seen as an accomplished sacrifice--is said to happen at Passover time, analogies with the story of Jesus are "discovered" by Christian commentators. The Epistle of Barnabas 7:3 describes Christ as fulfilling the type given in Isaac.[6] Irenaeus, Tertullian, and Origen all compare Isaac carrying the wood to Christ bearing his cross.[7] There is little doubt but that an answering echo of the Jewish exaltation of Isaac can be heard in Christian literature. But the echo reverberates between the two stone walls: in Agadat Bereshit 31, R. Abin is said to mock the claim that God had a son, since even in the case of Isaac God permitted no harm to come to the son of Abraham.[8] The curious thing is, of course, that even by the time Issac's blood (and even his ashes)[9] could be invoked, the standard story of Genesis 22, in which Isaac suffered no harm, could also be used. That is a point to which we must return. For the moment, what is at issue is the phenomenon of Jewish and Christian polemic in the case of Isaac. Just as Christ could be compared to Isaac, so Isaac could be depicted at the entrance to Gehenna,[10] and could be remembered for salvation by "Gentile or Jew, male or woman, slave or maid" (Leviticus Rabbah 2.11, cf. Galatians 3:28). Dr Hayward is ready enough to pick up my comments in regard to the polemical reaction of Judaism to Islam, but he passes in silence over my citation of

41

evidence regarding disputes between Jews and Christians in respect of Genesis 22. There appear to be some blind spots in the Oriental Institute at Oxford.

The most serious failure of vision, however, results in Dr Hayward's refusal to see any substantial development in the Targumim between the first century and the Islamic period. That there should be such an extensive hiatus in their evolution is, of course, quite unlikely. Indeed, the consensus is now against the older view that the extant Targumim derive from the first century.[11] Rather, cumulative composition over a period of centuries seems to have been what produced them.[12] In the light of that development, it is necessary--as I argued in 1978 and 1980--to read the Targums with due sensitivity to their juxtaposition of motifs from various periods, rather than as the works of single, heroically creative authors. Above all, it is necessary to bear in mind what R. Abin taught us (in the last paragraph): one might refer to the unadorned text of Genesis 22 long after the Aqedah (as an account of Isaac's actual death) became known. That is precisely the situation in the extant Targumim at Genesis 22. Dr Hayward quite correctly points out that the Aqedah, strictly defined as involving the death of Isaac, in which he sheds blood and is reduced to ashes, is not expressly mentioned in the passages (pp. 141, 142). But in Pseudo-Jonathan, for example, Abraham and Isaac go to the place of the Temple, where a cloud hovers, they bring figs and palm for the offering, Isaac explicitly asks to be bound, blessing is said to accrue from Isaac, and he is removed from the scene by angels. Why has all this attention been focused on Isaac as a sacrificial offering? On Dr Hayward's reconstruction, an early understanding, according to which Isaac was not actually sacrificed, was kept, from the point of view of essential development, hermetically sealed until the Islamic period, when a new aspect was introduced. I remain convinced that the influence of the rabbinic tradition from the second century onward, that Isaac did die, was no less influential than the traditions of the Koran. My explanation would account for the sacrificial portrayal of Isaac in the Targums; his would not.

My conviction is not merely based on common sense, although the readiness to admit that the Talmud might be more relevant to the study of Targums than non-Jewish traditions does at least seem apposite. As Dr Hayward acknowledges, the term "Aqedah" is actually found in the Pentateuchal Targums (p. 129 n. 13); he also admits that the noun is redolent of the manner of tying the Tamid (p. 136). Despite those indubitable facts, Dr Hayward resists seeing in them any knowledge of the view that Isaac actually died on Moriah as a completed sacrifice, and was resuscitated by God. That is, he denies that the rabbinic Aqedah is reflected in the Targumim. He does so, because the phrases "blood of Isaac," "ashes of Isaac," "blood of Isaac's Aqedah," and the like, do not appear in the Targumic references (p. 129). Indeed, that may be regarded as the main point of his article: he repeatedly insists that the Targums do not refer or allude to Isaac's death (pp. 141, 143), despite their use of the noun "Aqedah."

At this juncture, it becomes obvious why Dr Hayward is at pains to segregate Talmud and Midrash from Targum: the antiquity of the Targumic version of Genesis 22 can scarcely be maintained if the influence of the Tannaim and Amoraim be admitted. Time and research, of course, are steadily eroding the confidence of a previous generation that the Pentateuchal Targums are pre-Tannaitic. More importantly, Dr Hayward can offer no account of why these Targums speak in sacrifical language about Isaac (an observation he grants me), if the rabbinic notion that his sacrifice was completed was not current. Instead of proceeding from the known (the rabbinic doctrine of the Aqedah) to the unknown (the date of the Targumim), Dr Hayward enforces the dogma of early Pentateuchal Targums as a vow of silence upon rabbinic literature. By using the Targums to define rabbinic theology, the old fallacy of _ignotum per ignotius_ degenerates in his hands into _notum per ignotum_. Finally, and most obviously, Dr Hayward's analysis takes no account whatever of the nature of the Targums as translations. There is regularly in the Targums a tension between two constraints, the necessity of rendering the Hebrew Bible plausibly, and the desire to reflect those haggadic expansions which had become part of the community's life. For that reason, no Targumic rendering of Genesis 22 uses the precise language of Talmud or Midrash, on the one hand, or of the Masoretic text, on the other. Dr Hayward's expectation, that the Targums should represent the rabbinic "party line" (in his words, p. 145), seems naïve in the extreme.

Dr Hayward's failure adequately to discuss the "Poem of the Four Nights" appears particularly lamentable in this context. He acknowledges my finding that the reference to the Aqedah therein is secondary (pp. 140, 141, and the previous essay),[13] but contends that the addition is pre-Christian (p. 145). That he does so without argument makes it difficult to imagine why his confidence on this point is so great. Particularly, he does not explain why Isaac is explicitly described as "offered" in the Poem, unless it is because the notion that he had in fact been sacrificed was current. Similarly, Dr Hayward merely reasserts the old point of view, popularized by Dr Vermes, that the connection of Genesis 22 to Passover was pre-Christian (p. 145). In this case, his confidence is not only expressed without reference to evidence, but despite it. Dr Hayward knows very well that "the Aqedah has connections with _all_ lamb offerings" (p. 147), so that it seems reasonable to argue its natural association with the daily offering, the Tamid, which had been taken as paradigmatic of sacrifice since the time of Daniel (12:11). The very term, "Aqedah," supports that argument, and Dr Hayward cites the evidence from Mishnah without offering any explanation of it (p. 130).

Dr Hayward concludes that "the Targumists moulded ancient interpretations in the light of events of their own times" (p. 150). I can only agree, but would also express the hope that in future such a theoretical willingness to recognize the plasticity of the Aqedah during the period of the Tannaim and Amoraim might influence his exegesis of the Targums more directly. Above all, Midrash and Talmud must be permitted to reflect the rabbinic ethos and ideology which is part of the background of the Targums.

--3--

The means by which Aramaic renderings of the Hebrew text can allude to a rich haggadic lore are exemplified by the marginal reading of the Codex Reuchlinianus, beginning at Targum Isaiah 33.7, which presents a rather full reference to the Aqedah:[14]
(a) Behold, when I revealed myself to Abraham, their father, and I promised to give him Isaac, he believed in my Memra. And after that, the second time, when I commanded that he offer him up as a burnt offering, he did not delay, but went and built the altar on Mount Moriah, and offered him up as a burnt offering. (b) All the angels of the height arose, quaking messengers, shaking messengers, and were crying out back to their place, saying, Lord of the world, is this not Abraham, the righteous, for whose virtue the world is founded? To him you gave a son after one hundred years, and you promised him, "By Isaac sons will be named after you." But the messengers of peace which stood in the camp of the Shekhinah were weeping in bitterness until mercies were revealed, and I had pity on him. (c) Now the righteous are destroyed, who walked in the paths of the fathers of the world. The faithful have ceased, who walked in ways that are correct before me. They have changed the covenants of the law. Because when they were cast away from their cities and went into exile, the sons of men did not consider him. Those who dwelt in the land mourned the devastation, and the sanctuary was destroyed. The city of Jerusalem lies waste, as the wilderness; the walls are demolished; those who produced hard things are as Bashan and Carmel.
This is not the place to pursue a linguistic study of this passage, which would require reference to the whole of the alternative recension of the Targum which is represented in the margin of the Codex Reuchlinianus. It is, however, necessary to mention that certain saliant features appear to be late, e.g., the use of the participle for past continuous action (without the use of the verb "to be"), the Greek loan word "angel," and the use of 'rum for "that," as in Pseudo-Jonathan.[15] The mention of Pseudo-Jonathan might be apposite, because Abraham may be understood here to be told that Isaac, rather than Ishmael, will

44

represent his progeny (cf. Genesis 21:12). Indeed, the image of the Aqedah is here invoked by allusion, rather than reference. Genesis 22 is specified as the second test of Abraham, who is said to have "offered up" (slq) his son. The verbal usage implies that the action was actually carried out.[16]

The angelic witnesses of earlier representations, who merely attest the marvel of what unfolds,[17] become active mediators in paragraph "b"; by word or pathos they coax God to remember his promise. What they have to say, referring to Abraham's age, evokes the "Poem of the Four Nights," just as the bare statement that God "had pity" must allude to miraculous intervention (as well as to Genesis 22:12, 16), if Abraham actually offered up his son. It is precisely the themes of angelic mediation, and of Isaac's resurrection (even reconstitution) which is established by the Amoraic period.[18] The Targum does not establish the existence of these motifs, but it does operate on the basis of them. That is why the "Poem of the Four Nights" can be so laconically evoked, for example by means of a reference to the "second test."[19]

The intensity of religous insight in the passage becomes plainest when its literary transformation of antecedents is considered. The main text of the Targum of Isaiah 33.7 reads as follows:

> Behold, when it will be revealed to them, the messengers of the Gentiles will cry out in bitterness; those who went to announce peace return to weeping in soulful bitterness.

The innovative features of the main text (indicated in italics) indicate clearly that a transformation of meaning has already taken place at the level of the primary meturgeman(in) of the Targum. The Masoretic text refers simply to the cry of valiant ones, who are identified as the Gentiles in the Targum. The transformation is plausible as an account of the underlying Hebrew text, but it is also quite specific in its innovations. The margin of Reuchlinianus is, on the other hand, effectively a targum of a targum. The use of the verb gl' in the main text occasions "I revealed myself" and "mercies were revealed" in the margin, all by way of invoking the precise image of the second night in the "Poem of the Four Nights" (paragraph "a"). That leading idea is carried through the second paragraph, where "in bitterness" (albeit in differing forms) represents another point of contact between the main text and the margin of Reuchlinianus. The precise word for "messengers" ('zgdy) in the main text is not exactly mirrored in the margin, but the idea is reflected in 'ngly and ml'ky.

The third paragraph of the addition ("c") is better considered a transformation of vv. 8, 9 in the Targum than a part of the expansion of v. 7. The main text reads:

> The highways lie waste, the wayfaring men cease. Because they changed the covenant, they will be cast

45

away from their cities; the sons of men did not consider
that the evil was coming upon them. The land mourns and
is desolate; Lebanon is dried up and fades; Sharon is
like the desert; Bashan and Carmel are devastated.

The marginal text clearly represents a transformation of the specifically Targumic understanding of Isaiah 33.8, 9, with its
reference to exile in the verb "to be cast away," as well as the
normal idiom, "the sons of men."[20] But the transformation itself
is more striking than any borrowing. The reference to "the righteous" and "the faithful" passing away derives from no text but
experience, as the reader is told that the community's destruction, the physical ruin of the sanctuary (innovatively derived
from "Lebanon")[21] and of Jerusalem constitute Israel's
anti-Aqedah. What might have been, as in the case of Isaac, was
not, because there was none worthy of angelic pleading for the
divine mercy.

The terrible transformation of the text by the meturgeman
alludes, of course, to the complete destruction of Jerusalem at
the order of Hadrian. It is a stark reminder that an interpreter
of the main text had been disastrously wrong in his confident
assertion, "a temple of the nations shall never be built in
Jerusalem" (25.2). But the language of the margin, and (more particularly) its reversal of a highly developed appreciation of the
Aqedah, reflects the period after Muslim ascendance. A more precise designation of the marginal meturgeman(in) must await a
comprehensive treatment of the marginal additions. For the
moment, however, the point is amply demonstrated that the text of
the Aqedah, in its many forms, modulations, and reversals, is not
only Genesis 22, but the social experience of Israel.

NOTES

1   The section concerning "Intertestamental" literature was Davies's contribution to "The Aqedah: A Revised Tradition History," CBQ 40 (1978) 514-546. The previous essay in this volume represents the next step in discussion. C. T. R. Hayward's article, "The Present State of Research into the Targumic Account of the Sacrifice (sic) of Isaac," appeared in JJS 32 (1981) 127-150. Cf. also his brief appendix, "The Aqedah," in Sacrifice (ed. M. F. C. Bourdillon and M. Fortes; London: Academic Press, 1980) 84-87, and A. J. Saldarini, "Interpretation of the Akedah in Rabbinic Literature," The Biblical Mosaic. Changing Perspectives: Semeia Studies (Philadelphia: Fortress, 1982) 149-165; J. Swetnam, Jesus and Isaac. A Study of the Epistle to the Hebrews in the Light of the Aqedah (Rome: Biblical Institute, 1981); P. R. Davies, "Passover and the Dating of the Aqedah," JJS 30 (1979) 59-67, another version of which appears as "The Sacrifice of Isaac and Passover," Studia Biblica 1978 I (ed. E. A. Livingstone; Sheffield: JSOT, 1979) 127-132.

2   Cf. G. Vermes, "Redemption and Genesis xxii--The Binding of Isaac and the Sacrifice of Jesus," Scripture and Tradition in Judaism. Haggadic Studies: Studia Post-Biblica 9 (Leiden: Brill, 1961) 193-227.

3   Cf. F. H. Colson, Philo VI: The Loeb Classical Library (Cambridge: Harvard University Press, 1935).

4   Cf. M. L. Klein, The Fragment-Targums of the Pentateuch According to their Extant Sources: Analecta Biblica 76 (Rome: Biblical Institute, 1980); A. Diez Macho, Neophyti I. Targum Palestinense Ms de la Biblioteca Vaticana (Madrid: Consejo Superior de Investigaciones Científicas, 1968); D. Rieder, Pseudo-Jonathan: Targum Jonathan ben Uziel (sic) on the Pentateuch (Jerusalem: Salmon, 1974); M. Ginsburger, Pseudo-Jonathan (Thargum Jonathan ben Usiël zum Pentateuch) Nach der Londoner Handschrift (Brit. Mus. 27031) (Hildeshein: Olms, 1971).

5   Cf. J. Z. Lauterbach, Mekilta de-Rabbi Ishmael: The Schiff Library (Philadelphia: Jewish Publication Society, 1949) 56, 57. As Lauterbach's note, and the text itself, make unmistakably clear, the Mekhilta does not associate the Aqedah with Passover alone.

6   Cf. L. W. Barnard, "Is the Epistle of Barnabas a Paschal Homily?" Studies in the Apostolic Fathers and Their Background (Oxford: Blackwell, 1966) 73-85.

7   For citations, cf. Davies and Chilton (1978) 538, 539 For further discussion, cf. K. Hruby, "Exégèse rabbinique et exégèse patristique," Exégèse Biblique et Judaïsme (ed. J. E. Ménard;

Strasbourg: Faculté de théologie catholique, 1973) 187-215; J.
Daniélou, "La typologie d'Isaac dans le christianisme primitif,"
Biblica 28 (1947) 363-393; D. Lerch, Isaaks Opferung christlich
gedeutet. Eine Auslegungsgeschichtliche Untersuchung: Beiträge
zur historischen Theologie 12 (Tübingen: Mohr, 1950). The imagery
is taken up in Genesis Rabbah 56.3, cf. Davies and Chilton (1978)
539.

8   Cf. S. Spiegel (tr. J. Goldin), The Last Trial. On the
Legends and Lore of the Command to Abraham to Offer Isaac as a
Sacrifice: The Akedah (New York: Random, 1967) 83 n. 26.

9   Cf. Spiegel (1967) 38-50. For a discussion of such references, cf. Vermes (1961) 205-208. The curious thing about his
contribution is that, while Vermes emphasizes that the rabbinic
Aqedah was innovative in its treatment of Genesis 22, he insists
upon reading the Targumim in isolation from rabbinic thought.
Instead, he attempts to link the Targumic Aqedah of Genesis 22 to
a supposed theology of Isaiah 53 (pp. 202-204). Such a reading
of Isaiah 53, of course, is only possible if the Isaiah Targum is
ignored, and if the understanding of "the Suffering Servant" which
once reigned in biblical circles is accepted. Neither of those
conditions is tolerable within a critical approach.

10   Cf. Song of Songs Rabbah 8.9 and E. Lohse, Märtyrer und
Gottesknecht. Untersuchungen zur christlichen Verkündigung vom
Sühntod Jesu Christi: FRLANT (Göttingen: Vandenhoeck und
Ruprecht, 1963) 91.

11   Cf. Vermes (1961).

12   Cf. E. Levine, "La evolución de la Biblia aramea," Estudios
Bíblicos 39 (1981) 223-248.

13   See also M. McNamara, Palestinian Judaism and the New
Testament: Good News Studies 4 (Wilmington: Glazier, 1983) 226.

14   The text, with slight emendations, is as reproduced in A.
Sperber, The Bible in Aramaic III (Leiden: Brill, 1962) 65. For
Sperber's comments on the edition of Lagarde, and therefore of
Stenning also, cf. volume IVB (1973) 18, 19.

15   Cf. The Glory of Israel 7-11 for a discussion of such
issues. Similarity with the Fragmentary Targums is not, of
course, to be excluded on the grounds of a comparison with
Pseudo-Jonathan, and structurally the affinity of the marginal
recension with the former is much greater.

16   Cf. Leviticus 9:17 in Onqelos, and G. Dalman,
Aramäisch-neuhebräisches Handwörterbuch zu Targum, Talmud und
Midrasch (Hildesheim: Olms, 1967) 292. The usage of slq here may

be regarded as a development beyond that of qrb in the "Poem of the Four Nights."

17   For the feature of angelic praise, cf. Pseudo-Jonathan and the Fragmentary Targums, Genesis 22:9. This feature helps to establish the provenience of the reading, since Isaiah 33:7 was read in association with Genesis 22 within a cycle of lections, cf. Genesis Rabbah 56.5 and Spiegel (1967) 149 n. 68.

18   Cf. Spiegel, p. 44: "There is no doubt about it. The haggadah about the ashes of Isaac who was consumed by fire like an animal sacrifice, and of whose remains nothing was left except the sacrificial ash, is ancient indeed, and its traces are already visible in the first generation of the Amoraim..." Cf. especially pp. 42, 43 for the efficacy of these ashes, and pp. 28-37 for the resurrection of Isaac.

19   The references is at odds with the tradition which saw Genesis 22 as the tenth, and final, test, cf. Neophyti I and the Fragmentary Targum (V).

20   The theologumenon of exile, of course, appears ubiquitously in the Targum, cf. The Glory of Israel, 28-33.

21   Cf. G. Vermes, "Lebanon--The historical development of an exegetical tradition," Scripture and Tradition in Judaism (cf. n. 2) 26-39.

ESSAY 4 --
The Temple in the Targum of Isaiah

The term היכלא, which is cognate to היכל in Hebrew, appears in the Targum (Tg) only as a translation of its Hebrew equivalent in the Masoretic Text (MT). It does so when both terms evidently refer to the Temple in Jerusalem (6:1, cf. v. 4 in the Tg; 44:28; 66:4), and also--on one occasion--when the referent is the royal palace in Babylon (39:7).[1] In these passages, the meturgeman betrays no obvious interest in the Temple, much less anything like a theology of the Temple.

The case is globally different when we consider another locution, בית מקדשא "sanctuary house." The phrase appears some twenty-four times in the Tg; "my sanctuary house" occurs six times, "my sanctuary" once, "your sanctuary" once, and "sanctuary of the Mount of Zion" once. (The phrase "house of their sanctuaries" also appears.)[2] On one occasion (60:13), the meturgeman uses the phrase when there is a usage of מקדש (its cognate) in the MT, probably in the sense "sanctuary." But in two passages, the meturgeman does not render מקדש in the MT with בית מקדשא. In the first (8:14), the Hebrew term is used with "stone of offense" and "rock of stumbling;" the meturgeman evidently came to the conclusion that God's wrath, not his Temple, was at issue. He accordingly rendered מקדש as "an avenger." In the second passage (16:12), the meturgeman refused to use "sanctuary house" in respect of Moab's temple, despite the presence of מקדש in the MT. Instead, he spoke of "his idol house." Obviously, the significance of the meturgeman's בית מקדשא language lies not only in the fact that it is more frequent than the מקדש language of the MT. The fact that the meturgeman does not alwayts exploit the etymological possibilities of the latter shows that he is thinking rather precisely of God's own Temple when he uses the phrase. Given that this is his understanding of בית מקדשא, it is not surprising that the meturgeman used the phrase to render passages in the MT which speak of God's house either specifically (cf. 2:2; 6:4; 37:1, 14; 38:20, 22; 56:5, 7) or--as he thought--implicitly (cf. 10:32; 22:8; 38:2; 52:11).

There are, however, instances in which the meturgeman's use of the phrase is quite startling when one considers the corresponding passage in the MT. The reading at 30:20 offfers a suitable point of departure:

> And the LORD will give you the possessions of the adversary and the plunder of the one who distresses, and he will not any more take up his Shekhinah from the sanctuary house, but your eyes will see the Shekhinah in the sanctuary house.

If this passage rendered an explicit reference in the MT to the destruction of the Temple, or something associated with that event, one might conclude that it was simply a vivid way of speaking of the destruction of 587 B.C. The departure of the Shekhinah at that time is a convention within rabbinic theology.[21] As it happens, however, the MT refers to nothing of the kind:

And the Lord will give you bread of adversity and waters of affliction, and your teacher will no more be in a corner, but your eyes will see your teacher.

The removal of God's Shekhinah, his presence in the cult, appears to have been a preoccupation of the meturgeman's which no appeal to etymology or the vicissitudes of translating a difficult text alone can explain. There is within the Tg a tendency to see the eschatological Temple as a place of authoritative teaching (cf. 2:3), but that scarcely explains why the meturgeman here innovatively refers to the departure of the Shekhinah. A possible explanation of the meturgeman's practice is that, as he rendered a text which referred to the catastrophe of 587 B.C., the events of A.D. 70 came to expression. This suspicion is perhaps confirmed by the statement in the MT that "a citadel (אַרְמוֹן) is abandoned" is rendered by the meturgeman, "the sanctuary house is desolate" (32:14). The verb here translated "desolate" might also be reproduced in English as "ruined" or "destroyed;" the meturgeman normally employs חרוב to render the cognate verb in the MT, but also such verbal roots εs אחם ("scorch"), נבל ("wither"), אכל ("eat"), מלל ("fade"), נדך ("drive"), נשא ("take up), עזב ("forsake"), נפל ("fall"), and ערר ("strip"). There is no doubt but that physical desolation is in mind. The desolation of the Temple was sufficiently vivid in the meturgeman's awareness for him to render the MT in a creative manner, so as to call attention to it.

Whatever the past may have taught the meturgeman, his hope was no less vivid. At 24:16a, he felt able to write:

From the sanctuary house, whence joy is about to go forth to all the inhabitants of the earth, we hear a song for the righteous.

There follows a vision of the reward promised to the righteous and the punishment which is in store for the wicked. The MT reads differently here; songs are rather heard "from the end of the earth," and the idea of eschatological reward and punishment is absent from the argument. In practical terms, the Targumic rendering amounts to a reversal in the geographical sense of the Hebrew original. The idea of universal song in the MT has been transformed by the meturgeman's conviction into the hope that the sanctuary in particular is to be the epicentre of eschatological joy: the statement in respect of the sanctuary appears again in the prayer of Hezekiah (38:11) without any even remotely similar wording being present in the MT. Quite evidently, the meturgeman's expectation that the sanctuary would be the focus of a new movement of rejoicing was as strong as his awareness that it had been destroyed.

By implication, the sanctuary must be restored before the
desired end can come, and the meturgeman was not slow to spell out
how, and even by whom, restoration--including the return of the
Shekhinah (cf. 52:8)--would come (53:5):

And he (that is, the Messiah, cf. 52:13) will build the
sanctuary house which was profaned by our debts, handed
over by our iniquities; and by his teaching his peace
will increase upon us, and in that we attach ourselves
to his words our debts will be forgiven to us.

It is a well recognized feature of this "servant song" in the Tg
that the Messiah is pre-eminently an exalted and triumphant figure, while the reference to his weakness in the MT is transferred
to the exiled community.[3] Even given that principle of transformation, however, the reference to the rebuilding of the sanctuary
seems, on a purely linguistic basis, all but impossible to derive
from the MT:

And he was wounded for our transgressions, bruised for
our iniquities; the chastisement of our peace was upon
him, and by his stripes it is healed to us.

Certain features of this interpretation can be explained with reference to exegetical convention: healing is on other occasions
understood as forgiveness by the meturgeman (cf. 6:10; 57:18, 19).
There is also a degree of word play evident in this passage: "profaned" (אִיתַחֵל) takes up the cognate root of "wounded" (מְחֹלֵל) in
the MT, but in a different sense, and "handed over" (from the
Aramaic root מְסַר) is inspired by "chastisement" (מוּסַר) in the MT.
But such instances of play and habit are just that; they do not
explain how the original transformation of the Hebrew text took
place in the Tg. For such an explanation, one must have recourse
to the theology of the meturgeman.

The focus of the Isaiah Targum is on the messianic vindication
of Israel.[4] By means of various characteristic terms and phrases,
such as "law," "Jerusalem," "exile," "house of Israel," "repentance," "prophets," "Shekhinah," "righteous," and "Messiah," the
hope that the exiled house of Israel will be restored is
expressed. The restoration includes, in the expectation of the
meturgeman, an actual return of the chosen people to the promised
land, the rebuilding of the Temple by a Messiah who removes the
yoke of the Gentiles, and the descent of the Shekhinah. The engine
of this restoration is repentance. Repentance involves attending
to the words of the prophets and obeying the law: such are the
marks of the righteous.

Quite evidently, the בֵּית מִקְדְשָׁא theologoumenon which is under
discussion fits within the theology of messianic vindication which
has been described. Indeed, it is part and parcel of it. But at
this point, a qualification requires to be introduced. The theology sketched above comes to expression by means of the terms and
phrases cited, among others. They are repeatedly used throughout
the Tg, as is בֵּית מִקְדְשָׁא, and correspond to render various word-

ings in the MT. They have a life of their own, as does בית מקדשא,
in that their usage cannot be explained by reference to linguistic
and translational factors alone. I have called the entire edifice
of such characteristic language the exegetical framework of the
Isaiah Targum.[5]

By using the concept "exegetical framework," I do not mean to
assign a single theology, much less a single date, to the Tg. By
definition, Targums are a species of folk literature in their origin: translational practice in synagogues gradually coalesced
towards the production of literary works. But from an early stage,
rabbis expressed an active interest in the use of Targums, and
gradually came to exert a powerful influence on the wording
employed in them. The emergence of written Targums signals the
relative pre-eminence of the interpretations contained in them,
and also the attempt to produce a consistently exegetical account
of the biblical book concerned. The exegetical framework of the
Isaiah Targum represents precisely such an attempt at consistency;
it is the framework within which earlier material was presented,
and served also as an occasion for later developments. By its
nature, the exegetical framework does not represent a terminus a
quo, or ad quem, of Targumic development. It simply provides a
point at which our consideration and discussion may begin. Indeed,
I have been led to distinguish between an Amoraic level and
Tannaitic level within the framework of the Isaiah Targum.[6]
Although the two levels share the theology already described,
there seems to me to be a clear difference of emphasis between
saying, "a worship house of the Gentiles will never be built in
Jerusalem," as is said within the Tannaitic level of the framework
(25:2),[7] and saying, "I sigh for all those who are sighing from
before the king of Babylon," as is said within the Amoraic level
of the framework (21:2).[8] In that both renderings are quite innovative, it seems wise to explain them with reference to the
awareness of the meturgemanin. The first statement, an outstand-
ingly confident assertion, has a fairly obvious terminus ad quem,
since in A.D. 136 the temple of Jupiter Capitolinus was dedicated
in Jerusalem. On the other hand, the second statement would appear
to reflect difficulties experienced by the meturgeman under the
Sassanian régime in Babylon. Obviously, these are only examples of
a much larger body of evidence, but I believe they suggest, in
themselves, that we must reckon with the provenience of the Tg as
from distinct times and places, just as we must reckon with a plu-
rality of unknown interpreters.

The concentration of the framework on the בית מקדשא would
appear to belong to its earlier, Tannaitic level. In his classic
monograph, "Die Eschatologie der jüdischen Gemeinde," Paul Volz
describes a theology of return and vindication very much like that
of the Isaiah Targum, and he assigns it to the period of what we
would now call early Judaism.[9] Indeed, as Volz points out, the
hope for a glorious rebuilding of the Temple is already expressed

in Tobit 13:10; 14:5; only the clear reference to the situation after A.D. 70 in the Tg provides a later terminus a quo for its framework.

Within this generally comprehensible picture of בית מקדשא usage in the Tg, at least one passage appears perplexing. In 22:22, where in the MT Eliakim is promised "the key of the house of David," the Tg reads, "the key of the sanctuary house and the rule of the house of David." When one looks elsewhere in Rabbinica for a similar exegesis, the mystery of Eliakim's elevation to priestly status is confirmed, but not explained. In Leviticus Rabbah (5.5 [in respect of 16:32 in the MT]), the following comment is made of Shebna, Eliakim's predecessor:

> R. Eleazar said he was a high priest, R. Judah said he was a warden (אמרכול). For the opinion of R. Eleazar, who said he was high priest, there is the text, "and I will clothe him with your robe" (Is. 22:21a). For the opinion of R. Judah ben Rabbi, who said he was a warden, there is the text, "and your rule I will place in his hand" (v. 21b).[10]

In the case of both of the opinions cited in Leviticus Rabbah (cf. Exodus Rabbah 37.1), the assumption is that statements made in respect of Eliakim in the MT apply equally to Shebna. But while the emphasis of Leviticus Rabbah falls on Shebha, that of the Isaiah Targum falls on Eliakim. In the Tg, Eliakim is promised a "cincture" (v. 21), and the reliance on him of "the priests wearing the ephod," and "the sons of the Levites taking the harps" (v. 24). All this is consequent on the fact that "the turban" (v. 18), which is a seal of high priestly office for the meturgeman (cf. 28:1, 4), has been transferred to him. But we should not imagine that the meturgeman's interpretation coheres exclusively with the view of R. Eleazar. As in the explanation of R. Judah ben Rabbi (but in respect of Shebna), Eliakim is called a "warden" (אמרכל) in the Tg (22:23, 25, both times innovatively, for יתד ["peg"] in the MT).

Does the Tg represent a compromise, a synthesis of the two points of view expressed in Leviticus Rabbah? Or does it rather represent the sort of interpretation which occasioned the more qualified exegesis of the two rabbis at a later stage? Either alternative would appear viable. "Judah ben Rabbi" in Leviticus Rabbah is presumably the grandson of R. Judah ha-Nasi, known as "Rabbi."[11] That would place the speaker at the beginning of the Amoraic period, while he had a slightly earlier contemporary named R. Eleazar ben R. Elkeazar ha-Kappar, who is reckoned to have lived towards the end of the Tannaitic period.[12] This would place the expression of the two opinions in the later second, or early third, century. If, on the other hand, the "Judah" of the opinion is taken unqualified--as in the Yalkut Shim'oni-- then the opinion can be placed in the second century, with Eleazar taken as ha-Kappar himself, or any of the other rabbis of the time who bore this common name.[13] Because the exegetical framework of the Tg took shape over a long period, the opinions expressed in Leviticus Rabbah are explicable, both as its precedent and as its outcome, even in the face of the vagaries of rabbinic attributions.

The fact that it is possible chronologically to coordinate the opinions expressed in Leviticus Rabbah and the Tg should not, however, be taken to suggest they are exegetically homogenous. They pursue distinctive tendencies. The point of both exegeses in Leviticus Rabbah is that Shebna is and remains high priest or warden. The same can be said of the unattributed opinion in Exodus Rabbah 37:1. There, Zechariah 10:4 ("out of them shall come a peg [יחד]) is associated with the high priest who is "as a peg in a sure place" (Is. 22:23). The Tg would appear at first to follow a similar line, "And I will appoint him a faithful warden ministering in an enduring place" (v. 23). (The adjective "faithful" is equivalent to "sure" in the MT; only the shift from "peg" to "warden" occasions the slight change in sense.) But a radical change in tack occurs at v. 25:

> In that time, says the LORD of hosts, a faithful warden
> ministering in an enduring place will depart; and he
> will be cut down and fall and the oracle of prophecy
> that was concerning him will be void, for by the Memra
> of the LORD it is so decreed.

To some extent, this change is occasioned by the MT, which already speaks of the "peg" giving way. But the MT does not require the metaphor of the "peg" to be taken so directly of the "warden" Eliakim, and it provides no occasion on which to say that any prophecy concerning him will be void. These are innovations in the Tg which take it in the opposite direction from that pursued in Exodus and Leviticus Rabbah.

The conditions which brought about this seemingly odd innovation are to a limited extent evident from the Tg itself. In the first place, there is the reference, in both the MT and the Tg, to figures named Eliakim and Shebna in 36:3, 11, 22; 37:2, in connection with the embassy of Rabshakeh. The prophecy of Isaiah in 39:5-7 makes it plain that the house of Hezekiah is a temporary administration, and in this regard the exegesis of the Tg makes better sense of the entire book of Isaiah than do Exodus and Leviticus Rabbah. But a second condition of the Targumic innovation is perhaps the more important. In v. 18, the threat against Shebna is not only that his turban will be removed, but that the LORD "will encircle you with enemies as an encircling wall and he will exile you to a land of wide hands." (The MT reads: "he will whirl you around, a winding, he will throw you like the ball into a land wide of hands.") Quite evidently, the meturgeman did not absolutely require anything but a knowledge of the siege of 587 B.C. to write what he did. On the other hand, knowledge that another siege had recently been successful is perhaps a more plausible condition of the rendering. The use of the language of "encircling" (which involved the verb נקף) elsewhere in the Tg makes the latter alternative even more attractive. It is often used in the context of military conflict (15:8; 22:5; 29:2; cf. 3:16, 24; 5:8; 37:3). Of these usages, that at 29:2 is perhaps the most striking for the present purpose:

Yet I will distress the city where the altar is, and it will be desolate and evacuated, and it will be encircled before me with the blood of the slain as the encircling of the altar with the blood of holy sacrifices all around on the feast day.

The imagery of the bloody siege is far more vivid than the comparatively dry oracle concerning "Ariel" in the MT; indeed, it is so vivid that one is tempted to speak of the meturgeman's experience, not merely of his knowledge, of the siege. The previous verse in the Tg permits us to be more confident of this possibility:

Ho the altar, the altar which they build in the city where David settled, from before the gathering of armies which are gathered against it in the year the feasts cease in you.

In this case, etymological play is again evident in the Tg. The verb יסף in the MT is taken as "cease" (Hebrew סוף, Aramaic נבט) rather than "add;" נקף in the MT is used in the sense of running through a cycle, but its cognate appears in v. 2 to describe military encircling. But the especially significant feature is the link between the siege and the cessation of feasts. This is reminiscent of Josephus' report of the end of the Roman siege, which is associated with the cessation of sacrifice, in Bellum Judaicum 6.2.1 § 94.

In a recent study, Arie van der Kooij has argued that Shebna and Eliakim in the Tg represent Aristobolus II and Hyrcanus II, and that the Roman activity involved is that directed by Pompey.[14] This argument can only be sustained, however, by means of an atomistic reading of 22:15-25. As soon as 29:1,2 are taken into account, and it is remembered that frequent allusion is made to the destruction of the Temple in the Tg, Shebna and Eliakim seem not to refer merely to priestly figures from the first century B.C. But why are these biblical names used by the meturgeman at all? For him, it would seem that their very lack of validly priestly genealogy makes them appropriate types of the Temple system before A.D. 70: the entire point of the prophecy concerning them is that the prophecy will be annulled (22:25). That such an exegesis was developed later among the rabbis to refer to ordinary priesthood seems a more plausible progression than the reverse, that Shebna and Eliakim were first of all thought of as priests on a permanent basis, and that the meturgeman deliberately changed the received exegesis in order to speak of a limited régime. The latter progression would still leave open the question of why Shebna and Eliakim were chosen as priestly types in the first place, which our proposal would account for.

The image of a temporary régime which is under judgment is also evoked in 28:1,4, where woe is pronounced against one who "gives the turban to the wicked one of the sanctuary house" (MT: "fading flower of his glorious beauty"). A highly critical attitude is manifested against an evidently secular ruler who has the high priesthood in his gift. Such an attitude would be appropriate throughout the entire period of the Herodian settlement, that is, until the destruction of the Temple. Taking the evidence of chapter 22 together with that of chapter 28, it would appear that the Tannaitic framework of the Isaiah Targum includes attacks on the lax administration of the Temple, and so to some extent has a pre-A.D. 70 provenience. Indeed, the meturgeman of this early stratum called the high priest "wicked," which accords with the language of the Qumran group. W.H. Brownlee argued shortly before his death that "the wicked priest" could no longer be identified with an historical individual.[15] If the Tg is any analogy, perhaps no particular person was ever in mind.[16] The purpose of the meturgeman seems to have been first of all to attack the entire Temple system, and then to explain the success of the Roman siege with reference to that administration. The suggestion of an analogy to Essene language (if that is what it is) is not intended to imply that the meturgeman was himself a member of any group such as the Qumran community. The implication is rather that the meturgeman shared with some of his contemporaries an attitude towards the Temple which was critical. Indeed, his attitude was so hardened that the high priestly régime could be thought of as responsible for the success of the Roman siege. For the meturgeman of the Tannaitic framework, even the disaster of the Shekhinah's departure was a just punishment of "the wicked one of the sanctuary house" (28:1,4). And it was to be followed by repentance, the delight of the righteous in the rule of the Messiah, and the pilgrimage of all peoples to the restored Temple. As the meturgeman would have said--and often did say--"by the Memra of the LORD it is so decreed."

Essay 4 was first presented to a meeting of the European Association for Jewish Studies in Oxford (1984).

1 Cf. J.B. van Zijl, A Concordance to the Targum of Isaiah: Society of Biblical Literature Aramaic Series 3 (Missoula: Scholars, 1979) and A. Sperber, The Bible in Aramaic III. The Latter Prophets (Leiden: Brill, 1962).

2 Cf. van Zijl, 110, 111.

2' Cf. A.M. Goldberg, Untersuchungen über die Vorstellung von der Schekhinah (Berlin: de Gruyter, 1969).

3 Cf. P. Humbert, "Le Messie dan le Targoum des Prophètes," Revue de Théologie et de Philosophie 43, 44 (1910, 1911) 420-447, 5-46; R.A. Aytoun, "The Servant of the Lord in the Targum," Journal of Theological Studies 23 (1921-2) 172-180; H. Hegermann, Jesaja 53 in Hexapla, Targum, und Peschitta: Beiträge zur Förderung Christlicher Theologie 56 (Güterloh: Bertelsmann, 1954); S.R. Driver, A. Neubauer, The Fifty-Third Chapter of Isaiah according to the Jewish Interpreters (New York: Ktav, 1969); K. Koch, "Messias und Sündenvergebung in Jesaja 53--Targum. Ein Beitrag zu der Praxis der aramäischen Bibelübersetzung," Journal for the Study of Judaism 3 (1972) 117-148; S.H. Levey, The Messiah: an Aramaic Interpretation. The Messianic Exegesis of the Targum: Monographs of the Hebrew Union College 2 (New York: Hebrew Union College, 1974); P. Grelot, Les poèmes du Serviteur. De la lecture critique à l'herméneutic: Lectio Divina 103 (Paris: Editions du Cerf, 1981).

4 Cf. Chilton, The Glory of Israel. The Theology and Provenience of the Isaiah Targum: Journal for the Study of the Old Testament Supplement Series 23 (Sheffield: JSOT, 1982) 97-102. The substance of the monograph treats of characteristic terms and phrases in the Targum, some of which (including "sanctuary house") are mentioned here. It is on the basis of that treatment that the present generalizations in respect of the theology of the Targum are offered.

5 Again, reference may be made to The Glory of Israel, where the concept was developed. The history of the Tg's evolution is also discussed there.

6 In The Glory of Israel, I already made some reference to the distinctions between levels of the framework. I have attempted to trace them further in The Isaiah Targum: Translation, Apparatus, and Notes, which I have written for a project entitled The Aramaic Bible: A Modern Translation of the Targums (general editor, Martin McNamara; publisher, Michael Glazier).

7   This is one of the few passages in the Tg which have relatively evident termini ad quem. The date A.D. 136 is given for the
renaming of Jerusalem as Aelia Capitolina, and the dedication of
the temple of Jupiter Capitolinus there, by E.M. Smallwood, The
Jews under Roman Rule from Pompey to Diocletian: Studies in
Judaism in Late Antiquity 20 (Leiden: Brill, 1976) 459-464,
432-434.

8   Cf. P. Churgin, Targum Jonathan to the Prophets: Yale
Oriental Series--Researches XIV (New Haven: Yale University Press,
1927/New York: Ktav, 1983) 28, 29.

9   Cf. Die Eschatologie der jüdischen Gemeinde im neutestamentlichen Zeitalter (Hildesheim: Olms, 1966) 26, cf. The Glory of
Israel, 21, 22.

10   Cf. the edition published in Jerusalem by Lewin--Epstein
(1957), and the English rendering published by Soncino in London
(1939) under the general editorship of H. Freedman.

11   H.L. Strack (tr. Jewish Publication Society), Introduction to
Talmud and Midrash (New York: Atheneum, 1972) 120.

12   Strack, 119.

13   Cf. the Freedman edition for this emendation, and B. Lorje,
Jalkut Schimoni (Zolkiew: Madfis, 1858).

14   Cf. Die alten Textzeugen des Jesajabuches (Göttingen:
Vandenhoeck und Ruprecht, 1981) 161-164. The argument is made by
L. Smolar and M. Aberbach that the description of high priestly
combined with temporal power (v. 22a) uniquely applies to the
Hasmonean rulers (Studies in Targum Jonathan to the Prophets [New
York: Ktav, 1983] 65). It must, however, be borne in mind that the
innovative rendering concerns only the high priestly aspect, and
that the reference to the "house of David" need not be to secular
power. The meturgeman may simply have understood David's house as
an apposition to "sanctuary house" (cf. 2 Samuel 7:13,16). Smolar
and Aberbach (p. 66) refer the interpretation to Antigonus and
Aristobulus, and so contradict van der Kooij (cf. n. 14). The best
support for the general position represented by all three scholars
is v. 8 in the Tg: "He has taken away the hiding place of the
house of Judah, and he has looked in that time upon a weapon of
the treasure house of the sanctuary." This does appear to be a
clear, retrospective reference to Pompey's entering into the
Temple treasury (cf. Bellum Judaicum 1.7.6 § 152, 153). To this
extent, and to the extent he was exiled by Pompey (cf. v. 18),
van der Kooij's identification of Shebna with Aristobulus II seems
at least plausible. (It is, however, no more than that; "exile" in
the Tg is normally a typological description of punishment, and so

60

cannot be held unequivocally to refer to the particular fate of Aristobulus. Indeed, within Exodus Rabbah 5.5, perhaps in the name of Samuel bar NaDOman, v. 18 is interpreted as a figure of Babylonian exile, not as the ciphered reference to the banning of any particular individual). To the same extent, the reference of Smolar and Aberbach to the later Hasmonean figures appears less likely, although Antigonus was sent to Antioch prior to his execution, cf. Bellum Judaicum 1.18.13 § 347-357. But, against van der Kooij, the precise identification of Eliakim with Hyrcanus II in the mind of the meturgeman is not probable. The definitive annulment of the régime which enjoys the quasi-prophetic authority of this passage (v. 25) only occurs when sacrifice, the constitutive function of priesthood, comes to an end (29:1). Further, the nature of the annulment concerns less the person than the dispensation he represents.

15   "The Wicked Priest, the Man of Lies, and the Righteous Teacher--the Problem of Identity," Jewish Quarterly Review 73 (1982) 1-37.

16   It is notable that Eliakim is not claimed to be responsible personally for his fate; the problem lies in the order he belongs to. Indeed, he is clearly preferred to Shebna (cf. vv. 17-20). The implications of the distinction between Shebna and Eliakim are taken up in the next essay.

ESSAY 5 --
Shebna, Eliakim, and the Promise to Peter

A peculiar thing is promised Eliakim in the Isaiah Targum (22:22):
And I will place the key of the sanctuary and the
authority of the house of David in his hand: and he
will open, and none shall shut, and he will shut, and
none shall open.[1]
The peculiarity of this promise is to some extent superficial.
Eliakim and Shebna are taken in the Targum as priestly figures, so
that chapter twenty-two refers to a shift in cultic dispensations.
Shebna is accused of self-seeking (v. 16), and is told that shame,
the removal of the high-priestly turban, and mortal exile will be
the result (vv. 17-19). In his place, Eliakim will be exalted,
clothed in priestly garments, given full authority, and provided
with a full spectrum of assistants (vv. 20-24). Within that context, the fact Eliakim is promised the keys "of the sanctuary" in
particular comes as no surprise.

What is surprising, however, is that v. 25c removes from
Eliakim everything that has been promised to him:
...he will be cut down and fall, and the oracle of
prophecy that was concerning him will be void...
The perspective of the Targum generally helps, even here, to mol-
lify our surprise. The encircling of the altar with the blood of
the slain, and the cessation of festal celebration, are announced
(29:1, 2) in view of high-priestly wickedness (28:1-4). An interpretative presupposition of the Targum is that it is plain for the
world to see that Jerusalem is desolate, while Rome prospers
(54:1). High-priestly corruption has run its course, and the
Temple must pay the price, until messianic restoration results in
its rebuilding (53:5). That the present Temple, and its priest,
should pass, is therefore axiomatic within the Targum.

Even when v. 25 is viewed from the perspective of the Targum
overall, our surprise (however mollified) is not removed. No
accusation of any sort is raised against Eliakim in the passage;
he is (implicitly) a successor as worthy as his predecessor is
unworthy. Until v. 25, permanency appears to be promised, provided only that priesthood is properly conducted. Notably,
Leviticus Rabbah 5.5 relates a discussion (between R. Eleazar and
R. Judah) concerning the priestly office exercised by Shebna and
Eliakim, not concerning the transition of authority from one to
the other, and the same may be said of Exodus Rabbah 37.1 in its
citation of Isaiah 22:23.[2] It must, of course, be observed that
the Hebrew text to some extent controls the reading of the Targum,
but it does not entirely explain the interpretation. The "peg" of
the Hebrew text need not have been taken to refer to Eliakim,
and--once it was so taken--the reversal of a negative statement is
a targumic convention which might have been invoked here.[3]

63

Additionally, the reference to "an oracle of prophecy" is odd, since elsewhere (14:28; 14:1) that phrase refers to a promise which is kept, not broken.[4] Apparently, the meturgeman has not only reproduced the negative note of v. 25 (which any rendering of the Hebrew text might have caught), but has intensified it.

It is the purpose of this essay (1) to consider attempts to explain the oddity of the promise to Eliakim, and on that basis to offer a fresh suggestion. In order to explain how Eliakim functions as a literary figure, and at the same time express a distinctly social perspective, attention will also be paid (2) to the definition of the "exegetical framework" of the Isaiah Targum. The thesis that the promise was developed within the first century becomes more plausible (3) when comparable usages from the period are also considered. At the close of the last section, our attention will focus on Matthew 16:18, 19. A quotation of Isaiah (in Targumic form or otherwise) within the saying attributed to Jesus cannot be proven, but its usage of language associated with the promise to Eliakim may offer a new prospect for construing Jesus' ministry.

1) The Identity of Eliakim

Arie van der Kooij has offered a suggestion which would help to account for the surprising discontinuity between v. 25 and the preceding material in the Tg. He suggests that Shebna and Eliakim should be identified with Aristobulus II and Hyrcanus II.[5] Similarly, Leivy Smolar and Moses Aberbach refer the interpretation to Antigonus and Aristobulus III.[6] Of course, neither of these explanations, which involve merely the transfer of power to "Eliakim," can be accepted as interpreting the Targum as it presently stands, since they do not account for v. 25, which is the point at issue of the entire chapter, the climax of the transition which is described. The present form of the text, of course, might refer in retrospect to the foundation of what is soon to be annulled, by means of an earlier targumic paraphrase, according to which Shebna was Aristobulus II (or Antigonus) and Eliakim was Hyrcanus II (or Aristobulus III).

It appears unwise, however, to insist on the particular identifications of Shebna and Eliakim which haved been posited. Certainly, the contention made by Smolar and Aberbach, that the passage can "only refer to" Antigonus and Aristobulus III, is extreme.[7] Antigonus was exiled and killed (cf. Tg Is. 22:18 and Bellum Judaicum 1.18.2, 3 § 353-357), but the same fate befell Aristobulus II, albeit within a series of hectic developments (cf. Bellum Judaicum 1.6.6. § 138-141; 1.7.1 § 141; 1.8.6 § 171-174; 1.9.1 §183, 184; van der Kooij [1981] 163). The very fact that both sets of identifications are plausible, when they are viewed from the perspective of how Shebna's fate is handled in the

64

Targum, vitiates any exclusive claim to credibility. Moreover, both identifications suffer from the lack of any reference in v. 18 to the violence of Shebna's death. To the extent that Pompey's entry into the treasury of the Temple seems to be alluded to in v. 8 (cf. Bellum Judaicum 1.7.6. § 152-154 and van der Kooij [1981] 166, 167), van der Kooij's appeal for a reference nearer to that period than Smolar and Aberbach would allow does seem preferable, but no more than that.

Van der Kooij's identification is superior to that of Smolar and Aberbach only insofar as Shebna is concerned: both exegeses do far less justice to Eliakim. Even if we accept that, before its present incorporation within the exegetical framework of the Targum, the interpreter used Shebna as a cipher of attack against Aristobulus II (or Antigonus), we must ask whether support for a faction of Hyrcanus II (or Aristobulus III) was actually expressed by the passage at any stage. Such support is precisely what both interpretations require, but none of the scholars involved asks whether it is in fact there.

The difficulty of van der Kooij, and Smolar and Aberbach, is that they confuse the possibility of allusions to the last gasp of the Hasmonean period with a specifically Hasmonean perspective. The easy equation between Josephus' programme and that of the meturgeman can distort our understanding of the Targum. The meturgeman could allude to Pompey's entry into the treasury without providing anything like a specific identification of that general; the uncovering of treasure is itself emblematic of defeat (v. 8). If so, how much more might he have thought of Shebna as the image of priestly corruption, without having a specific priest in mind? In that case, Eliakim is only a tragic emblem, a decent functionary who must pass with the decadent régime of which he is a part, not a precisely identifiable figure of history.

Moreover, if we approach the passage from a later Herodian, rather than a Hasmonean, perspective, we might think of Eleazar, the "captain" (stratêgôn) of the Temple who lead the refusal to sacrifice on behalf of the Emperor (see Bellum Judaicum 2.17.2 § 409, 410),[8] and who might well be described as an "officer" ('mrkl, cf. vv. 23-25) in Aramaic,[9] rather than as a priest (khn'). He was, moreover, the son of Ananias, so that his priestly pedigree is sound, and his fall was as evident as the burning of the Temple. The purpose here, however, is not to trump a Hasmonean reading with a later Herodian reading, but to suggest that, in the face of so many possible identifications of Shebna and Eliakim, which the checkered history of the high priesthood might be used to augment (cf. Bruce [1982] 53-64), it is unwise to suppose that any given set of them has an exclusive claim on the meaning of the text.

Some pair of identifications from the Hasmonean and/or late Herodian period might have been intended by the originating meturgeman, or meturgemanin, who looked forward to the replacement of a wicked priest with a faithful one. But by the time the Targum as we know it was transmitted, the end of that cultic dispensation which was in effect in the Temple had become an inescapable reality (v. 25)

Who, precisely, in the minds of those who composed and transmitted the Targum, were Shebna and Eliakim? In order to answer that question, one must do more than choose two likely candidates from the general period during which the Targum took shape. One must ascertain the particular provenience of the passage as a traditional interpretation taken up within the Targum. The traditional pedigree of our passage is not in question, but to type the provenience of a traditional unit, as distinct from the document in which it is incorporated, is notoriously difficult. In the present case, whether we are dealing (for example) with a partisan of a Hasmonean group, who favored "Eliakim" over "Shebna," or with a sect altogether hostile to the contemporary administration of the Temple, or with an anti-Roman phalanx which despised any tendency towards accommodation, cannot be determined with any confidence. Each option seems plausible, and for precisely that reason, none is entirely convincing.

The insistence on determining which (if any) of the above options is preferable derives from that form of historical curiosity which might be described as genetic.[10] History is commonly regarded as the explanation of past events on the basis of earlier events. As a result, the rhetoric of history, and even its assumptions about reality, tend to become causational. When and where that occurs, any historical statement will be found wanting which does not explain how any given event is the product of some group of antecedents. In the present case, any dissembling as to the identities of "Shebna" and "Eliakim" will frustrate the genetically curious historian.

However frustrated he might become, the fact remains that our uncertainty grows as more evidence is adduced, rather against what we might hope. But that uncertainty only obtains at the level of history as a genetic account of past events. What becomes increasingly clear about our passage is that it celebrates the demise of Shebna, a figure of priestly corruption, and the ascendancy of Eliakim, a figure of corresponding rectitude. As social history, the text is far more eloquent than as genetic history.

The passage, both as an instance of literature and as a specimen of history, conveys a certain stance in respect of the Temple. The attempt to understand its meaning cannot succeed, if it is construed in purely literary, or in purely historical, terms. As has been suggested already, the passage is patient of historical curiosity only to a limited extent, and even then, with the provision that curiosity of the appropriate sort is in effect. "Shebna" and "Eliakim" convey, not information about specific persons and the programmes of identifiable groups, but an attitude of hostility towards priestly administration, and then the conviction that the Temple will (or already has) suffered as the result of that administration. That is, the text articulates its socially historical perspective when its literary affect is taken into account. If it is approached as if every image within it were a code to be deciphered, the result is that its meaning dissolves into a series of plausible, but competing, possibilities. On the other hand, there is no question here of dispensing with the understanding that the text is possessed of a historical dimension. A literary approach which allowed of reference only to "the final form of the text," as if literature were incapable of retrospective or prospective reference, would yield an exegesis of the passage which is no more satisfactory than a genetically historical interpretation. Such a reading would simply leave us with the anomaly with which we began, that Eliakim is elevated, only to fall. By allowing the text to speak within its socially historical idiom, in which traditional material has been taken up and revised, its literary integrity is not violated, but confirmed: it speaks coherently of the concerns of varying times and circumstances.

2) The Framework of the Isaiah Targum

The consideration up to this point would suggest that our passage is susceptible of the technique of analysis developed and advocated in The Glory of Israel (see note 4). In that volume, the "exegetical framework" of the Isaiah Targum was isolated and described. The phrase "exegetical framework" was chosen in order to convey two crucial features which a critical reading of the Targum reveals. The first is that, however surprising the translation of a given pericope might be, at each point the Targum is to be understood as an instance of exegesis, in which the meturgeman was proceeding on the basis of the (or a) Hebrew text, if not solely on that basis. To this extent, even if the constituents of the Targum be judged to be of varying provenience, as a whole it is an extended exegesis. The second feature is closely related to the first. The Targum, in its assemblage of varying traditions, is no disjointed farrago of exegeses: there is a demonstrably controlling framework of themes, manifested by a coordinated use of vocabulary, which articulates a coherent theology.

The development of this exegetical framework represents a considerable achievement in the evolution of early Judaism into rabbinic Judaism. At the same time, the framework itself manifests stages in its own growth, as I described in The Glory of Israel:

67

Before proceeding to distinguish between one framework and the other, one must have some grasp of the overall framework to which the framework interpreters contributed, because the contribution of the individual meturgemanin becomes more distinctive when viewed within the context of the total edifice they built with their colleagues. The coherent usages of various terms in the overall framework centre on the restoration of the house of Israel. This restoration involves a return from the dispersion to the land appointed by God, and therefore victory over the Gentile dominion. The entire earth will have to recognize that true glory which is uniquely God's. The Temple and Jerusalem, the designated geographical associates of the Shekinah itself, are very much at the heart of the restoration, and the sanctuary features particularly both as the locus of divine power and the focus of Israel's obedience. For obedience to the law is the sine qua non of divine favour, just as rebellion occasions God's wrath. But in the wrath or favour of his memra, God remains constant in his choice of Israel, to whom he issues the call to repent through the prophets, the agents of his holy spirit. Israel may accept or reject the divine work, but God's choice of Abraham is unchanging. Still, it is righteousness akin to Abraham's which the interpreters demand from their people in the prophet's name; a return to the law and correct Temple service were to them the content of repentance. Only such repentance could put Israel in a position to receive the vindication willed him by God. That is why the messiah's programme--of restoring law so as to occasion forgiveness--is so crucial in the Targum.

The principal and most striking feature of this overall Targumic framework is its perennial relevance to Israel. This is what permitted the Amoraic framework meturgeman to incorporate the contribution of his Tannaitic predecessors into his own work, what enabled the rabbis of Babylonia to authorize the transmission of the Targum itself, and what encouraged medieval scholars to make enough copies to ensure (substantively) the textual integrity of the Stenning and Sperber editions. Here is a message, in the name of the greatest literary prophet, which speaks to a dispersed and disoriented Israel living on the sufferance of Gentile officials, without a cult and yet expectant of a messiah who will restore the Temple and the autonomy of Israel. The Targum acknowledges these circumstances--indeed it speaks (at one level) from an immediate experience of them--and it also articulates these hopes. But the Targum is no broadsheet whose purpose is to foment the uncritical expectation for vengeance among those who lived under various forms of oppression; hope is appropriate only for those who repent to the law; the promises of Abraham belong to whose who behave as Abraham; the memra is always with Israel, but it might support or punish. The Targum has addressed all dispersed Israel in the time since the desolation of Mount Zion seemed final, and it has done so--not as generality--but as comfort and challenge. To those for whom rabbinic literature is nothing more than academic legal discussion and speculative haggadah, the Isaiah Targum is a most eloquent answer, and the dearth of accessible modern language editions is unfortunate.

Yet the very success of the Targum in its extant form as a contribution to the spiritual life of dispersed Israel (that is, Israel as disoriented by the desolation of the cult, not only as geographically scattered) means that it is problematic to assign the overall framework to a single given period. Indeed, the usage by different framework meturgemanin of the same characteristic terms often makes it impossible with any certainty to decide when the work of one leaves off and that of another takes up, and the echoes between the Targum and the Shemoneh Esreh (for example) demonstrate that rabbis might responsibly have encouraged the use of such a paraphrase in almost any period between the dissolution of cultic practice and the medieval attestation of the document.

By itself, the Targum's understanding of the law as the central means of Israel's approach to God and the secret of his communal identity serves only to highlight the coherence of the interpreters' faith with the spiritual movement which found its voice in the Seleucid challenge and culminated with the rabbis. But the specific and emphatic association between the law and the cult in the Targum, and the expectation that a messianically restored Israel would attend to teaching which comes from the Temple, seemed especially (although not exclusively) similar to the fervent, literally expressed hope in Intertestamental literature. Such similarity was far more apparent in respect of "sanctuary" usage, because-- while the concrete restoration of the Temple is a prominent expectation shared by the Targum, Intertestamental literature and early rabbis--the Amoraim appeared less eager to emphasize the building of the Temple as an immediate and central hope. At this point also, the internal evidence of the Targum suggested that two strata within the earlier framework should be distinguished, the first of which takes restoration to be a matter of regulating the cult properly, and the second of which assumes that physical rebuilding is necessary. The early framework meturgemanin hoped as passionately for Jerusalem's consolation as did one of their contemporaries, the author of the fifth Sibylline book, and their attitude was contrasted in our study with the tendency of rabbinic exegesis to see Jerusalem's vindication in ethical terms. Moreover, the Targumic descriptions of Jerusalem's oppression made it clear that the hope of the interpreters was articulated in critical circumstances: the Roman campaign against the city (stratum one) and its eventual success (stratum two) seem to have influenced the choice of language. A cognate differentiation between the attitude manifest in Intertestamental literature, the early Targumic framework, and the Shemoneh Esreh on one hand, and rabbinic opinion from the second century onward on the other was made in respect of "exile" usage: a development from a literal hope for immediate, militarily triumphal return to the land to a more positive approach to exile as a condition endured by God with his people seemed apparent. At the same time, "exile" within the early framework is both a threat (at stratum one) and a reality (at stratum two). All usages of the term "Shekinah" in the Targum cohere with the primary type of idiom isolated by A.M. Goldberg ("Gegenwartsschekhinah") and suppose an identification with the Temple such that the Shekinah is either sinned against by cultic abuse (stratum one) or removed because of such sin, but soon to return (stratum two). A more attentuated use of the term characterizes the Amoraic period. "Kingdom" in the Targum is associated with Zion, as is consistent with the viewpoint of the early meturgemanin. Their usage represents a development in the meaning of the term (which is evident in comparison with the usage of other Prophetic Targumim and the Mekhilta), in that the earlier understanding saw the kingdom in less restricted terms. But the connection of the kingdom with the sanctuary is also attested in the musaf prayer for pilgrimages, and is only a step in the direction of a nomistic understanding of the kingdom which was achieved at or near the end of the first century. The early framework interpreters' view of righteousness is, as in Intertestamental literature, communal and motivated by the hope of vindication; the Amoraim were no less emphatic in their call to be righteous, but they understand righteousness as a more individual duty and associate it more with obedience to the law (an association which is presupposed in their demand for right behaviour) and less with the teaching of the law (which was a crucial necessity in the days of the early meturgemanin).

70

For the Amoraic framework meturgeman(in), sin in general, rather than specifically cultic abuse, is the cause of exile to Babylon, and his hope for the eventual end of the Babylonian tyranny is linked more to individual than to ethnic repentance. In the sense that exile is the situation in which the individual is to cultivate righteous behaviour, the Amoraic acceptance of exile as the status quo seems presupposed, and we found a near parallel to an "exile" reading from the later framework (Targum Is. 43.14) in the Pesiqta Rabbati (30.2), and many Amoraic parallels to a later and individualistic "repentance" reading (at Targum Is. 57.19). Moreover, Israel for this interpreter is more a "congregation" than a "house" (again, cf. Pesiqta Rabbati 37.3); a post-nationalistic perspective seems evident. On the other hand, it must be acknowledged and stressed that the Amoraic interpreter was an ardent traditionalist. He was willing, for example (at Targum Is. 48.15, 16), to let the work of his predecessors stand and transmit to his readers an imperative to follow Abraham in a vocation of cultic service rather than voice the call, fashionable in his day, for scholars to be heard with the respect due to Moses. Likewise, the Amoraic Isaian framework meturgeman (unlike his, or another's, practice in Targum Micah) effaced his own kingdom theology in favour of the viewpoint of a Tannaitic framework meturgeman. Interpreters at both the Tannaitic and Amoraic levels availed themselves of the introductory phrase, "The prophet said." The former typically employed it to articulate the demand for communal repentance and the hope for the renovation of prophecy thereafter; the latter used it to insist on right conduct in view of eschatological judgement (cf. Targum Is. 21.12 with Numbers Rabbah 16.23). The Amoraic meturgeman also developed the earlier picture of the messiah ben David who, with a priestly counterpart, gives the law from the Temple he restores into a figure who is proleptically active (Targum Is. 43.10, and not in name only) as a witness to God's sole efficacy as God.

What we have postulated to explain the growth of the Isaiah Targum is not a series of mechanical redactions, but the unfolding of an interpretative continuum. There is no way of determining the number of meturgemanin who were responsible for each of the individual readings contained in the extant manuscripts, and yet the evidence has substantiated our hypothesis, developed in the introduction, that the repetition of characteristic terms manifests an organizing framework. We have collated that evidence against selected data from

Intertestamental literature, the Qumran finds, ancient Jewish prayers, Rabbinica and the New Testament, and we have been led by our exegeses to differentiate between the applications of these characteristic terms within the Targum itself. We have come to the conclusion-gradually, as the inquiry progessed, and term after term appeared to bear now one meaning, now a distinct (albeit related) meaning--that we must think of the framework as a developing, organizing principle which permitted more ancient readings to be transmitted even as their theological significance was adapted to the points of view of the meturgemanin and their readers. As rings on a tree, the two strata of the Tannaitic level and the single, although less substantial, Amoraic level stand out as witnesses to stages of growth. The shape of the tree was at each stage distinctive, but related to its shape at the next stage, and at every point it was recognizably the same tree that was growing....[11]

This passage has been quoted at length, in order to avoid giving any misimpression as to what is meant by "exegetical framework." The phrase designedly avoids the language of "source" and "redaction," at least as those terms have come to be employed. The perception of a framework of governing themes does not warrant the conclusion that all thematically similar exegeses in the Targum were taken up as a source into the framework, or that every exegesis was collated by a single "redactor" who thought these themes a good idea. One can only say, in literary terms, that the framework imputes coherence to the whole. Similarly, the historical information which can be gleaned from the framework is meager. My description of the provenience of the framework(s) is not out of keeping with the traditionally rabbinic understanding that both Jonathan ben Uzziel and Joseph bar Ḥiyya were involved in the formation of the Prophetic Targumim, but it offers no particular support to that understanding. The fact remains, however, that the literary profiles of thematic frameworks can be collated with evolving patterns in other instances of Jewish literature. In other words, the exegetical framework of the Isaiah Targum is the plane of intersection between literary and socially historical approaches.[12]

Misunderstanding regarding the nature of the exegetical framework, as I have defined it, has resulted in an inaccurate assessment of my work, at least on the part of one reviewer.[13] Peter Nichols poses the question, "What is an 'exegetical framework'?" He does not cite from the extensive passage quoted above, which would have answered the question in my own words, but attempts inductively to state my position:

...one has the impression that he has done no more than relate (uncertainly in many cases) specific passages to specific historical and literary settings...

72

That impression is justifiable, if one reads my book as a sequence
of isolated paragraphs (much in the way that critics of a certain
generation have read the Bible). But the passages treated were
chosen, as any serious reader of my book will know, in view of
their representative usage of terms and phrases which recur char-
acteristically in the Targum. Lest there by any doubt, I should
like to repeat what I said on p. 12:

> While historical and literary allusions might guide us
> to an understanding of the date and provenience of a
> given passage or motif, and language (if that were an
> established criterion) would help to establish the time
> and place of the final redaction of the whole, Targums
> as such are not farragos of tradition or de novo compo-
> sitions, but specimens of extended exegesis. To
> discover the provenience and date of a Targum one must
> ask, first, what exegetical terms and phrases are so
> frequently used as to constitute characteristic conven-
> tions, and then, how do these conventions relate to
> historical circumstances, to the New Testament and early
> Jewish literature generally? Such conventions, when
> repeatedly used in a given work, would provide the
> ordering principle for traditional interpretations and
> for the inclusion of subsequent insights. This exegeti-
> cal framework belongs to the esse of a Targum: without
> it, targumic readings are only a pot pourri, while with
> it even the addition of material does not constitute a
> recension, only an addendum.

The intention of the definition was to formulate an alternative to
"source" or "redaction," as the italized portion of the passage
cited previously makes unmistakably (as I once hoped) plain.[14] The
point, as I still think is evident, is to avoid the language of
mechanical compilation.

A friend in the field of English Literature warned that my sim-
ile of a tree, in the passage from the conclusion which was cited
earlier, might seem too obvious to some; he felt it was already
plain that my programme did not involve anything that could be
taken as a metaphor of the inorganic. He did not reckon with Fr
Nichols, who actually imputes to me the idea that my "exegetical
framework" is to be identified with a "redaction." He rightly
states, "'Redaction' would seem to indicate a more thorough edit-
ing than C. has claimed or demonstrated..."; for precisely that
reason, "C." never used the word "redaction." Because I said I
had used "a modified form of redaction criticism" (p. 110),
Nichols decided I thought all along that an "exegetical framework"
was the same thing as a "redaction."[15]

It is, of course, annoying to have one's book reviewed on the
basis of what it did not say, and I am happy to see that other
reviewers have more clearly seen the point of my method.[16] But
Nichols's confusion does betray the common assumption of genetic

history within allegedly literary approaches. Despite my care in defining "exegetical framework," he concluded it must be a hypostasized entity, a "redaction" or a "source." He then compounded the confusion by suggesting that the term "trajectory" might serve better than "exegetical framework."

The notion of trajectory, as developed by Helmut Koester and James Robinson, was designed to describe the development of theologoumena used in various documents, with the aim of assessing early Christian ideology.[17] It has been criticized for creating its own hypostasis, a supposed entity out of the relationship among documents which happen to speak on similar subjects, and for being inherently teleological.[18] These criticisms must be met before the language of "trajectory" can be used precisely, and to refer to its usage in a review, as if it were an accepted part of critical usage, is most curious. Moreover, "trajectory," evocative though the term might be, is quite irrelevant to literary analysis. In assessing a Targum, the crucial issue is to appreciate the stance of the document generally in its presentation of disparate exegeses. The "trajectory" of any series of those exegeses might be traced, but that would not characterize the Targum as a whole.

The present purpose is not to claim inviolability for the phrase "exegetical framework" as a norm of Targumic criticism. But before a replacement can be suggested, it is necessary to comprehend what the phrase does, and does not, seek to describe. In the absence of a method for locating the exegetical frameworks of Targums within Judaism, the way will be open to use selected readings to characterize entire compositions. Three recent studies of the Isaiah Targum manifest just this tendency. Smolar and Aberbach place the exegesis of the Targum in the Tannaitic period, and especially within the school of Aqiba.[19] Unfortunately, they do so without considering the body of evidence adduced by Churgin[20] and myself for a substantive Amoraic phase in the development of the Targum. Even within their own terms of reference, the authors' attempt to limit the period of the Targum's development seems strained: they acknowledge allusions to the period after Aqiba (pp. 48, 80, 81, 82, 83, 88, 120).[21] Quite a different understanding of the Targum is assumed by Pierre Grelot in his study of the interpretation of the "servant songs."[22] His starting point is the Amoraic phase of Targumic development, and he claims that the understanding of the text is designed in part to counter Christian exegesis (pp. 220-223). He argues that the religious nationalism and the emphasis on the law in the Targum, as well as its picture of the Messiah in classically Davidic terms, betray an apologetic interest. In effect, he has seized on one possible strand in the tapestry of Targumic development, and used it to characterize the whole as an anti-Christian tract. Lastly, Arie van der Kooij[23] takes the Targumic emphasis on prophecy to betray a priestly interest (pp. 198-203), and decides that the hero of the piece is Eleazar, the colleague of Bar Kokhba, whom van der Kooij identifies with Eleazar of Modiim (pp. 205-208). The argument is speculative in the extreme, and can be questioned at each point in its development; it scarcely bears the weight of the claim that the Targum did not grow out of the translational practice in synagogues, and instead reflects specifically priestly interests.

When one keeps a view to the exegetical framework of the Isaiah Targum, varying stances are seen to be in tension, but the artificial programme of forcing all of them into a single mould is avoided. That is the methodological point of The Glory of Israel. It may seem elementary, but previous, and even contemporary, practitioners of Targumic investigation apparently have not grasped it. In the case of the present passage from the Targum, the first, Tannaitic level of the framework, with its keen focus on the Temple, is most in evidence. Indeed, it is precisely the sort of tension which is apparent between v. 25 and the foregoing material which makes it advisable to speak of strata within that initial level. Because we are dealing with exegetical frameworks, and not thorough-going redactions, the seams created by juxtaposing traditions of varying provenience sometimes remain visible.

3) The Promise to Eliakim
in Christian literature of the first century

Our finding in respect of the attitude conveyed in the Targumic paraphrase of Isaiah 22 would be strengthened if a similarly voiced promise to Eliakim could be found elsewhere, but in the relevant period. As is happens, a generally recognized reference to Isaiah 22:22 is to be found in Matthew 16:19, where Peter is promised that, whatever he binds on earth will be bound in heaven, and that whatever he looses on earth will be loosed in heaven.[24] Despite the distinction of the diction from the Masoretic Text and the Targum, the syntactical similarity has been taken to be enough to warrant the judgement.[25] Rather more significantly for the present purpose, Isaiah 22:22 is also cited in Revelation 3:7. There, one like son of man (1:13) identifies himself as "The holy one, the true one, who has the key of David, who opens and none will shut, and shuts and none will open." That usage establishes quite clearly that the promise to Eliakim could be taken as a permanent one, as we posit for the earliest form of the Targumic tradition within its framework.[26]

The Septuagintal version of Isaiah 22:22 may also have been influenced by such an understanding:.
    And I will give David's glory to him, and he will rule,
    and none will contradict.
As might be expected, that reading is supplemented or replaced elsewhere with a more literal rendering,[27] but as it stands it is

a plainer, and therefore more emphatic, version of the promise to Eliakim than is found in the Masoretic Text.

When the Targumic interpretation of Isaiah 22:22 is understood as we have suggested, a fresh approach to the promise to Peter in Matthew 16:18, 19 becomes possible. Those verses, of course, have been subjected to a great deal of discussion; for the present purpose, we are interested only in the degree of agreement between them and the Targum.[28]

Since the publication of Joachim Jeremias' classic study, Golgotha,[29] the argument has been considered that the "rock" upon which Jesus promises to build his congregation is the cosmic foundation, Mount Zion. The suggestion of some allusion to Mount Zion is, in itself, not implausible, especially on the understanding that Isaian diction is used in the promise to Peter. Reference is frequently made to it in all of the ancient versions of Isaiah, the nearest references in the Masoretic Text being 18:7 and 24:23. The latter of those is of particular interest, since in the Targumic interpretation a reference to the kingdom of God appears, a theologoumenon which also features in the promise to Peter.[30]

The difficulty with Jeremias' suggestion, however, is that it relies on taking petra in the promise as the cosmic rock, the antithesis to the "gates of Hades." That is, the saying is viewed as cultic only because, and insofar as, it is cosmological. Such a primary interest in cosmology is supported only by the reference to Hades; petra, in Greek or Aramaic, must be taken as a neutral term.[31] Generally, of course, the corpus of Jesus' sayings is not characterized by a cosmological interest, and it must be remembered that "the gates of Hades" might be understood as an immediately existential threat (cf. Isaiah 38:10) and need not be taken cosmologically. For all of these reasons, Jeremias' suggestion has not won wide support.

The notion that a promise in respect of the Temple is in effect here, however, is in some ways attractive. Elsewhere in Matthew, Jesus is presented as developing halakhoth in respect of the Temple. His teaching includes the taking of oaths (23:16-22), instructions for the offering of sacrifice (5:23, 24), and a more elaborate story relates to the payment of the half shekel (17:24-27, cf. 23:23, 24/Luke 11:42). All of those passages are uniquely Matthean, and yet are widely accepted as relating to the substance of Jesus' attitude towards the Temple, as evidenced in the multiply attested accounts of his teaching about the widow's example of providing for the Temple (Mark 12:41-44/Luke 21:1-4), of his occupation of the holy precincts (Matthew 21:12, 13/Mark 11:15-17/Luke 19:45, 46/John 2:13-17), of his discourse regarding the destruction of the Temple (Matthew 24:1-25:46; Mark 13:1-37; Luke 21:5-36), and--most famously--his prediction against the Temple (John 2:19; Matthew 26:61; Mark 14:58). It would be quite coherent with this pattern of evidence if, as the similarity to the Targumic interpretation would suggest, Jesus in Matthew 16:18, 19 were establishing the mechanism for articulating the cultic halakhah. He would be doing so by assuming an attitude not unlike that of the meturgeman of Isaiah 22:22, and by using the theological language his time to stake out his position. That language appears to have focussed on Eliakim, and to have been influential in the formation of the Targum of Isaiah as it can be read today.[32]

NOTES

Versions of this essay were read at the yearly meetings of the Society of Biblical Literature (1985) and of the New Testament Colloquium of Harvard and Yale.

1   Renderings are based on my forthcoming translation, with apparatus and notes. It is to appear in a series to be entitled, "The Aramaic Bible," and the volume presenting the Isaiah Targum is now in proof.

2   Both of these passages are discussed at some length in "The Temple in the Targum of Isaiah," the previous essay in the present volume.

3   The reversal of statements, from negative to positive, and vice versa, is a well known convention in Targum Jonathan. Instances of this, and related phenemona, are provided in J. F. Stenning, The Targum of Isaiah (Oxford: Clarendon, 1949) xvi.

4   For related usages, cf. The Glory of Israel. The Theology and Provenience of the Isaiah Targum: JSOTS 23 (Sheffield: JSOT, 1982) 52-56.

5   Arie van der Kooij, Die alten Textzeugen des Jesajabuches. Ein Beitrag zur Textgeschichte des Alten Testaments: Orbis Biblicus et Orientalis (Göttingen: Vandenhoeck and Ruprecht, 1981) 161-164. Van der Kooij makes his claims on the basis of collations of Targumic passages with Josephus' work, cf. H. St. J. Thackeray, Josephus II: The Loeb Classical Library (New York: Putnam, 1927).

6   Leivy Smolar and Moses Aberbach, Studies in Targum Jonathan to the Prophets: The Library of Biblical Studies (New York: Ktav, 1983) 65, 66.

7   Smolar and Aberbach, 65, 66. Cf. van der Kooij, 162 for the same claim, in respect of his own, quite different, identification.

8   Cf. F. F. Bruce, New Testament History (London: Pickering and Inglis, 1980) 359, 360. Thackeray, 482 relates the function to that of the sgn, but cf. n. 9.

9   See Gustaf H. Dalman, Aramäisch-neuhebräisches Handwörterbuch zu Targum, Talmud und Midrasch (Hildesheim: Olms, 1967) 24, who refers both to "Oberster" and "Priesteroberster" as possible meanings. It is notable that in the Targum of Jeremiah 1:1, where the sense is evidently priestly, the 'mrkly' are specifically located in Jerusalem. See also J. Levy, Chaldäisches Wörterbuch über die Targumim (Köln: Melzer, 1959) I, 38, 39. In the Jeremiah Targum 52:24, the 'mrkly' are mentioned after the high priest and the sgn they correspond to the three keepers of the threshold in the Masoretic Text. A position in the priestly hierarchy, which is already implicit contextually in Targum Isaiah 22:22, does seem evident.

10   The critical stance taken in this section was developed in Beginning New Testament Study (London: SPCK, 1986), and in a forthcoming article on Mark 1:21-28 in Gospel Perspectives 6 (Sheffield: JSOT).

11   Cf. The Glory of Israel, 97-102. A more precise allocation of material in the Targum, according to the framework to which it belongs, is available in the introduction of my commentary (cf. n. 1).

12   By "social history," the record and accounts of attitudes, beliefs, and practices in societies of the past is meant. For recent, albeit varied, applications of the discipline, see Howard Clark Kee, Miracle in the Early Christian World. A Study in Sociohistorical Method (New Haven: Yale University Press, 1983); Abraham J. Malherbe, Social Aspects of Early Christianity (Philadelphia: Fortress, 1983); Wayne A. Meeks, The First Urban Christians. The Social World of the Apostle Paul (New Haven: Yale University Press, 1983). In the study of Judaism, the literature itself is more directly susceptible of socially historical investigation, since it is of a more communal nature than that of the Hellenistic world.

13   In CBQ 47 (1985) 514, 515.

14   The earlier passage is taken from the conclusion of The Glory of Israel. The italics have been added for the purpose of the present discussion. At the same time, I have taken the opportunity to make certain corrections which were introduced at the proof stage of producing the book; unfortunately, they were not properly entered.

15   Cf. The Glory of Israel, 125 n. 49.

78

16 See the reviews of D. Bourget, ETR 59 (1984) 255; R. Coggins, JTS 36 (1985) 275; R.P. Gordon, SOTS Book List (1984) 44; B. Grossfeld, JBL 104 (1985) 138, 139; O. Kaiser, ZAW 96 (1984) 300; S. C. Reif, VT 34 (1984) 124; J. Ribera, Estudios Bíblicos 42 (1984) 230-234; R. Tournay, BR 91 (1984) 465-466; R. White, JJS 35 (1984) 106-108.

17 Cf. Trajectories through Early Christianity (Philadelphia: Fortress, 1971).

18 Cf. "'Not to Taste Death': A Jewish, Christian, and Gnostic Usage," Studia Biblica 1978 II. Papers on The Gospels: JSNTS 2 (ed. E. A. Livingstone; Sheffield: JSOT, 1980) 29-36.

19 Smolar and Aberbach, 1, 29.

20 Pinkhos Churgin, Targum Jonathan to the Prophets: Yale Oriental Series (New York: Ktav, 1983).

21 Further criticism of their position, together with those of van der Kooij and Grelot, is available in "Three Views of the Isaiah Targum," JSOT 33 (1985) 127, 128.

22 Cf. Les poèmes du Serviteur. De la lecture critique à l'herméneutique: Lectio Divina 103 (Paris: Les éditions du Cerf, 1981).

23 Cf. n. 5.

24 See, above all, John A. Emerton, "Binding and Loosing--Forgiving and Retaining," JTS 13 (1962) 325-331. The observation of the allusion to Isaiah 22:22 does not, however, rest on the particulars of Emerton's argument, cf. the editions of F. H. A. Scrivener (Cambridge: Deighton, Bell, 1891) and of the Nestles, Kurt Aland, et allii (Stuttgart: Deutsche Bibelstiftung, 1981).

25 Isaiah 22:22 is, quite correctly, not listed as quoted in Matthew 16:19 in the editions of B. F. Westcott and F. J. A. Hort (London: Macmillan, 1901) and the United Bible Societies (Stuttgart: Württemberg Bible Society, 1968).

26 The association of Rev 3:7 with Matthew 16:18, 19 becomes even closer according to 2050 (dated 1170 in Nestle-Aland) and certain other minuscules. There, "of Hades" replaces "of David." But the association (even in the mind of the scribe of 2050) may only be apparent, since the son of man is already identified in Revelation 1:18 as holding the keys of death and Hades (cf. Job 38:17).

27 Cf. Alfred Rahlfs, Septuaginta II (Stuttgart: Württembergische Bibelanstalt, 1935) and Joseph Ziegler, Isaias: Septuaginta 14 (Göttingen: Vandenhoeck and Ruprecht, 1967).

28 I hope elsewhere to develop a fuller explication of the passage generally.

29 In the series Angelos 1 (Leipzig: Pfeiffer, 1926) 68-77. Jeremias repeats and summarizes his arguments in the article on Hades in the Theological Dictionary of the New Testament (eds G. Kittel and G. W. Bromiley; Grand Rapids: Eerdmans, 1978) 146-149.

30 Cf. The Glory of Israel, 77-81 and A Galilean Rabbi and His Bible. Jesus' Use of the Interpreted Scripture of His Time: Good News Studies 8 (Wilmington: Glazier, 1984, and, with the subtitle, Jesus own interpretation of Isaiah, London: SPCK, 1984) 58-63. A more technical consideration of Jesus' use of the theologoumenon of the kingdom, and its relation to Targumic usage, appears in God in Strength. Jesus' Announcement of the Kingdom: Studien zum Neuen Testament und seiner Umwelt 1 (Freistadt: Plöchl, 1979).

31 It has become something of an axiom in modern interpretation that the term kyp' was used twice in the original form of the saying, cf. Max Wilcox, "Peter and the Rock: A Fresh Look at Matthew XVI.17-19," NTS 22 (1976) 73-88, 74. Ptr', however, is a term (borrowed from Greek) which appears in Aramaic with the meaning "foundation," cf. Dalman, 332 and Charles Taylor, Sayings of the Jewish Fathers (Cambridge: Cambridge University Press, 1897) 160.

32 The present case of dominical reliance on Targumic tradition might be associated with those presented in A Galilean Rabbi. It was not included in the original study because it does not present the more straightforward dictional or contextual connections between the Targums and Jesus' diction which are manifest in the other instances.

In the January 1977 issue of Novum Testamentum, Mr Brian McNeil suggests that the conviction voiced in John xii 34 that ho khris-tos menei eis ton aiôna is mirrored in Targum Isaiah ix 5 in the proximity of the phrase qyym `lmy' to a mention of "Messiah."[1] The Targum in question is a compendium of the exegetical work of centuries, so that it is indeed possible that some of its readings reflect the first-century haggadic diction of which the Johannine passage is a more certain representative.[2] But it is inappropriate to conclude on this basis that John had this Targum "in mind" when he wrote.[3] A haggadah that the Messiah stands forever could have circulated for generations before it was applied exegetically to this passage in the book of Isaiah. Mr McNeil would have to show a positive allusion by the crowd to Is. ix before his entire suggestion could be considered tenable. The probability that elements in the Targums are early is no reason to assume that the Targums in their present form underlie the New Testament.[4] On the contrary, care must be taken in N.T. exegesis to refer only to those Targumic passages which have a demonstrable, verbal kinship to the pericope in question, and to apply the rabbinic notion preserved by the Targum to the N.T. only insofar as the verbal relationship extends. If we do not follow this principle, we will be in danger of repeating the error of the nineteenth century in using post-Christian Rabbinica to interpret the N.T. Repetition of this error could, in turn, bring back the reaction against the use of Targums in N.T. exegesis which prevailed earlier in this century, a reaction in which the possible pertinence of Targumic diction to the N.T. was largely ignored.[5]

According to this principle, Mr McNeil's suggestion is useful insofar as it relates to the haggadah contained in Targum Is. ix 5, and misleading insofar as it reads the extant Targum into the Gospel according to John. On the other hand, there is evidence that Jesus' assertion (as cited here by the crowd: that the Son of Man must be lifted up) reflects the Targumic understanding of another passage in Isaiah. In Targum Is. lii 13, it is "my servant the Messiah" who will be exalted (yr'm).[6] The specifically Targumic association of the Messiah with the idea hupsôthênai (Jn. xii 32, 34) is what stands behind the crowd's assumption that Jesus is speaking of the Messiah, just as the phrase "sons of men" in Is. lii 14 corresponds to their use of it in the singular. Likewise, it is not a coincidence that Is. lii 1 is explicitly cited in Jn. xii 38. Of course, it is not likely that a use of hupsôthênai alone would trigger the association in such a crowd's mind between the Messiah and Isaiah's servant. They heard Jesus refer to the Son of Man, although John does not report he said it, and by taking this hint we can guess that he was understood also to refer to the Messiah.

Jesus, then, is understood by the crowd to have used a messianic haggadah on what we would call a servant song, and the Targum Isaiah transmits a similar exegesis. In the absence of evidence that the Targum is influenced by Christian formulations, we are left to infer that Targum Is. lii 13 preserves a first-century turn of phrase and thought with which Jesus was familiar. If we fully accepted Mr McNeil's suggestion, we would say that the crowd counters Jesus' citation with another haggadah from the same document. But, aside from the weakness in such an interpretation which I have already mentioned, we come up against the exegetical problem that the crowd says they have heard that the Messiah remains forever ek tou nomou. W. C. van Unnik has demonstrated that it is oral law which is cited here and which John thinks of as related to the book of Psalms;[7] this militates against taking the crowd's objection as a specific allusion to Targum Isaiah. The crowd is rather in the position (cf. vii 40-43) of objecting to Jesus' exegetically articulated claims with a common sense and slightly muddled acquaintance with contemporary haggadha. I agree with Mr McNeil that Targums should be combed for early material (even if expressed in the language of a later age) which might illuminate the N.T., but I fear the optimistic assumption that the Targums predate the N.T. may lead us seriously astray.

Mr McNeil follows the translation of J. F. Stenning, "his name has been called from of old, Wonderful counsellor, Mighty God, He who lives for ever, the Anointed one (or, Messiah)..."[8] As the rendering makes plain, to associate the messiah with the phrase "living for ever" requires also that he be named as God. Stenning's translation accomplishes that identification by taking mn qdm to mean "from of old." That is also the interpretative line taken by C. W. H. Pauli, who has the messiah's name called "from eternity."[9] Pauli's translation as a whole is still worth consulting in respect of possible, grammatical construals, but a propagandistic purpose in his writing can scarcely be ignored. He observes on p. vi:

> The unprejudiced Jew by reading this Paraphrase will
> see, that we Christians believe in no other salvation,
> than that which their fathers expected the Messiah
> should bring.

On the same page, he also makes the bland comment, inexplicable from a critical point of view, that the terms "messiah" and "Shekhinah" express the same meaning. Pauli dedicated his work to its publishers, the London Society for Promoting Christianity amongst the Jews, and it would seem that, in matters even faintly christological, fervour got the better of his judgment.

Of course, to observe the intent of Pauli, which may derivatively have influenced the interpretation of Stenning, does not falsify their rendering of Targum Is. ix 5 in particular. Samson H. Levey, however, has vigourously suggested that the doctrine of an eternal, explicitly divine messiah is not that of the Targum.[10]

Without explanation, he insists we should take the clause as, "his name has been called by the One who gives wonderful counsel..." (p. 45). At this point, the dispute seems largely a function of the presuppositions on the basis of which reading takes place, and the renderings of Pauli and Stenning at least have the virtue that they correspond well to the Masoretic Text, where the messianic figure enjoys such titles as "mighty God" and "everlasting father."[11] Levey's rendering, on the other hand, itself falls within the genre of targum.

Just this problem of meaning occupied me in my production of a fresh translation of the Targum, together with an apparatus and notes, a project in which I had access to van Zijl's concordance.[12] It became plain to me that the rendering should be, "his name will be called before the Wonderful Counselor, the Mighty God, existing forever, 'The messiah in whose days peace will increase upon us.'" Had mn qdm been intended in the sense, "from of old," I should have expected to find a form of qdm'h, not qdm. The latter form may occasionally bear the sense ascribed to it by Pauli and Stenning (cf. xxiii 7), but only in association with unequivocally temporal phrases. In other words, the Targum in its extant form rejects the notion of messianic eternity such as the crowd refers to in John xii 34. A premise of McNeil's argument, that the Targum "is an explicit statement in a scriptural text that the Messiah lives for ever" (p. 24) is therefore false. Whatever the crowd in the Johannine passage had in mind, it was not the Targum as it can be read today.

NOTES

Essay 6 first appeared in Nov T 22 (1980) 176-178.

1   "The Quotation at John XII 34," pp. 22-33.

2   In his monograph, Targum Jonathan to the Prophets (New Haven: Yale, 1927), P. Churgin cited passages in the Isaiah Targum which he thought stem from the period from before the destruction of the Temple (p. 23) until the Sassanid persecution (p. 28). S. H. Levey, "The Date of Targum Jonathan to the Prophets," V.T. XXI (1971), pp. 186-196, argues for a tenth century terminus ad quem. While he does show a continuing interest in the prophetic Targums in the period of the Geonim, his argument is vitiated by the fact that his most convincing datum (the "Romulus" cipher for Rome at xi 4, which Saadia also used) is only a variant reading (see Sperber's edition). Since, however, the line between editorial redaction and textual transmission is almost indistinguishable in Targum studies, his contribution is a useful warning against assuming the antiquity of Targum readings.

3   A point eloquently made by P. Grelot in his review of M. McNamara, The New Testament and the Palestinian Targum in the Pentateuch (Rome: Pontifical Biblical Institute, 1966), in Biblica XLVIII (1967), pp. 302-306. He says on the last page, "Je poserais cependant une question: la mise en écrit du Targoum sous la forme et dans la langue où il nous parvient a-t-elle été fait avant le temps du NT? Ne voudrait-il pas mieux envisager au 1er siècle une tradition orale, substantiellement fixée, mais non encore 'recensée'?." For further discussion, see the Targum bibliographies of P. Nickels (Rome: Pontifical Biblical Institute, 1967) and B. Grossfeld (New York: Ktav, 1972).

4   Especially when, according to J. A. Fitzmyer, the language of the Targums is later than that of the first century. See his review of the third edition of Black's Aramaic Approach, in C.B.Q. XXX (1968), pp. 417-428, and "The Languages of Palestine in the First Century A.D.," C.B.Q. XXXII (1970), pp. 501-531.

5   See McNamara, pp. 5-37.

6   McNamara, pp. 145-149, suggests that slq lies behind hupsoun in John.

7   "The Quotation from the Old Testament in John XII 34," Novum Testamentum III (1959), pp. 175 f. (citing x 34; xv 25).

8   J. F. Stenning, The Targum of Isaiah (Oxford: Clarendon, 1949) 32.

9   C. W. H. Pauli, The Chaldee Paraphrase on the Prophet Isaiah (London: London Society's House, 1871) 30, 31.

10   S. H. Levey, The Messiah: An Aramaic Interpretation - The Messianic Exegesis of the Targum: Monographs of the Hebrew Union College 2 (New York: Hebrew Union College, 1974) 153 n. 31.

11   Cf. The Glory of Israel, p. 87, where this observation influenced me in favour of Stenning's translation, as compared to Levey's. Since that time, my work on the commentary has caused me to develop a third rendering.

12   J. B. van Zijl, A Concordance to the Targum of Isaiah: SBL Aramaic Studies 3 (Missoula: Scholars Press, 1979). For the translation and commentary noted here, cf. Essay 5, n. 1.

ESSAY 7 --

Gottesherrschaft als Gotteserfahrung
Erkenntnisse der Targumforschung für den neutestamentlichen
Begriff "Königsherrschaft Gottes"

Die Bedeutung der Königsherrschaft Gottes in der Predigt Jesu ist
in der einschlägigen Literatur dieses Jahrhunderts vor allem als
eine literarisch-historische Frage behandelt worden. Trotzdem lassen sich auch bestimmte theologische Tendenzen erkennen, die sich
innerhalb der wichtigsten Beiträge der Forschung,[1] nämlich der von
Johannes Weiss, Albert Schweitzer, C. H. Dodd und Joachim
Jeremias, leicht aufzeigen lassen.

Im Vorwort der zweiten Auflage seines berühmten Buches "Die
Predigt Jesu vom Reiche Gottes" hatte Weiss erklärt, dass seine
Stellungnahme das "Ergebnis eines" ihn "bedrängenden persönlichen
Conflictes" sei.[2] Nicht nur als Schüler, sondern auch als
Schweigersohn Albrecht Ritschls wurde Weiss stark von der libera-
len Auffassung seines Lehrers über das Reich Gottes beeinflusst,[3]
das mit Ritschls Worten "das höchste Gut, welches Gott uns
Menschen verwirklicht, und zugleich ihre gemeinschaftliche
Aufgabe" ist, "da die Herrschaft Gottes nur an der Leistung von
Gehorsam durch die Menschen ihren Bestand hat."[4] Weiss hatte also
noch die Überzeugung, dass Ritschls System Bedeutung und Wert für
das moderne Leben habe. "Aber schon früh," schrieb er, "beunru-
higte mich die deutliche Empfindung, dass Ritschls Gedanke vom
Reiche Gottes und die gleichnamige Idee in der Verkündigung Jesu
zwei verschiedene Dinge seien."[5] Wilhelm Baldensperger hatte schon
in einem Buch, das im selben Jahr wie Ritschls "Christliche Lehre"
erschienen war, versucht, das messianische Selbstbewusstsein Jesu
von den Hoffnungen und der programmatischen Zuversicht der jüdischen Apokalyptik her zu begreifen.[6] "Apokalyptik" wurde das
Lieblingswort mancher Leben-Jesu-Forscher, aber Weiss selbst gab
freimütig zu, dass die Königsherrschaft Gottes in der Predigt Jesu
kein eigentlicher apokalyptischer Begriff sei. Denn "seiht man
sich in der einigermassen gleichzeitigen apokalyptischen Literatur
nach directen Parallelen zu dem Ausdruck und Begriff 'Reich
Gottes' um, so findet man ausserordentlich wenig."[7] Weiss hatte
also bereits erkannt, was T. F. Glasson später noch deutlicher und
nachdrücklicher sagen sollte, dass es nämlich in der uns heute
bekannten Literatur keine Verwendung des Begriffs
"Königsherrschaft Gottes" in einem apokalyptischen Zusammenhang
gibt. In der zweiten Auflage seines genannten Buches hat sich
Weiss beklagt, dass die achtjährige Auseinandersetzung seit dem
Erscheinen der ersten Ausgabe 1892 sich zu sehr mit "einer
unfruchtbaren Fragestellung" beschäftigt habe, nämlich "inwieweit
Jesus das Reich Gottes als noch zukünftig oder schon gegenwärtig
angesehen habe."[8] Nur in _einer_ Hinsicht wollte er die
Königsherrschaft Gottes als apokalyptisch gekennzeichnet wissen,
als sie nämlich "das messianische Selbstbewusstsein Jesu" verdeut-

85

liche.[9] Dieser messianische Gehalt der Verkündigung vom Reiche Gottes, von der perspektivischen Ansicht Jesu her betrachtet, sei eigentlicher apokalyptischer Bestandteil. Jesus sei getrieben, Heil und Gericht der Welt zu verkünden, "weil er die Nähe des Reiches Gottes mit Sicherheit vorausempfand und weil er sich in besonderer Weise als der Vertraute und Beauftragte Gottes wusste."[10] Der Gedankengang bei Weiss ist deutlich: Weil das Selbstbewusstsein Jesu seinen Grund in seinem Glauben an das Reich Gottes hat, ist dieses Selbstbewusstsein der Schlüssel, mit dem die Bedeutung dieses Wortes zu erschliessen ist. Für Weiss ist es eindeutig (so nach Baldensperger), "dass Jesu für sein Person ebenso wie für sein Werk die entscheidende Wendung erst von der Zukunft erhoffte."[11] Diese Ausrichtung des Selbstbewusstseins Jesu auf die Zukunft besage also, dass das Reich Gottes wesentlich ein zukünftiger bzw. apokalyptischer Begriff sei.

Es ist notwendig, diese Struktur der Darstellung bei Weiss zu verstehen. Sie zeigt uns, dass für ihn das "Apokalyptische" nicht die eigentliche Ursache für das Reich Gottes ist, sondern aus Jesu eigenem Selbstbewusstsein erwächst. Darum sei der temporale Aspekt der Gottesherrschaft unwichtig, ja sogar geradezu irreführend. Ohne diese christologische Auffassung bleibt dem, der sich mit Weiss' Werk beschäftigt, nur die wenig glaubhafte These, Jesus habe eine apokalyptische Herrschaft, aber keine zeitliche Abfolge der letzten Dinge gelehrt.[12] Bei Weiss darf das Reich Gottes nicht absolut betrachtet und vom "eigenartigen religiösen Bewusstsein Jesu" getrennt werden, dem der Religionsforscher "als vor etwas schlechthin Gegebenem" gegenüberstehe.[13] Der letzte Satz der zweiten Auflage erklärt Jesu Verständnis des Reiches Gottes als Auswirkung seiner Demut, weil er es "erst von dem Eingreifen seines himmlischen Vaters erwartet hat."[14]

Albert Schweitzer hat zwar die Apokalyptik als eine Quelle der Predigt Jesu über das Reich Gottes akzeptiert, aber doch in einer eingeschränkten Weise. In der "Vorrede zur sechsten Auflage" seiner "Geschichte der Leben-Jesu-Forschung" schrieb er: "Im Verlaufe dieser Forschung stellt sich immer mehr heraus, dass das fundamentale Problem dieses ist, ob Jesus die Vorstellungen der spätjüdischen Eschatologie von dem Kommen des Reiches Gottes und dem des Messias voraussetzt, oder ob er eine nicht eschatologische an ihre Stelle setzt."[15] Es braucht kaum gesagt zu werden, dass seine Neigung in Richtung jener Alternative ging, doch ist die Vehemenz bemerkenswert, mit der er betont, dass das Problem des Lebens Jesu "im wesentlichen gelöst" werde "durch die aus der spätjüdischen Eschatologie gewonnene Erkenntnis."[16] Die Interpretation durch Weiss bildet auch die Grundlage seiner Darstellung, auch wenn er - völlig abweichend von ihm - schreiben konnte: "Die primitive, spätjüdische Metaphysik, in der Jesus seine Weltanschauung ausspricht, erschwert die Übersetzung seiner Ideen in die Formeln unserer Zeit in ausserordentlicher Weise."[17] Denn Weiss selbst hatte darin, wie wir schon gesehen haben, kein eigentliches Problem gesehen, weil für ihn Jesu Predigt vom Reich Gottes Ausdruck seines Selbstverständnisses war. Trotzdem hat Schweitzer bekanntlich auf ihn das "dritte grosse Entweder- Oder" in der Leben-Jesu-Forschung zurückgeführt: "entweder eschatologisch oder uneschatologisch."[18]

Warum hat Schweitzer die These von Weiss so radikal angewandt? Zwei Gründe sind dafür anzuführen. Zuerst hat Schweitzer den Beitrag seines Vorgängers am Werk Reimarus' gemessen. Bei der Darstellung der "Predigt Jesu" von Weiss sah sich Schweitzer veranlasst, auch Reimarus einzubeziehen: "Hier ist der Ort, sich des Reimarus zu erinnern. Er war der erste und einzige vor Johannes Weiss gewesen, der es erkannt und ausgesprochen hatte, dass Jesu Predigt nur eschatologisch war."[19] Schweitzer wurde so stark von Reimarus beeindruckt, dessen Vorstellung von der Absicht Jesu, die apokalyptischen Ereignisse zu verkürzen, er akzeptierte, dass Weiss in seiner Darstellung mehr als Reimarus' denn Ritschls Schwiegersohn erscheint. Der zweite Grund ist der wichtigere. Wie schon angedeutet, veranlasste die These, Jesus habe eine apokalyptische Metaphysik vertreten, Schweitzer zu der Schlussfolgerung, dass es fast unmöglich sei, die Predigt Jesu in eine moderne Denkweise zu übertragen. Versuche in dieser Richtung von liberaler Seite erschienen ihm vergeblich: "Der Jesus von Nazareth, der als Messias auftrat, die Sittlichkeit des Gottesreiches verkündete, das Himmelreich auf Erden gründete und starb, um seinem Werke die Weihe zu geben, hat nie existiert."[20] Die eschatologische Art und Weise der Predigt Jesu, wie Schweitzer sie verstand, macht es unvermeidlich, dass Jesu nur "als ein Unbekannter und Namenloser" zu uns kommt, um die häufig zitierten Worte des letzten Paragraphen seines Buches anzuführen.[21]

Es bliebe oberflächig, Schweitzers christologische Denkweise auf diesen Satz zu beschränken. Nach ihm ist die Fremdartigkeit Jesu nicht nur eine Folge unseres geschichtlichen Abstandes, sondern gleichzeitig auch die Möglichkeit, den richtigen Zugang zu seiner Persönlichkeit zu finden. Die historische Forschung zeige, dass die Wirkung Jesu auf unser Leben nicht nur geschichtlich begriffen werden könne: "Jesus ist unserer Welt etwas, weil eine gewaltige geistige Strömung von ihm ausgegangen ist und auch unsere Zeit durchflutet. Diese Tatsache wird durch eine historische Erkenntnis weder erschüttert noch gefestigt."[22] Jesus wird in Schweitzers Denk-System zu einer geistigen Grösse, die angenommen werden kann, nicht durch den Versuch, zwischen dem Vergänglichen und dem Bleibenden in seiner eschatologischen Lehre zu unterscheiden, sondern durch "eine Übertragung des Urgedankens jener Weltanschauung in unsere Begriffe."[23] Diese Übertragung sei "ein Verstehen von Wille zu Wille:"[24] "In Wirklichkeit vermag er für uns nicht eine Autorität der Erkenntnis, sondern nur eine des Willens zu sein. Seine Bestimmung kann nur darin liegen, dass er als ein gewaltiger Geist Motive des Wollens und Hoffens, die wir und unsere Umgebung in uns tragen und bewegen, auf eine Höhe und zu einer Klärung bringt, die sie, wenn wir auf uns allein angewiesen wären und nicht unter dem Eindruck seiner Persönlichkeit ständen, nicht erzielen würden, und dass er so unsere Weltanschauung, trotz aller Verschiedenheit des Vorstellungsmaterials, dem Wesen nach der seinen gleichgestaltet und die Energie wachruft, die in der seinigen wirksam ist."[25] Die Eschatologie Jesu wird also für Schweitzer zur Gewähr dafür, dass keine Identität innerhalb einer nur geschichtlichen Entwicklung angenommen werden muss. Jesus werde nur verstanden, sofern man seine sittliche Handlungsweise übernehme: "Es handelt sich um ein Verstehen von Wille zu Wille, bei dem das Wesentliche der Weltanschauung unmittelbar gegeben ist."[26] Weil das "Wesentliche" der Eschatologie Jesu nur sittlich zu erfassen sei, ist unsere Beziehung zu ihm "mystischer Art,"[27] und dieses mystische Verhältnis bedeutet einen Ruf zur Umkehr an unsere moderne abendländische Gesellschaft, die nach Schweitzers Ansicht "das grosse Ziel einer sittlichen Endvollendung der gesamten Menschheit"[28] verloren habe: "Die eschatologische Auffassung Jesu ist also nicht, wie man es oft annimmt, eine Erschwerung seiner Verkündigung an unsere Zeit. Wenn wir nur das Zwingende in seiner Person und seiner Predigt vom Reich Gottes zu Worte kommen lassen, so kann das Fremdartige und Anstössige ruhig festgestellt werden."[29] Schweitzer glaubte, dass er die historische und geistige Chiffre, die die Persönlichkeit Jesu entziffere, gefunden habe. Das konnte auch den überraschenden Anspruch haben, dass jeder, der von dieser eschatologischen Auffassung abweiche, "die starke Ausprägung des Wollens und Hoffens auf die sittliche Endvollendung der Welt, die für Jesus und seine Weltanschauung entscheidend sind," verfehle.[30]

Weiss und Schweitzer haben beide - jeder auf seine Art - die Königsherrschaft Gottes im Blick auf die Christologie erklärt. Bei Weiss ist die Demut Jesu in seinem Hoffen auf das zukünftige Eingreifen Gottes bestimmend; bei Schweitzer ist die eschatologische Predigt Jesu charakteristisches Gewand seines Strebens nach einer sittlichen "Weltvollendung." Im wesentlichen war die christologische Orientierung dieser beiden Gelehrten, deren Einfluss noch in der gegenwärtigen Diskussion gross ist, bestimmend für ihr Verständnis der Königsherrschaft Gottes. Nachdem die Eschatologie Jesu ihre christologische Absicht erreicht hatte, hielten sie sie für abgeschlossen. Weiss gar hat die erste Ausgabe seines Buches mit den Worten beendet: "Wir warten nicht auf ein Reich Gottes, welches von Himmel auf die Erde herabkommen soll und diese Welt vernichten, sondern wir hoffen, mit der Gemeinde Jesu Christi in die himmlische <u>basileia</u> versammelt zu werden."[31]

Ganz ähnlich hat Schweitzer formuliert: "Nur darauf kommt es an, dass wir den Gedanken des durch sittliche Arbeit zu schaffenden Reiches mit derselben Vehemenz denken, mit der er den von göttlicher Intervention zu erwartenden in sich bewegte...."[32] Solange die Demut, die die Eschatologie Jesu einschliesst, anerkannt war, neigte Weiss dazu, die Gottesherrschaft ins künftige Leben hineinzuverlegen. Schweitzer erklärte sie als eine sittliche Bewegung, eine übertragene Deutung, die ihm angemessen erschien, solange die Predigt Jesu nicht in eine liberale Skizze umgestaltet würde. Die Eschatologie wird bei beiden Forschern zu einen Schirm, der den historischen (und wirklichen) Jesus vor einer liberalen, ganz diesseitigen Analyse beschützt; sie ist eine "Dienstmagd" der Christologie und hat, für sich betrachtet, keinen unverändert bleibenden Gehalt.

C. H. Dodd hat in seinem Buch "The Parables of the Kindom" grundlegende Schwierigkeiten für "konsequente Eschatologie" Schweitzers und seiner Nachfolger aufzeigt. Ihm war bewusst, wie Weiss vor ihm, dass die apokalyptische Literatur mit nur einigen Ausnahmen den Gebrauch des Wortes "Reich Gottes" meidet.[33] Aber er betonte, dass solche Stellen wie Mt 12, 28 (und ihre Parallele Lk 11, 20) das Reich Gottes nach Jesu Auffassung als schon gekommen charakterisieren.[34] Aus diesem Grund erklärte er die Thesen von Weiss und Schweitzer für widerlegt; in den Evangelien werde das schon gekommene Reich Gottes mit Jesus selbst und seinem Auftreten verknüpft.[35] Mit diesen und ähnlichen Erwägungen bestritt er die rein zukünftige Erwartung vom Reich Gottes und ersetzte sie durch den Begriff der "realisierten Eschatololgie," der erfahrenen Gottesherrschaft:[36] "The eschaton has moved from the future to the present, from the sphere of expectation into that of realized experience. It is therefore unsafe to assume that the content of the idea, 'The Kingdom of God,' as Jesus meant it, may be filled in from the expectations of apocalyptic writers. They were referring to something in the future, which could be conceived of only in terms of fantasy. He was speaking of that which, in one aspect at least, was an object of experience."[37]

Die exegetische Sorgfalt, die Dodd zu seinen Ergebnissen geführt hat, wirkte so überzeugend auf Joachim Jeremias, dass er ebenfalls die Idee vom Reich Gottes als etwas schon Erfahrenem in seiner Darstellung der Gleichnisse übernommen hat. Er kam, fast übereinstimmend mit Dodd, zu dem Schluss, dass die Gleichnisse "alle erfüllte von dem 'Geheimnis der Königsherrschaft Gottes' (Mk 4, 11)" seien - "nämmlich der Gewissheit der 'sich realisierenden Eschatologie.'" Die Botschaft der Gleichnisse fasst er wie Dodd so zusammen: "Die Stunde der Erfüllung ist da, das ist ihr Grundton."[38] Die Einsicht Dodds in die diskursive Art des Reiches Gottes wurde durch die weiter entwickelte, formgeschichtliche Methode, die Jeremias anwendet, bestätigt.

Dodd hat nicht nur statuiert, dass die Königsherrschaft Gottes eine gegenwärtige Erfahrung sei, sondern er schritt weiter voran und beschrieb den Inhalt dieser Erfahrung. Bei den Gleichnissen wird nach seiner Beobachtung das Reich Gottes mit natürlichen Prozessen verglichen, und zwar in einer ganz unterschiedlichen Weise von der Denkweise des apokalyptischen Judentums.[39] Hier beginnt die These Dodds problematisch zu werden. Weil einige Gleichnisse innerweltliches Geschehen und das Reich Gottes nebeneinander stellen, kam Dodd zu dem allgemeinen Schluss, dass die Göttlichkeit der Natur der gesamten Lehre Jesu zugrunde läge.[40] Gegen Ende seines Buches sprach Dodd beinahe im Sinn der Inkarnation über die Königsherrschaft Gottes: "It appears that while Jesus employed the traditional symbolism of apocalypse to indicate the 'other-worldly' or absolute character of the Kingdom of God, He used parables to enforce and illustrate the idea that the Kingdom of God has come upon men then and there. The inevitable had happened: history had become the vehicle of the eternal; the absolute was clothed with flesh and blood."[41] Dieser Anklang an die "Fleischwerdung" ist kein Zufall: Auf den vorhergehenden Seiten hatte Dodd Jesus selbst, nicht die Gottesherschaft, zu dem erfahrenen Inhalt realisierter Eschatologie gemacht. So sagt er, dass das Reich Gottes neben Jesus selbst komme,[42] und ferner, dass in der Wirkung Jesu die göttliche Kraft gegenüber dem Bösen unbehindert erscheine.[43] Zuletzt nennt er die Wirkung Jesu selbst realisierte Eschatololgie.[44] Wie bei den Arbeiten von Weiss und Schweitzer, wenn auch auf eine neue Weise, wird hier das Reich Gottes zum Mittel der Christologie. Darüberhinaus wird für die Christologie Dodds eine ontologische Ausprägung innerhalb der Lehre Jesu beansprucht, die jedoch die Exegese nicht gesichert hat.

Es ist deshalb verständlich, dass Jeremias diesen zweiten Gesichtspunkt der These Dodds nicht übernommen hat. Aber auch, wenn er die ontologische Christologie Dodds in bezug auf das Reich Gottes ablehnt, wird Jesus bei ihm zum eigentlichen Gegenstand der Predigt vom Reich Gottes. Nachdem Jeremias vom Geheimnis des Reichs Gottes mit den oben zitierten Worten gesprochen hat, schliesst er den letzten Satz seines Buches an: "Denn erschienen ist Der, dessen verborgene Herrlichkeit hinter jedem Wort und jedem Gleichnis aufleuchtet, der Heiland."[45] Jeremias konnte diese Behauptung aufstellen, weil er fest davon überzeugt ist, dass Jesus in dem Gebrauch des Begriffs "Reich Gottes" "ihn (sc. den Terminus) darüber hinaus mit einem neuen Inhalt gefüllt hat, der analogielos ist."[46] Die Schlussfolgerung, die hier - wie bei seinem Verständnis der "Abba"- und "Amen"-Worte, dem seit kurzem hart widersprochen wird[47] - gezogen wird, wird auf der Voraussetzung aufgebaut, dass die Eigentümlichkeit des Gebrauchs der Aussagen vom "Reich Gottes" durch Jesus mehr auf seiner obersten Autorität beruhe, als auf dem tatsächlichen Inhalt des Terminus. Der Begriff "Reich Gottes," der in der Predigt Jesu erscheint, ist aber - wie wir sehen werden und andere hier erwähnte Forscher einräumen - kaum eigentümlich für Jesus. Des weiteren ist es mindestens zweifelhaft, ob der Inhalt der Königsherrschaft Gottes, die so sehr und notwendig im Zentrum der Verkündigung Jesu steht, an den Rand unseres Verständnisses seiner Predigt gerückt werden darf.

90

Insofern die Kyrios-Logien die Königsherrschaft und die Persönlichkeit Jesu in direkter Bezugnahme auf Gott erwähnen, ist die Annahme berechtigt, dass die zwei Gruppen von Aussagen in einem Zusammenhang miteinander stehen. Dieser Zusammenhang ist aber nur stillschweigend gegeben, weil die Aussagen (ausser Mt 12, 28 und Lk 11, 20, die eine bedeutsame Ausnahme dazu bilden) normalerweise eine formale Beziehung zwischen Jesus und dem Reich Gottes nicht ausdrücken. Wenn die Königsherrschaft Gottes und das Konzept von der Persönlichkeit Jesu in den Aussagen in eins gefasst würden, könnte der Exeget beide in ihrer eigentlichen Verbindung belassen und eine Darstellung der Theologie der Aussagen insgesamt entwickeln. Die Grundaufgabe, ohne die solche Synthese unerreichbar bleibt, ist zu begreifen, was die Königsherrschaft Gottes selbst in den Logien exakt bedeutet. In allen Evangelien - zuerst den Synoptikern (vgl. Mt 4, 17; Mk 1, 14.15; Lk 4, 43), aber auch bei Johannes (vgl. 3, 3-5) - wird die Königsherrschaft Gottes nicht wie eine christologische Chiffre, sondern wie ein Entwurf, den Jesus ganz allgemein verstanden wissen will, vorgestellt.

Warum aber haben die modernen Gelehrten, deren Arbeiten wir erwähnt haben, dazu geneigt, die Königsherrschaft Gottes mit Jesus gleichzusetzen? Schweitzers Buch schloss eine ideologische Antwort auf diese Frage ein. Er hat in der Vorrede seines Buches festgestellt: "Die Leben-Jesu-Forschung ist eine Wahrhaftigkeitstat des protestantischen Christentums;" doch auf derselben Seite kann er behaupten, dass dieses Christentum "Nicht kirchgläubig, sondern christgläubig ist."[48] Innerhalb solcher systematischer Begrenzung ist die christologische Auslegung der Königsherrschaft Gottes vielleicht unabwendbar, aber das ist noch keine Gewähr für ihre exegetische Richtigkeit. Wenn wir rein exegetisch vorgehen, legt sich eine praktischere Antwort auf unsere Frage nahe. Die Forscher haben bei ihren Versuchen, den Inhalt der Predigt vom Reich Gottes zu bestimmen, kein zeitgenössisches jüdisches Konzept finden können, durch das die Bedeutung des Begriffes für Jesus verständlich werden Könnte. Die apokalyptische Literatur - wie Weiss und Dodd erkannt hatten - bietet keinen eindeutigen Anhaltspunkt dafür. Die verschiedenen rabbinischen Aussagen, die vom Aufnehmen des Joches der Königsherrschaft der Himmeln sprechen, scheinen - wie Jeremias erörtert hat - eine Gesetzesorientierung widerzuspiegeln, die seit der Zeit von Jabne vorherrschend geworden ist. Die Neigung, die Königsherrschaft Gottes auf eine christologische Darstellung zu reduzieren, ist also verständlich, aber der Schluss ist unausbleiblich, dass die Predigt vom Reich Gottes durch Jesus damit noch nicht in ihrem Kern verstanden ist. Weil der Entwurf vom "Reich Gottes" den Mittelpunkt seiner Predigt und Wirksamkeit bildet, ist eine Erfassung seiner Lehre ohne das Verständnis dieser Königsherrschaft Gottes ausserordentlich schwer und vielleicht auch, kritisch gesehen, unmöglich.

In recht sonderbarer Weise scheinen die Redewendungen "Gotteskönigsherrschaft" und "Herrenkönigsherrschaft" in jüdischen Urkunden, die, wie nachgewiesen worden ist, auf vorchristliches Gedankengut zurückgehen, wenigstens in einem bestimmten Mass Entsprechendes zu enthalten. Die aramäischen Paraphrasen des Alten Testaments, die Targume, verwenden einigemal diesen Ausdruck (vgl. Onkelos zu Ex 15, 18; Jonathan zu Jes 23, 24; 31, 4; 40, 9; 52, 7; zu Ez 7, 7.9; zu Ob 21; zu Mi 4, 7; zu Sach 14, 9). Jeremias hat zwar diese Belege erwähnt, sie aber im Zusammenhang der allgemeinen rabbinischen Auffassung über die Königsherrschaft Gottes belassen.[49] Folglich hat er die besondere Bedeutung dieses Begriffes in den Targumen übersehen. Wir werden uns in dem nächsten Aufsatz mit den Targumen und ihrem Gebrauch des Begriffs der Königsherrschaft näher beschäftigen, können aber schon hier einige Bemerkungen vorwegnehmen, die die Königsherrschaft Gottes in der Predigt Jesu vorläufig verdeutlichen können. Da der hebräische Text, der in den Targumen paraphrasiert wird, im wesentlichen zugänglich ist, können wir auf diesem Hintergrund gut erkennen, wie die Übersetzer das Wort von der Königsherrschaft benutzt und verstanden haben. Es bezieht sich zunächst auf das eigene Dasein Gottes um seiner Menschen willen; es hat mit irgendeiner Regierungsform ohne Gott nichts zu tun. Der Blick ist folgerichtig auf Gott selbst gerichtet. Die Targume sprechen von der Königsherrschaft dann - und nur dann - , wenn die hebräischen Bibelstellen das persönliche Eintreten Gottes aussagen. Der targumische Begriff von der Königsherrschaft Gottes ist kein starres apokalyptisches Konzept. Obgleich die Herrschaft Gottes in den Targumen wie eine zukünftige Offenbarung angesehen werden kann (und meist auch wird, vgl. zu Jes 23, 24; 31, 4; Ob 21; Mi 4, 7; Sach 14, 9), wird sie auch bei der konkreten Ankündigung des Herannahens Gottes gebraucht (vgl. zu Jes 40, 9; 52, 7; Ez 7, 7) und ebenso - an einer Stelle - in Verbindung mit einem zeitlichen Ereignis gesehen (vgl. zu Ex 15, 18). Übrigens ist die gesetzliche Orientierung des rabbinischen Begriffs der Gottesherschaft hier nicht zu finden. Die Targume verwenden Aussagen über die Königsherrschaft nachdrücklicher als andere jüdische Urkunden, die möglicherwiese Überlieferungen tradiern, die gleichzeitig zu der Entstehung des Neuen Testaments sind. Ausserdem ist der targumische Gebrauch, wie der Jesu, frei von zeitlichen und geseltzlichen Beschränkungen.

Im Zusammenhang einer redaktions- und traditionsgeschichtlichen Darstellung habe ich vorgeschlagen,[50] dass der Gebrauch des Begriffs Königsherrschaft in den Targumen zu einem Verständis des Begriffs "Reich Gottes" bei Jesus führen könne. Die Einschätzung dieser Arbeit als einem exegetischen Beitrag sei anderen überlassen. Der Zweck hier ist mehr theologischer Art - zu Bedenken zu geben, dass der targumische Begriff wichtig ist für den Versuch, die Predigt Jesu darzustellen. Unsere Einwände gegen die Arbeiten von Weiss, Schweitzer, Dodd und Jeremias gehen gegen ihre Neigung, die Predigt Jesu in moderne theologische bzw. christologische

Konzepte einzuzwängen. Die praktischen und ideologischen Aspekte dieser Neigung sind eindrucksvoll. In beiden Richtungen könnte der targumische Gebrauch unser Problem lösen helfen. In praktischer Hinsicht geben die Targume eine klare und häufig ausgesprochene Auffassung der Königsherrschaft wieder. Wenn diese Auffassung schon in den Targumen der Zeit Jesu vorauszusetzen ist, wird die Zuversicht Jesu, dass die Hörer, denen er verkündigte, ohne Erklärung seine Predigt vom Reich Gottes begreifen konnten, leicht zu verstehen. In ideologischer Hinsicht zeigen die Targume einen Begriff der Königsherrschaft, der unberührt von christologischen Tendenzen ist.[51]

Johannes Weiss hatte bereits erkannt, dass die Predigt Jesu die theologischen Moden der nachreformatorischen Zeit in Frage stellte,[52] und die Herausforderung, die davon ausging, so möchte ich sagen, ist radikaler, als er dachte. Wann die Targume von der Königsherrschaft reden, beziehen sie sich auf Gott als einer dynamischen Gewalt in Vergangenheit, Gegenwart und Zukunft um seiner Menschen willen. Wenn Jesus diese Königsherrschaft Gottes verkündigte, können wir zwar unsere Christologie innerhalb der Aussagen vom Reich Gottes erklären - aber nicht umgekehrt, denn die Christologie ist keine Bedingung der targumischen Königsherrschaft. Um dies zu verdeutlichen, wollen wir im nächsten Aufsatz die Königsherrschaft in den prophetischen Targumen untersuchen.

ANMERKUNGEN

1   Vgl. die beiden Publikationen von N. Perrin bzw. G. Lundstrom, die 1963 unter dem Titel The Kingdom of God in the Teaching of Jesus veröffentlicht wurden, und B. D. Chilton, The Kingdom of God, 1984.

2   Die Predigt Jesu vom Reiche Gottes, 2, Aufl. 1900, S. V. Die erste Auflage war 1892 erschienen.

3   W. G. Kümmel, Das Neue Testament. Geschichte der Erforschung seiner Probleme, 1958, S. 286.

4   Die christliche Lehre von der Rechtfertigung und Versöhnung, Bd. III, 3. Aufl. 1888, S. 30. Es ist bemerkenswert, dass diese Bestimmung auf der "Gleichartigkeit der Begriffe Reich Gottes und Rechtfertigung" basiert.

5   Die Predigt Jesu, S. V.

6   Kümmel, Das Neue Testament, S. 275; vgl. W. Baldensperger, Das Selbstbewusstsein Jesu im Lichte der messianischen Hoffnung seiner Zeit, 1888.

7   Die Predigt Jesu, S. 19; vgl. auch S. 11: "Es ist nämlich geradezu überraschend, wie selten uns diese Bezeichnung für die messianische Zeit oder das Heil der Endzeit im AT und im Judentum begegnet."

8   Die Predigt Jesu, S. 69.

9   Die Predigt Jesu, S. 175.

10   Die Predigt Jesu, S. 176.

11   Die Predigt Jesu, S. 178.

12   Vgl. z.B. N. Perrin, Jesus and the Language of the Kingdom: Symbol and Metaphor in New Testament Interpretation, 1976, S. 77.

13   Die Predigt Jesu, S. 176.

14   Die Predigt Jesu, S. 178.

15   Geschichte der Leben-Jesu-Forschung, 6. Aufl. 1951, S. V. Die erste Auflage war 1906 erschienen.

16   Geschichte, S. XII. Vgl. S. XVII zur Parusieverzögerung.

17   Geschichte, S. 635. Vgl. T. F. Glasson, Schweitzer's Influence - Blessing or Bane?, in: JThSt 28, 1977, S. 289-302.

18   Geschichte, S. 232.

19   Geschichte, S. 234.

20   Geschichte, S. 631; auf derselben Seite deutet sich schon der berühmte letzte Satz des Buches an: "In der besonderen Bestimmtheit seiner Vorstellung und seines Handelns erkannt, wird er für unsere Zeit immer etwas Fremdes und Rätselhaftes behalten."

21   Geschichte, S. 642.

22   Geschichte, S. 632.

23   Geschichte, S. 635.

24   Geschichte, S. 639.

25   Geschichte, S. 636.

26   Geschichte, S. 639.

27   Geschichte, S. 641.

28   Geschichte, S. 637-638.

29 Geschichte, S. 640.

30 Geschichte, S. 636.

31 Die Predigt Jesu, 1. Aufl., S. 67.

32 Geschichte, S. 639; auf derselben Seite bemerkt er fast lakonisch: "Dass er eine übernatürlich sich realisierende Endvollendung erwartet, während wir sie nur als Resultat der sittlichen Arbeit begreifen können, ist mit dem Wandel in dem Vorstellungsmaterial gegeben."

33 Erste Aufl. 1935. Ich zitiere nach dem Neudruck (1965) der 2. revidierten Aufl. 1961, S. 24 Anm. 2. Die erste revidierte Auflage erschien 1936.

34 Parables, S. 30.

35 Parables, S. 55.

36 Parables, S. 35: "The impact upon this world of the 'powers of the world to come' in a series of events, unprecedented and unrepeatable, now in actual process." Vgl. Kümmel, Das Neue Testament, Anm. 459 zum späteren Wortgebrauch Dodds: "inaugurated eschatology."

37 Parables, S. 34.

38 Die Gleichnisse Jesu, 9. Aufl. 1977, S. 227, auch S. 5. Vgl. auch Kümmel, Das Neue Testament, Anm. 459 und J. Jeremias, Neutestamentliche Theologie. Teil I: Die Verkündigung Jesu, 1971, S. 26f.43.105f.110.

39 Parables, S. 10f. : "...the Kingdom of God is intrinsically like the processes of nature." "This sense of the divineness of the natural order is the major premise of all the parables, and it is the point where Jesus differs most profoundly from the outlook of the Jewish apocalyptists, with whose ideas He had on some sides much sympathy."

40 Vgl. "the diviness of the nature order" im Zitat der vorigen Anm.

41 Parables, S. 159.

42 Parables, S. 30. In Anm. 2 zitiert Dodd die äusserst wichtige Behauptung Rudolf Ottos, die er dann aber nicht berücksichtigt: "Nicht Jesus 'bringt' das Reich - eine Vorstellung, die Jesus selber ganz fremd ist - sondern das Reich bringt ihn mit." Zu der Stellungnahme Ottos s. Kümmel, Das Neue Testament, S. 496. Dodd

(Parables, S. 24 Anm. 2) bestreitet zurecht die religionsgeschichtliche Ausführung Ottos, die vor allem in seinen 1934 erschienenen Buch "Reich Gottes und Menschensohn. Ein religionsgeschichtlicher Versuch" ausgeführt wird. In der Tat tritt jedoch bei Otto ein philosophisches Motiv stärker hervor. Es wird in seiner Darstellung des Systems von Jakob Friedrich Fries "Die Kantisch-Fries'sche Religionsphilosophie und ihre Anwendung auf die Theologie. Zur Einleitung in die Glaubenslehre für Studenten der Theologie," 1921, gründlicher entwickelt. In ihm beschäftigt sich Otto mit dem Gefühl von etwas Erfahrenem als Grund religiöser Erkenntnis: "Aus unserer religionsphilosophischen Grundlage heraus haben wir das Mittel, dieses seltsame Phänomen, das in Wahrheit das Zentrum des religiösen Erlebens ausmacht, allgemein zu deuten: es ist das im Gefühl lebendig werdende dunkle Erkennen des Ewigen überhaupt und der ewigen Bestimmung des Seins. Und als Christen glauben wir, dass diese in Wahrheit 'Gotteskindschaft' und 'Gottesreich' ist" (S. 198f). Vgl. noch S. 105.110.122. Diese teleologische Auffassung (S. 122) liegt seiner Darstellung des "Reichs Gottes" zugrunde, während ihre religionsgeschichtliche Bestimmung, die durch die Apokalyptik einer persischen Art betont, nur als eine methodologische Ausprägung anzusehen ist. Fries selbst hat sich mehr ästhetisch als teleologisch ausgesprochen: "Wir glauben nicht an das tausendjährige Reich..., sondern allein an das Gottesreich unter der Herrschaft der ewigen Schönheit und der heiligen Liebe..." (Die Religionsphilosophie oder die Weltzwecklehre. Sämtliche Schriften Bd. XII, 1970, S. 144). Bemerkenswert sind auch seine Bezugnahme auf "den heiligen Ernst der sittlichen Ideen," die mit dem Gottesreich gleichzusetzen sind (S. 143, vgl. Schweitzer!) und auf die "Ahndung" dieser ewigen Ideen (S. 198, vgl. das "Heitlige" bei Otto).

43   Parables, S. 35.

44   Ibid.

45   Gleichnisse, S. 227; vgl. S. 226: "Sie (sc. die Gleichnishandlungen) zeigen, dass Jesus die Botschaft der Gleichnisse nicht nur verkündigt hat, sondern dass er sie lebte in seiner Person und verkörperte."

46   Theologie, S. 43; vgl. S. 105f.110.

47   Vgl. G. Vermes, Jesus the Jew, 1973; B. D. Chilton, "Amen:" an Approach through Syriac Gospels, in: ZNW 69, 1978, S. 203-211, und S. 15ff. in diesem Band.

48   Geschichte, S. XVIII.

49   Jeremias, Theologie (2. Aufl. 1973), S. 105 Anm. 23.

50   God in Strength: Jesus' announcement of the Kingdom, 1979; vgl. Regnum Dei Deus Est, in: SJTh 31, 1978, S. 261-270, und S. 99ff. in diesem Band.

51   Vgl. M. Lattke, Zur jüdischen Vorgeschichte des synoptischen Begriffs der "Königsherrschaft Gottes," in: P. Fiedler - D. Zeller, Gegenwart und kommendes Reich, 1975, S. 9-25, spez. S. 12.

52   Die Predigt Jesu, 1. Aufl., S. 5.

"The Kingdom of God" is central in the proclamation of Jesus, the
reality to which his preaching points and which the parables are
designed to explicate;[1] the student of the New Testament must
understand this concept if he is to appreciate dominical theology,
and the ecclesial theology which developed from it. Since Albert
Schweitzer's well-known study, it has been taken as a matter of
course that Jesus' kingdom concept was "apocalyptic."[2] Yet just
this assumption has necessitated crucial qualifications. To take
two notable examples of this, Rudolf Bultmann assserted that Jesus
rejected "the whole content of apocalyptic speculation,"[3] and
Norman Perrin went a step or two further by saying that "the difference between Jesus and ancient Jewish apocalyptic is much
greater than Bultmann will allow."[4] At this point, the term "apocalyptic," as applied to Jesus' preaching, is practically evacuated of content. On purely logical grounds, the propriety of its
continued usage in this connexion is seriously to be questioned.

A serious historical objection to the consensus was voiced in
1964, when T. F. Glasson challenged the presupposition that the
"kingdom" is of apocalyptic provenience by pointing to "the striking fact that while the apocalypses and pseudepigrapha often deal
with the end-time and Messianic age they do not make use of the
precise phrase 'the kingdom of God'".[5] Glasson followed the lead
of T. W. Manson by turning to the Rabbinic phrase, "the kingdom of
the heavens;" here the kingdom can refer to the divine authority
which one takes on oneself by obedience.[6] But this position had
already been undermined by Norman Perrin who, in a critique of
Manson and Gustav Dalman, observed that these references in classical Rabbinic literature could not be used to establish
first-century diction.[7] Effectively, the present situation is one
of stalemate: apocalyptic usage fails to provide sufficiently
exact parallels to dominical kingdom diction, while the Rabbinic
passages in question come too late in the day for their parallels
to be conclusive. Strangely enough, then, a dearth of evidence is
the principal obstacle to our understanding Jesus' preaching, and
this nearly a century after Johannes Weiss.

Further evidence is presently available and, at the outset, the
possibility presents itself that some of it at least represents
first-century diction. I refer to exegeses contained in the
Latter Prophets Targums; these Aramaic documents are paraphrases
of the prophetic books occasioned by the decline in the ability of
some Jews (even some of those resident in Palestine) to understand
classical Hebrew. The Targums incorporate the exegetical understanding and vocabulary of the communities in which they were
used, and they appear to be the products of centuries of translation, discussion and selection.[8] In his magisterial study of the

prophetic Targums, P. Churgin found allusions to circumstances in the period ranging from before the destruction of the Temple to the persecution of the Jews in Sassanian Babylon much later.[9] This suggests that the Targums achieved their present form as part of the same process which gave us Mishnah, Midrash, and Talmud, a process dedicated to the preservation and evaluation of tradition. It is therefore possible that Jesus was familiar with diction presently contained in these documents, and even that he came to know it in association with the biblical passages which it presently explicates. How can we know if this is in fact, or even probably, the case?

For two reasons, our approach to this question must be circumspect. In the first place, these Targums are, as extant, too late to permit us to interpret Jesus' preaching as if he were directly and intimately familiar with them. Indeed, so far as the date of a given reading is concerned, the balance of probability must be tipped in favour of the view that it is later, rather than earlier, than a given New Testament passage, simply because these Targums had centuries of development in front of them by the time the Church's canon had achieved a fixed form. In the second place, Targumic renderings do not have the names of Rabbis attached to them, as is commonly the case in classical Rabbinic literature. Since this labelling is usually taken as a guide (however rough and ready) to the dating of Rabbinic traditions, Targumic passages cannot be dated by means of the standard procedure.

A different procedure is called for, one which can operate on the basis of the diction of the Targums alone, because this is the only evidence which they present. To speak of the date of an extant Targum, it would be necessary to place its characteristic exegeses in the context of other, datable Rabbinic pronouncements. In this way, the theology of a Targum, or a section thereof, would reasonably be associated with the Rabbinic circle to which it has the greatest affinity. The systematic application of such a method is clearly desirable, but it would constitute a major project and results should not be expected in the near future.[10] Fortunately, the student of the New Testament need not await the conclusive dating of extant Targums and their traditions; he is concerned only with those exegeses which display positive coherence with the New Testament passages with which he is concerned, because the Targums may on occasion provide evidence of the vocabulary and thought on which the canonical tradition is built. I have said "positive coherence" because a merely notional connection would not be enough to suggest that a Targumic rendering underlies a New Testament reading. After all, both bodies of literature take the Old Testament as read. Positive coherence may only be posited where there is a strong similarity in language which is not explicable on the supposition that the Hebrew and Greek Old Testaments have influenced the diction of the New Testament. If that is the case, further analysis is warranted. If the same thought is expressed by this similar language, coherence is established, but the possibility that the Targum represents pre-Christian diction must be weighed against the possibility that it is a deliberate riposte to Christian teaching. That is, the substance, as well as the language, of a rendering must be evaluated in order to determine its pedigree in relation to the New Testament. Only such methodological evaluation can avoid the Charybdis of interpreting Jesus' preaching in terms of later developments and the Scylla of discounting prematurely a potentially significant body of evidence.

So far as mere language is concerned, on eight occasions the Prophetic Targums make use of the precise phrase "kingdom of God" or "of the Lord."[11] This means that we are on to much harder linguistic parallels to dominical usage than we would be if we were to limit ourselves to apocalyptic material. Moreover, the Targumic usage is nearer to Jesus' phrase than the periphrasis, "the kingdom of the heavens," which both the Gospel according to Matthew and classical Rabbinic literature prefer. Given the principles of investigation set out in the previous paragraph, the identity between Targumic and dominical diction requires us to look more closely at those passages in the Prophetic Targums in which the usage occurs. To set out the evidence, I have translated first the Masoretic Text (MT) counterpart of the Targumic passage in question, and then the Targum (Tg) reference itself, underscoring its differentiae so that they are apparent at a glance.

It is convenient to begin with Targum Zechariah 14:9, because the use of kingdom diction in connexion with this verse can be dated with reasonable accuracy:

MT   and the LORD will be king upon all the earth
Tg   and the kingdom of the LORD will be revealed upon all the dwellers of the earth

"Kingdom" (mlkwt') appears in place of the corresponding MT term (mlk) and it takes the predicate "will be revealed" (from gl', which is familiar from Rabbinic usage)[12] to convey an emphasis on disclosure. It is not just that the LORD will reign: his kingdom, already a reality, will be manifest. At the same time, there is no question of the kingdom being separate from God because the clause as a whole renders an assertion in MT of what God himself will be. An allusion to Zechariah 14:9 in association with a statement about the kingdom is contained in material ascribed to the first-century Rabbi Eliezer ben Hyrcanos.[13] This Rabbi was the student of Rabbi Yohanan ben Zakkai, who according to Jacob Neusner was active in Galilee at about the same time Jesus was.[14] It is therefore conceivable (but no more than that) that Jesus and Yohanan shared a then current kingdom vocabulary which has been preserved in both the New Testament and the Targums. Be that as it may, R. Eliezer's statement forces us seriously to consider the possibility that Targumic references akin to Tg Zechariah 14:9 reflect a first-century conception.

So far we have considered only the first _differentia_ in Tg Zecharia 14:9 (the kingdom of, revealed), and not the second (the dwellers of). In itself, the latter addition does not alter the meaning of the Hebrew text. It tells in favour of the relative antiquity of this reading, however, that it is reproduced verbatim at Tg Obadaiah 21:

MT   and the kingdom will be the LORD's
Tg   and the kingdom of the LORD will be revealed upon
      all the dwellers of the earth

This suggests that the rendering at Zechariah 14:9 was practically a catchword for the interpreter of Obadaiah 21. Of course, the rather universalistic "dwellers" reading (which had no part in R. Eliezer's statement) might well have been introduced after the kingdom diction was already established; I only wish to suggest that Tg Obadaiah 21 shows that Tg Zechariah 14:9 was considered to be a conventional assertion of the divine kingship.

To recapitulate: the exegesis preserved in our passages accords with a first-century conception of the kingdom. We have also seen that "the kingdom of God" refers to God himself, as it were, personally. This pattern is also evident at Tg Isaiah 31:4:

MT   so the LORD of hosts will descend to fight upon
      Mount Zion
Tg   so the kingdom of the LORD of hosts will be
      revealed to dwell upon Mount Zion

What we have called a personal reference to God is especially evident here because "kingdom" does not represent a mlk-root word. This makes it undeniable that we must see more in "kingdom" than slavish translation; it refers in context to God's activity on behalf of his people. The question now is, does such a view of the kingdom coincide with that of Jesus? Recent research indicates not only that the understanding of the kingdom as God himself is consistent with Jesus' preaching, but that in the interpretation of certain parables it is difficult to see what Jesus meant if he did not have such an understanding (Matthew 18:23-35; 22:1-14; Mark 4:26-29).[15] In other words, the Targumic kingdom passages are substantively, as well as linguistically, coherent with Jesus' preaching of the kingdom.

The case for coherence could be rested here, because the evidence already indicates that Jesus' language and thought is similar to that of the Targums in the matter of kingdom diction, and there is not a whisper of anti-Christian apologetic in the Targumic passages so far discussed. The evidence, however, will bring us a bit further: Jesus used "the kingdom" in contexts similar to those in which it appears in the Isaiah Targum. Jesus applied festal imagery to the gathering of many from east and west in the kingdom (Matthew 8:11, 12/Luke 13:28, 29), and this imagery is reminiscent of the LORD's banquet in Isaiah 25:6-8. The connexion becomes more than a reminiscence when we read an explicit reference to the kingdom in Tg Isaiah 24:23:

MT   because the LORD of hosts reigns on Mount Zion

102

Tg   because the kingdom of the LORD of hosts will be
revealed on Mount Zion.
Since the connexion between this passage and Jesus' preaching is
linguistic, substantive, and contextual, it is worth noting that
it is virtually repeated at 31:4 (with the addition of "to dwell,"
representing MT "to fight," and with "upon," again following MT,
instead of "on"), and worth repeating that "kingdom" in the latter
passage represents the very activity of God. This is also the case
in the next passage to be cited. It is one of two in the Isaiah
Targum in which kingdom usages occur as announcements; their contexts indicate that they are to be proclaimed (40:9; 52:7):
    MT   behold your God
    Tg the kingdom of your God is revealed
    MT   your God reigns
    Tg the kingdom of your God is revealed
Since Jesus is also described as consistently preaching the kingdom (Mark 1:14, 15; Matthew 4:17, 23; 9:35; Luke 4:43; 8:1) and as
sending others to do so (Matthew 10:7; Luke 9:2, 60; 10:9, 11), we
have another contextual link between his view and that represented
in Tg Isaiah. The near identity of the above two Targumic passages, despite variation in the Hebrew, again suggests that the
interpreter's kingdom vocabulary was somewhat stereotyped, and
therefore that it is part of a definite view, we might almost say
a theology, and not an ad hoc translation. Finally, Tg Isaiah 40:9
is of particular interest because it is followed by a clause which
says that God reveals himself "in power" (btqwp). It is not
likely a coincidence that, in a unique phrase in Mark's Gospel,
Jesus speaks of the kingdom of God "in power" (en dunamei, 9:1).[16]

There is kingdom diction in other prophetic Targums, but it
appears to reflect later locutions, and such positive associations
with dominical logia as we have seen are not evident. Since this
is the case, it seems convenient to summarise our findings for Tg
Isaiah before proceeding. The kingdom here is not separable from
God, nor again is it simply a periphrasis for the verb mlk: it is
neither an autonomous regime nor does it merely refer to the
LORD's assertion of sovereignty. What is at issue is God's action,
his very being as God. It is permissible at this stage to suggest
that the dominical "kingdom" ought also to be seen as inalienable
from God. Seen in this way, the "kingdom of God" is not a distinct
entity which arrives apart from God, so that one need not pose
what   Johannes   Weiss   already   called   "die   unfruchtbare
Fragestellung" concerning the time of the kingdom.[17] Jesus' eschatology has been variously described as, e.g., "consistent,"
"realised," "self-realising" and "inaugurated,"[18] but the evidence
from Tg Isaiah shows that all the time we have been talking about
aspects of God's activity, which cannot be limited by time.
Because the kingdom is the self-revelation of God, it can be taken
as having various temporal dimensions, but none of these can be
taken to be the exclusive domain of the kingdom. Jesus announced
to his hearers the self-disclosure of the King; for him, as in Tg
Isaiah, regnum dei deus est.

For the sake of completeness, we may now turn to Targumic passages which apparently stem from a later period. Once the full phrase, "the kingdom of God," is familiar, one is inclined to use the term "kingdom" alone by way of abbreviation (as in the present paper). Such a usage occurs in the Gospel according to Matthew (see especially the summary statements 4:23; 9:35) and also in Tg Ezekiel 7:7(10):

MT   the crown(?) has come to you

Tg   the kingdom is revealed upon you

The usage in the Targum need not have any connexion with that in Matthew; we are speaking here of a natural development in the use of vocabulary in which dependence need not be postulatd. There is a further usage in Tg Micah which reflects a highly systematised theology (4:7b, 8):

MT   and the LORD will reign upon them in Mount Zion from now and forever, and you, tower of the flock, hill of the daughter of Zion, to you it will come, even the former dominion will come, the kingdom of the daughter of Jerusalem

Tg   and the kingdom the LORD will be revealed upon them in Mount Zion from now and forever, and you Messiah of Israel that is hidden from before the sins of the congregation of Zion, to you the kingdom is about to come, even the former dominion will come to the kingdom of the congregation of Jerusalem.

The Mount Zion-kingdom connexion is already familiar to us from Tg Isaiah 24:23; 31:4; Obadaiah 21, but there is a startling departure here in the progressive narrowing of the kingdom concept. The first use of the term simply replaces the root verb: the interpreter does not seem concerned substantially to alter the meaning of this clause. What does consume his interest is the scope of the revelation. The Targum announces that the kingdom is about to come to the messiah addressed, and this kingdom is subsequently associated with the "former dominion." This practical equation between God's kingdom and Jerusalem's autonomy is underlined in the last clause, in which the "congregation" (not presently a national unit) becomes the recipient of the blessing. Such a limited kingdom conception is not that of the New Testament, and it even disagrees with Tg Zechariah 14:9. Relatively speaking, then, this passage appears to be a late-comer to the Targumic tradition which corrects earlier notions. The idea that the messiah is hidden because of "the sins of the congregation" may permit us to date this passage. Generally speaking, the repeated use of "congregation" presupposes the Jewish loss of national status; more specifically, the rendering coheres with the fourth-century dictum that one day of Israelite repentance would bring the messiah.[19]

Targumic kingdom diction, then, is a rich seam for students of Christian and Jewish origins. These passsages provide specimens of a turn of phrase of which Jesus availed himself, and they illustrate that Rabbinic theology was not monolithic, but developed markedly after the formation of the New Testament. Historically speaking, Jesus' proclamation is an important event in the development of Judaism which cannot be appreciated until it is placed in its proper context. Once that is done, it appears that the dominical "kingdom of God" was no cipher in an esoteric view of history. Rather, a contemporary catch-phrase which referred to God was taken up by Jesus to serve as the key term in his vivid assertion that God is active among us.

NOTES

Essay 8 first appeared in SJT 31 (1978) 261-270.

1   This is an opinio communis, shared by, e.g., Norman Perrin, "The Kingdom of God," in Rediscovering the Teaching of Jesus (New York, 1967).

2   (Tr. W. Montgomery), The Quest of the Historical Jesus (London, 1910, 1963 from the 1906 German edition), see p. 365, "The eschatology of Jesus can therefore only be interpreted by the aid of the curiously intermittent Jewish apocalyptic literature of the period between Daniel and the Bar-Cochba rising."

3   (Tr. L. H. Smith and E. H. Lantero), Jesus and the Word (New York, 1934, 1958 from the 1926 German edition), p. 36; the italics are not my own.

4   Cf. Jesus and the Language of the Kingdom (London, 1976) p. 77.

5   "The Kingdom as Cosmic Catastrophe," in F. L. Cross (ed.), Studia Evangelica, III, part ii: Texte und Untersuchungen 88, pp. 187-8. In fairness, it should be noted that Psalms of Solomon 17:3 ("The kingdom of our God is eternal...') provides a near equivalent to our phrase, but the passage in question could not be called apocalyptic. Cf. the Testament of Moses 10:1, where the noun may mean no more than "rule," despite its usage within an eschatological scenario.

6   Glasson, p. 190; Manson, The Teaching of Jesus (Cambridge, 1931), pp. 130-2.

7   Cf. The Kingdom of God in the Teaching of Jesus (London, 1963, 1966), pp. 95, 24-7.

8   Two readable introductions to this subject: J. W. Bowker, The Targums and Rabbinic Literature (Cambridge, 1969); R. Le Déaut, Introduction à la littérature targumique (Rome, 1966). All citations from the prophetic Targums are taken from the Aramaic text of Alexander Sperber (Leiden, 1962). The Isaiah Targum has

been translated into English by J. F. Stenning (Oxford, 1949), cf. the seventeenth-century translation of all the prophetic Targums by Bishop Brian Walton in his monumental Biblia Sacra Polyglotta.

9   Cf. Targum Jonathan to the Prophets (New Haven, 1927); he cites Targum Isaiah 28:1, where reference is made to a wicked high priest (p. 23), and 21:9, where a second judgment on Babylon is predicted (p. 28). S. H. Levey, "The Date of Targum Jonathan to the Prophets," Vetus Testamentum 21 (1971), pp. 186-96 argues for a tenth-century terminus ad quem. While he does show a continuing interest in the prophetic Targums in the period of the Geonim, his argument is vitiated by the fact that his most convincing datum (the "Romulus" cipher for Rome at 11:4 which Saadia also used) is only a variant reading (see Sperber's critical apparatus). Since, however, the line between editorial redaction and textual trans-mission in Targum studies has not yet been clearly drawn, his contribution is a useful warning against assuming the antiquity of any reading.

10   A recent contribution to this field which is very impor-tant, if preliminary, is offered by M. Aberbach and B. Grossfeld, Targum Onkelos on Genesis 49: Society of Biblical Literature Aramaic Studies I (Missoula, 1976). For the treatment of render-ings which appear to cohere with New Testament passages, see M. McNamara, The New Testament and the Palestinian Targum to the Pentateuch (Rome, 1966) and Targum and Testament (Shannon, 1972).

11   Isaiah 24:23; 31:4; 40:9; 52.7; Ezekiel 7:7, 10; Obadaiah 21; Micah 4:7, 8; Zechariah 14:9, cf. the Masoretic text and Septaugint.

12   See, e.g., G. Dalman (tr. D. M. Kay), The Words of Jesus (Edinburgh, 1902), p. 97, and G. F. Moore, Judaism II (Cambridge, Mass., 1946), p. 374.

13   Mekilta Exodus 17:14 (p. 186, lines 4-7, of the Horovitz and Rabin edition (Jerusalem, 1960): "and the Place will be alone in eternity and his kingdom will be forever;" a citation of Zechariah 14:9 follows).

14   Cf. A Life of Rabban Yohanan ben Zakkai (Leiden, 1962), pp. 27-32.

15   See Perrin, The Kingdom, p. 184, and Joachim Jeremias (tr. S. H. Hooke), The Parables of Jesus (London, 1972), pp. 210-14; 176-80; 151-3. Chapter III of Perrin's Jesus and the Language updates Jeremias with a competent review of the recent discussion (and see pp. 195, 196).

16   In "An evangelical and critical approach to the sayings of Jesus," Themelios 3 (1978) 78-85, the verse is analysed in detail.

17 In the preface of the 1900 edition of <u>Die</u> <u>Predigt</u> <u>Jesu</u>.

18 For a handy review of this controversy, see O. Knoch, "Die eschatologische Frage," <u>Biblische</u> <u>Zeitschrift</u> 6 (1962), pp. 112-20.

19 H. L. Strack and P. Billerbeck, <u>Kommentar</u> <u>zum</u> <u>Neuen</u> <u>Testament</u> <u>aus</u> <u>Talmud</u> <u>und</u> <u>Midrasch</u> I (München, 1926), p. 164, citing the Jerusalem Talmud, Taanith I.I.

Jesus, the King and His Kingdom (1985)
by George Wesley Buchanan

The idea that Jesus was a political activist, whose aim was to
overthrow Roman rule in Israel, has received active attention for
more than two hundred years. H.S. Reimarus championed such a picture of Jesus during the eighteenth century, and he has attracted
some (usually qualified) support ever since. Robert Eisler portrayed Jesus as a military insurgent in a book which first
appeared in 1929, and his work was taken up by S.G.F. Brandon in
Britain. Brandon's Jesus and the Zealots (1967) remains the best
defence of the thesis in the modern period, largely by virtue of
the nuances it develops. Brandon believed Jesus was not himself a
Zealot, but remained independent of a revolutionary cell. That
qualification helps to explain why references to armed organization do not feature in the Gospels. It also gets over the
embarrassment, suffered by many accounts of Jesus as a revolutionary, that the Zealots are only mentioned (by Josephus) as a
military party long after Jesus' death, in connexion with the
Jewish revolt which resulted in the burning of Jerusalem in 70
C.E. Brandon argued, too, that the Gospels were written in order
to exculpate Jesus from the charge of insurrection. Once the documents are read in that way, of course, their silence about Jesus'
militarism can be taken to support the view that he was, in fact,
a revolutionary.

Brandon's subtle argumentation provoked a considered response,
Jesus and the Politics of His Day (1984), edited by Ernst Bammel
and C.F.D. Moule. No person who wishes seriously to entertain the
portrait of Jesus as a revolutionary can responsibly ignore that
volume; it reflects the careful historical and exegetical discussion which has cast the shadow of deepest doubt on the hypothesis.
As so often happens in biblical study, however, popular publications have been produced in cheerful ignorance of scholarly
inquiry, with the result that all manner of political complexions
are ascribed to Jesus in books of wide circulation. The more radical Jesus is made to appear, the better the market is likely to
be, according to the evident logic of some publishers. The affect
of such marketing on exegesis, the discipline of discovering what
texts mean in their own terms, seems to be a secondary consideration.

George Buchanan's book evidences wide reading, and represents
scholarly work of great complexity, but it also puts the case for
a revolutionary portrait of Jesus in a bald fashion. The author's
favorite comparison is between Jesus and the Ayatollah Khomeini:
"While the Shah ruled Iran, there was a kingdom of the followers
of Khomeini forming quietly within Iran...it was in the midst of
Iran and it did finally come into being. In a political resistance

movement, as one expects who is in quest of a kingdom, such a response as the one Jesus gave to the Pharisees seems fitting..." (p. 40, see also pp. 14, 217). The clarity of Buchanan's thesis is not marred by any tendency towards understatement. Jesus is said to have referred to God's kingdom "as a name or code word for a distinctly political monarchy" (p. 38); his disciples joined him in the "goal of acquiring the Kingdom of Heaven" (p. 102) by means of a "political movement" (p. 119), an "undercover government" (p. 217), a "military-religious enterprise" (p. 222).

The diverse contents of Buchanan's book cannot be summarized in the space allowed here, but two foundational arguments, on which the logic of his case rests, can be surveyed. The first foundation is the understanding of God's kingdom in early Judaism. Buchanan contends that "the term 'Kingdom of Heaven' could be used as a code word for the restoration of the promised land" (p. 24); "It takes place when the promised land is under Jewish control" (p. 25). If such were the case, Jesus might indeed be expected to have used the phrase in a similar way. The second foundation of Buchanan's case consists of Jesus' own sayings, particularly those the author calls "chreias," which are brief reminiscences of what characters from the past said, sometimes which an indication of setting. Although the khreia is a category of Greek rhetoric, Buchanan applies it to Jewish and Christian literature, as well, and he argues that "The scribes -- whether Greek rhetoricians, Jewish rabbis, or Christian leaders -- seemed (sic) to have been very conscientious in their respect for basic messages of speakers" (pp. 71, 72). And Buchanan is convinced that Jesus' basic message was militantly political.

Buchanan's first foundation is constructed from his reading of the Targums, which are paraphrases of the Hebrew Bible in Aramaic. Targumic research has attracted much interest in recent years, to some extent because they help us to see how the Bible was understood by Jews during the period in which the New Testament was formed. The phrase "kingdom of God" (or its equivalent), for example, was used innovatively by those who produced the Targums, without the warrant of the Hebrew text. The Aramaic translators brought to expression their hope for God's dynamic intervention on behalf of his people, and there can be no question but that the restoration of Israel features prominently in the Targums, sometimes when the language of God's kingdom is employed. But the kingdom in the Targums is certainly not merely nationalistic, as is evident when it is said to be revealed "upon all the dwellers of the earth." On p. 20, Buchanan omits that crucial phrase when he cites passages in which it in fact appears. Because he takes no account of that aspect of the evidence, and does not consider Jewish prayer texts which mention the kingdom in detail, his first foundation is exegetically shaky.

110

In his partial review of the relevant evidence, Buchanan is up against those who have commented upon the Aramaic texts. Rather than discussing their opinions, he dismisses the scholars concerned. Dalman is accused of deliberately slanting his translations (p. 19); Jeremias is said wilfully to have ignored evidence (pp. 20, 31); I am criticized for "wishful thinking" (p. 32). Unless the author has some special gift of divination, the basis of his claims would appear wholly subjective. I have no pretensions to being classed with Dalman and Jeremias, but I have made out an exegetical argument for my position in two books. A study of Jesus' announcement of the kingdom, God in Strength, appeared in 1979, and an analysis of the Isaiah Targum, The Glory of Israel, was published in 1982. Neither of these works is cited by Buchanan, and such omissions permit him to make up in rhetoric what is lacking in exegesis.

Buchanan's second foundation, the existence of kheiai, is rather more solid. They were indeed spoken of and described as scribal conventions in antiquity. Whether they were consciously employed within Jewish and Christian literature, however, remains an open question. An oral phase in the composition of Rabbinica and the Gospels needs to be considered; not all Jewish and Christian teachers were scribes. But, by whatever technique, some of Jesus' sayings were faithfully handed on by his followers; that is Buchanan's main point, and it is a reasonable one.

The meaning Buchanan discovers in his khreiai is developed, not from their form, but from his own understanding of Jesus' political ministry. Jesus is presented in the Synoptic Gospels as justifying his fellowship with tax collectors and sinners (Matthew 9:10-13; Mark 2:15-17; Luke 5:29-32). As Buchanan has it, Jesus had "to go where the money" was (p. 133, see also pp. 111, 117, 146). Jews who had contacts with Gentiles were viewed as unclean, but they had wealth and influence; to such outsiders, Jesus appealed for support, since "he needed lots of money for an effective revolution against Rome" (p. 133). Within the pages which discuss this passage (130-133), other views are not discussed, and no attempt is made to integrate the interpretation with Jesus' stance towards the Jewish law in other sayings. Unless the reader has some prior liking for the thesis, which is presupposed, he or she will probably not be convinced by the argument.

Buchanan's thesis does not progress beyond that of Brandon. While the latter admitted that the militarism he posited quickly died out, Buchanan boldly maintains that "Like other Jews, Christians did not give up their political aspirations with the defeats of A.D. 70 and 135 but continued their subversion right up until the time of Constantine" (p. 245). The sheer vigour of this book is attractive, and it is a provocative incentive to think again about many passages, and Jesus' orientation. Morever, a wealth of information is cited within it, which might lead

"Targum" is not merely the appropriate designation for certain documents; it implicitly refers to the process by which those documents were produced. This process (as well as the fact that they are written in Aramaic) distinguishes Targumim from other translations. In these Aramaic paraphrases, popular piety and rabbinic theology meet in a uniquely informative way. The synagogue was certainly the home of the interpretation which led to the evolution of the documents called Targumim. The Hebrew Bible was too difficult in its language, and often too obscure in its imagery, to be left untranslated for the congregation. The interpreter (meturgeman) therefore rose to translate after the Hebrew reading, and a passage in the Babylonian Talmud (Megillah 21b) indicates that such interpretation was so popular that some congregations desired to hear more than one targumic rendering of the same Hebrew passage.[1] Some of the translations were so firmly fixed in folk memory that rabbis, we are told, consulted with speakers of Aramaic to recover the proper phrasing in their versions.[2]

With the mention of rabbis, we are brought to the second and equally crucial element in the process of targumic formation: it is obvious that the evolution of synagogue practice alone cannot explain the existence of written, authoritative Targums. The usage of centuries produced a measure of consolidation and common custom, but the step from rendering those passages which happen to have been read in public worship to translating an entire corpus was a considerable one. The passage cited from tractate Megillah shows that some variety in practice was countenanced by the rabbis for good, pastoral reasons; it also displays the rabbinic concern for and involvement with targumic tradition. The rabbis proscribed some renderings and accepted others, handed on complete targumic versions in the names of certain rabbis, and claimed Onqelos as "our Targum".[3] The rabbinic influence on the actual content of Onqelos has been established in a recent monograph by Moses Aberbach and Bernard Grossfeld.[4] The evidence quite clearly indicates, then, that while Targums might be characterized as "popular paraphrases" in respect of their liturgical function,[5] substantively they are products of a dialectical relationship between synagogue and academy. Put in another, perhaps overly simplified way, Targums are popular in origin but scholarly in their presentation.

Once Targums are understood in this fashion, their importance for the student of early Judaism becomes obvious. Mishnah, Midrash, and Talmud evidence, in the main, intramural rabbinic discussion. Targums provide us with some insight into how those discussions found expression (and qualification) in a more public, less expert context, i.e., in the worship of the faithful. We may

113

say this without being so rash as to imagine that the standard rabbinic translations were everywhere or consistently accepted, or that there was an exclusive norm among the rabbis themselves. The large number of extant Targums militates against the propriety of such a supposition. The Targums better represent a process than an ideal, and the process is distinct from, even though related to, that which produced Mishnah, Midrash, and Talmud.[6]

Inasmuch as the reader of the New Testament is by definition a student of early Judaism, the recent explosion in Targum studies is to be welcomed even if it is somewhat daunting to those who attempt to keep abreast of the literature.[7] But despite, or perhaps because of, the diligence of many skilled scholars, the dating of Targums remains a matter of dispute. This is a cause for concern, because our understanding of when a Targum, as we know it, was in circulation determines how we use it (and whether we use it) in exegeting the New Testament. Were Jesus and Paul, for example, familiar with the Targums we can read today, or are the Targums actually products of rabbinic retrenchment in the post-Yavneh period and therefore designed in part to refute Christian claims?

The evidence of the Targums themselves and cf other rabbinic literature is notoriously ambiguous in this regard. The Pseudo-Jonathan Pentateuch Targum, for example, alludes to the majesty of John Hyrcanus on one hand, and mentions relatives of Mohammed on the other.[8] We read in Talmud that Jonathan ben Uzziel, a disciple of Hillel, composed the Prophets Targum which bears his name, but he is described as a follower of Haggai, Zechariah and Malachi;[9] as if just to compound the confusion, renderings of Prophetic passages which are clearly related to readings in the Targum Jonathan are transmitted in the name of Joseph bar Ḥiyya the fourth century sage of Pumbedita.[10] An attempt has been made to cut through the Gordian knot by asserting that the failure of a Targum to abide by mishnaic regulations proves that it is pre-mishnaic.[11] The Targums do sometimes render passages in a way forbidden by the rabbis and interpret what the rabbis said should not be translated at all,[12] but does this evidence justify an early dating? The divergence from Mishnah might be explained in terms of the dissimilar purposes of targum and mishnah, or by the influence of non-rabbinic, popular, but not necessarily primitive opinion, or by divisions within rabbinic discussion about which we may or may not be informed. All such divergences prove only what we already know, that Targums are the products of a distinctive process: the Targums can no more be measured by mishnah alone than synodical proceedings could be said to furnish an adequate criterion for dating parochial sermons.

Research into the language of the Targums has proceeded at an intense level during this century, so one might have hoped that it would shed some light on their date and provenience. If so, the expectation has not been met; in order to explain the situation as briefly as possible, an almost schematic introduction to the work of the major contributors in this field will be offered.

Towards the end of the last century, Zacharias Frankel developed a view of the linguistic relationship between Onqelos, the official Babylonian Targum, and Pseudo-Jonathan, styled the "Jerusalem" or "Palestinian" Targum since, it was supposed, it did not derive from Babylonia. Frankel noticed that Onqelos and Pseudo-Jonathan sometimes agreed in using words not found in the later Targums to the Hagiographa, while at other times Pseudo-Jonathan parted company with Onqelos and employed the usage of later centuries.[13] Largely following Frankel, Gustav Dalman added that the defective orthography of Pseudo-Jonathan reflected the common speech of Galilean and Babylonian Aramaic from the fourth to the seventh century. The language of Onqelos was characterized as "scholarly" and "artful," a "Hebraized Aramaic",[14] but more primitive than that of Pseudo- Jonathan.

Paul Kahle and his famous student, Matthew Black, presented an alternative reconstruction. Kahle's study of the Cairo Geniza material (dated to a period between the seventh and the eleventh century) led him to conclude "that Onkelos was without importance in Palestine, indeed, that it had not even existed there till it was introduced from Babylonia, and then scarcely before 1000 A.D."[15] For earlier renderings, he thought, one had to look to the Fragment Targum, Pseudo-Jonathan and the Geniza Fragments. The obvious difficulty here is that the documentation of these sources is relatively late: the textual attestation of Pseudo-Jonathan and the Cairo Geniza finds is post-Islamic, and that of the Fragment Targum is medieval.[16] To account for such evidence a Palestinian Targum in what Black calls its "fluid state" has been postulated as the matrix of what is alleged to be primitive material in the later Targums.[17] So far as the testimony of the documents discussed can take us, this source is little more than a cipher; earlier attestation to the "Palestinian Targum" was necessary to make the hypothesis viable and thereby to overturn the analysis of Frankel and Dalman.

In 1956, the late Alejandros Díez Macho publicly identified the Vatican manuscript he had been working on for some years as an early representative of the Palestinian Targum. Since it belongs to the collection of the Library of Neophytes, he named it Codex Neophyti I. That this new and important discovery further evidences non-Babylonian targumic renderings is a matter of consensus. But, while admitting that Neophyti's Aramaic is that of seventh and eighth century manuscripts, Díez Macho asserts that substantively his text is pre-mishnaic in content.[18] We have already observed that anti- or non-mishnaic is not to be equated with pre-mishnaic, and one of Díez Macho's most important followers, Martin McNamara, has not always agreed with the early dating.[19] Doubt has also been cast on Díez Macho's claims linguistically, in that the language of the Targum presents signs of a Greek influence which is so strong as to raise suspicions about the provenience of the translation, and textually, in that the manuscript is the victim of poor scribal handling.[20] In sum, while the importance of this sixteenth century document is not to be minimized, neither will it serve as the vindication of Kahle's thesis. The recent investigation of Qumran Aramaic, pioneered by Joseph Fitzmyer, suggests that the language of Onqelos stands closest to the literary dialect of the first century.[21] Díez Macho's rejoinder, that the Qumran finds employ a literary Aramaic contaminated by the spoken Aramaic better attested in the Palestinian Targum,[22] remains to be substantiated.

The circular path of recent discussion of the language of the Targums reminds one, if not of the tower of Babel, then of a plateau of discordant opinions from which continued ascent is difficult. Nor should it be thought that this discussion, even should it lead to agreement, would definitively settle the literary question of the relationship between the Pentateuch Targums. As Díez Macho reminds us, "the content might be older than the language."[23] In the end, it appears premature to base Targumic exegesis - especially in respect of the New Testament - on any single theory of how the Aramaic language evolved: there seem to be more variables than any of them can comfortably accommodate.

It has nonetheless proved possible to isolate heuristically certain Targumic passages which antecede the New Testament. This possibility has long been recognized, as selected examples from only the recent literature will show. T.W. Manson demonstrated that the form of Jesus' citation from Isaiah as reported in Mark 4:12 is closer to what we read in the Isaiah Targum than it is to the Masoretic or Septaugintal versions of that book.[24] Among the many similar instances adduced by Martin McNamara in his two tradition critical treatments of the relationship between the New Testament and the Targums, Pseudo-Jonathan on Leviticus 22:28 is quite striking in respect of Luke 6:36:[25]

My children, children of Israel, as our Father is merciful in heaven, so shall you be merciful on earth.

Investigations of this kind, whether or not all their conclusions are accepted, have indicated that some of the material which we can read in extant Targums - whatever their dates of compilation - was known and used by those who contributed to the formation of the New Testament. When a Targumic passage parallels or appears to provide the logical antecedent to a New Testament passage, the natural inference is that the Targum in question informs us of the basis on which the New Testament tradents were operating. I have argued elsewhere, briefly and at length, that such an inference is reasonable in respect of the phrase, often attested in the Targums, "kingdom of God" or "kingdom of the LORD".[26] Since the phrase is most frequently found in the Isaiah Targum (24:23; 31:4; 40:9; 52:7), I have devoted a study to that Targum in particular in which I posit some fifteen instances in which sayings of Jesus appear to reflect Targumic diction and themes.[27] For the present purpose, perhaps a single instance will suffice by way of example. In terms of Matthew 7:2 and Mark 4:24, the following statement, found in Targum Isaiah 27:8, is surely of note:

With the measure with which you were measuring they will measure you....

In evaluating all such work, it must be borne in mind that it does not establish the date of any Targum as a whole, and there is no realistic prospect that the tradition critical approach can succeed in this regard: the Targums as a whole are too disparate in the material they preserve and too dissimilar to the New Testament and to Mishnah, Midrash, and Talmud for every Targumic pericope to be dated relative to those documents. The point is worth emphasizing, because there is a tendency to assume the antiquity of Targumic readings. The most notable example of the tendency is recent discussion of the understanding of Genesis 22 in the New Testament. Because some Targums present Isaac as dying on Moriah in a way which was efficacious for Israel, we are encouraged by such scholars as Geza Vermes and Roger Le Déaut to assume that the Aqedah influenced New Testament soteriology. The fact is, however, that the Aqedah is not mentioned in the New Testament, and some evidence indicates that the rabbis actually embellished Genesis 22 and referred to their haggadah at Passover time in order to reply to Christian claims about the Passion.[28]

Recent discussion makes it obvious that the Targumim need to be described by means of an approach which permits them to convey their character as complete documents within the context of rabbinic Judaism. In The Glory of Israel, I have attempted to apply a modified form of redaction criticism to the Isaiah Targum in an attempt to determine its theology, provenience and date. Recognizing that historical allusions and literary parallels might guide us to an understanding of the date and provenience of a given passage or motif in a Targum, and that language (if it were an established criterion) would help us to suggest the time and place of the final compilation of the document as a whole, we know that Targums as such are not farragos of tradition or compositions de novo, but specimens of extended exegesis. To discover the provenience and date of a Targum one must ask, first, what exegetical terms and phrases are so frequently used as to constitute characteristic conventions, and then, how do these conventions relate to historical circumstances, to the New Testament and rabbinic literature? Such conventions, when repeatedly used in a given Targum, would have provided the ordering principle of traditional interpretations and for the inclusion of subsequent insights. This exegetical framework belongs to the _esse_ of a Targum: without it, targumic readings are only a _pot pourri_, while with it the later addition of material does not constitute a recension, only an addendum. An analysis of some fifteen characteristic terms and phrases in the Isaiah Targum reveals a theology of messianic vindication centered on the return of dispersed Israel and the re-establishment of cultic integrity. This theology coheres with the cherished desire of the Babylonian rabbinate in the Tannaitic period "to avenge the sanctuary and make possible its restoration" in the words of Jacob Neusner.[29] Very recent treatments of the language of the Prophetic Targum and its cousin, Onqelos, have tended towards a corroborative finding,[30] though for the reasons discussed earlier it would be wrong to see therein a proof of the thesis.

The somewhat inconclusive results of intensive Targum study perhaps explains why students of the New Testament have been less than enthusiastic about referring to these documents in their exegeses. But if research has not yet shown when precisely the Targums were compiled, the "why" and "how" of their formation have become increasingly clear. They were designed to hand on and interpret the Law, Prophets, and Writings. In principle, they were oral: the meturgeman was forbidden to look at a text as he translated, lest there be any confusion between the paraphrase and the written canon in the mind of the congregation.[31] Whatever the practice in the synagogue, the Targums did come to be fixed in writing, and that froze their wording at a moment of their development in a way which has permitted posterity to consider their formation. The Hebrew text is the primary datum of all Targums, to which they consistently do justice,[32] but they also deviate from that written tradition for the sake of clarity or exposition.[33] The workings of the process are particularly apparent in the case of Pentateuchal Targums, where we can compare several renderings of the same Hebrew corpus. Among these Targums (especially those styled Palestinian) we have verbatim agreements and marked deviations; Martin McNamara has rightly observed, "we do have a synoptic problem."[34]

The more famous synoptic problem in the New Testament presents an obvious possible analogy, and all the more so as at least a restricted period of oral transmission must be postulated in respect of dominical tradition. J.M. Rist's recent study resuscitates the oral gospel hypothesis to explain the relationship between Matthew and Mark,[35] but just what was this oral gospel like? Various models have been suggested. Form criticism gave us pericopae - discrete pearls threaded on a redactional string by the Evangelists, and each pearl a community formation over (at best) a dominical piece of sand.[36] Thorleif Boman has attacked this model, showing quite convincingly from the orally developed literature of many cultures that we must think rather of longer, continuous epics at the point of origin which were woven together in the course of time.[37] The evident weakness in Boman's analogy is that the gospel of Jesus was not preached in some anthropological abstract, but - in the first instance - in a specifically Jewish culture. Birger Gerhardsson has shown how much might be learned from that fact and has used the Mishnah as a model for understanding the development of the New Testament. But Morton Smith has rightly complained against Gerhardsson that, in adition to being quite late, Mishnah is too specialist, to the point of being sui generis, to be of direct relevance in understanding the formation of the New Testament.[38] Targums, however, provide a possible analogy for four reasons, (1) they are oral in one sense and written in another, (2) they are specifically Jewish, (3) they are designed for popular consumption, and (4) they manifest a synoptic relationship.

As a test case, to assess the possible analogy further, I propose to compare the Synoptic Temptation with the Poem of the Four Nights in the Palestinian Targums. These passages are chosen because they are each self-contained, and because both are constructed from Old Testament citations and allusions. (N.b., the Poem refers to more than Exodus 12:42, of which it is the rendering). It is to be stressed that any literary dependence between the Targums and the Synoptic Gospels forms no part of our argument; their qualitative difference in subject matter immediately precludes such an implication. Moreover, the Aqedah reference in the Poem seems quite late, as I have argued elsewhere.[39] We are attending to the simple task of asking if the structure of these passages and the alterations which occur through their transmissions might justify the claim that Synoptic tradition is cognate with Targumic tradition.

A consideration of the Poem as found in the Fragment Targum will show the structural importance of Old Testament references, of which the most major are identified in brackets:

> It is a night to be observed and set aside for redemption before the LORD when he brought forth the sons of Israel, freed from the land of Egypt. Because four nights are written in the book of memorials.

> [The "watching" of the LORD and of Israel is already mentioned in Exodus 12:42 MT.]

> The first night, when the LORD's memra was revealed upon the world to create it, when the world was without form and void and darkness was spread on the face of the deep, and the LORD's memra illuminated and enlightened; he called it the first night.

119

[Genesis 1:1-5, quite obviously, paraphrased, one might note (given that "memra" might be translated as "word"), in a manner reminiscent of the Johannine prologue.]

The second night, when the LORD's memra was revealed upon Abraham between the parts. Abraham was a hundred years old and Sarah was ninety years old, to establish what scripture says, is Abraham, a hundred years old, able to beget, and is Sarah, ninety years old, able to bear? Was not Isaac our father thirty-seven years old at the time he was offered on the altar? The heavens descended and came down and Isaac saw their perfections and his eyes were darkened from the heights, and he called it the second night.

[The second night is identified with various moments in salvation history, arranged in a sequential pattern: Abraham's convenant sacrifice (Genesis 15:17), the removal of the obstacle to the covenant promise (Genesis 17:17), and the confirmation of the promise in respect of Isaac (Genesis 22:1-18 cf. 27:1).]

The third night, when the LORD's memra was revealed upon the Egyptians at the dividing of the night; his right hand killed the firstborn of the Egyptians and his right hand spared the firstborn of Israel, to establish what scripture says, Israel is my firstborn son, and he called it the third night.

[Primarily, this refers to Exodus 12:29, cf. vv.12, 13, 23, 27 and 4:22.]

The fourth night, when the end of the age is accomplished to be redeemed, the servants of wickedness are destroyed and the iron yokes broken. Moses comes from the desert, but the king messiah from above. One leads in the head of the cloud, and the other leads in the head of the cloud, and the LORD's memra leads them both, and they will go together.

This is the night of passover before the LORD, to be observed and set aside by the sons of Israel in their generations.

[Eventually, we get back to Exodus 12:42, but the Moses-messiah eschatology is not biblical in the same sense that the references included in the texts attached to the first three nights are.]

While the Neophyti Poem does deviate from this version, its most striking feature is its similarity to the Poem as we have cited it.[40]

The Fragment Targum's Poem obviously differs signally from the Matthean Temptation. The Targum opens and closes with a reference to the Hebrew text it renders, while Matthew refers first to the temptation by the devil (4:1) and finally to the support of the angels (4:11). Structurally, Matthew presents a three-tiered dialogue or repartee between biblical passages as spoken by the principals, while the Targum straightforwardly offers the reader biblical exposition of the four nights. But two significant similarities should be observed at the outset. First, in each, a clear associative chain links the citations. The LORD's memra is a primary agency in each Targumic explication of the nights. The Matthean interplay of citations centers on the proper place of the Son in relation to God. Second, the climactic point in both (in the Targum, the Moses-messiah haggadah, in Matthew, the devil's invitation to apostasy) is not a direct biblical citation, but is immediately followed by one. The structural patterns of these two very different passages are therefore distinctive, and yet they are similar enough to hint at the possibility that they were transmitted in much the same way.

When we turn to Luke's Temptation, we see another structural similarity to the Targumic Poem: Luke opens and closes (4:2, 13) with a reference to the devil's tempting, which he treats as if it were his "text." The Lukan order, however, insures that the pattern of a climactic departure from scripture is broken. But this may not be used as evidence that Luke here disrupts any analogy to Targumic transmission. On the contrary, variations in order are well known to students of the Targums, and two instances can be cited in respect of the Poem: (1) in Neophyti, which generally follows the Fragment Targum more closely than Luke follows Matthew, the reference to Exodus 4:22 ("his firstborn son is Israel"), which the Fragment Targum cites in the context of the third night, is attached in the margin to the second night, (2) the ancient Exodus midrash, Mekhilta de R. Simeon b. Yoḥai, actually presents a poem of three nights, omitting the messianic fourth night.[41] The Lukan alteration appears a median between the slighter change of Neophyti (margin) and the radical excision of the Mekhilta (which also, of course, omits the departure from direct scriptural reference altogether).

The Markan compression of the Temptation into two verses (1:12, 13) is so stark as to suggest to some scholars that it does not come from the same stable as the "Q" account.[42] But the relation of Mark to Matthew and Luke in this matter is perhaps more explicable when we compare the following version of the Poem, from Targum Pseudo-Jonathan, to those of the Fragment Targum and Neophyti:

> Four nights are written in the book of memorials before
> the Lord of the world. The first night, when he was
> revealed to create the world; the second night, when he
> was revealed upon Abraham; the third night, when he was
> revealed against Egypt, his left hand killing all the
> firstborn of Egypt and his right hand sparing the first-
> born of Israel; the fourth night, when he will be
> revealed to redeem the people of the house of Israel
> from among the nations....[43]

It is true that the version in Pseudo-Jonathan at least maintains
the four night structure, while Mark does not do any justice to
the three specific temptations, and that there is little new in
Pseudo-Jonathan as compared to the Fragment Targum and Neophyti,
while the beasts mentioned by Mark constitute an odd deviation
from Matthew and Luke. But having said that, the fact remains that
the scriptural references in the Poem as found in Pseudo-Jonathan
are so attenuated as to be nearly non-existent, the second night
passage lacks a reference to Isaac and the fourth night passage is
no longer explicitly messianic. The analogy to Mark in relation
to his colleagues is certainly not exact, but it is also not
entirely uninstructive.

Literal agreement and frustrating variety in diction pose a
major difficulty to theories of documentary dependence. Why should
Mark follow his scroll of Matthew verbatim (or vice versa) in one
passage and pick up a different scroll when he comes to write
another? Even if it is credible that the Evangelists had libraries
at their disposal, why should an author use a predecessor's material when writing up a passage and then, before he gets to the end,
suddenly go his own way by adding, deleting, abbreviating, expand-
ing, conflating, separating, and/or changing its context? "Literal
agreement" is still the battle cry of those who argue literary
dependence, but the latter is not a necessary inference from the
former.[44] The relationship between the Fragment Targum and
Neophyti already suggests that documents which were oral in origin
- and were always so in principle - might agree literally. But the
phenomenon in the Synoptic Gospels for which we are seeking an
analogy is agreement and variety together; for this purpose, we
may leave Mark and Pseudo-Jonathan aside, because both documents
present the passages in question in such a relatively compressed
form that they are idiosyncratic from the point of view of the
words they employ. We are therefore left to compare Matthew and
Luke on the one hand with the Fragment Targum and Neophyti on the
other.

The present inquiry does not require that we observe all the
variations manifest in the two sets of documents. We will restrict
ourselves to selecting a sample of substantive deviations between
Matthew and Luke, and then see whether or not analogous deviations
can be found between the Fragment Targum and Neophyhti. Because we

use one of a pair of documents as our starting point for collation, we will speak of its partner as "changing" or "adding" or "omitting" words, but such language is only used as a convenience in order to describe the linguistic relations at issue, not as an assertion of literary or oral priority. The deviations between Matthew and Luke selected for analysis are as follows:

1. Luke 4:1 (cf. Matthew 4:1) adds "Full of the holy spirit he returned from the Jordan."

2. Luke 4:2 (cf. Matthew 4:2) adds "And he ate nothing in those days and when they were ended he hungered."

3. Luke 4:3 (cf. Matthew 4:3) changes "the tempter" to "the devil" and "these stones" (nominative) to "this stone" (dative).

4. Luke 4:4 (cf. Matthew 4:4) omits "but by every word proceeding from God's mouth."

5. Luke 4:5, 6 (cf. Matthew 4:8, 9) adds "in a moment of time" and "for it is given to me and to whom I wish to give it."

6. Luke 4:13 (cf. Matthew 4:11) omits "And behold angels came and ministered to him."

As will be seen, each of the deviations selected is distinctive from the others, so we are not considering a mere multiplication of the same sort of variant. Each deviation will be described briefly, and a Targumic analogy posited.

Deviation 1 is of a narrative order, linking the Lukan Temptation to the Baptism (3:21, 22). The resumptive clause is appropriate, serving to take the story line up again after the long, parenthetical genealogy (3:23-38).

Analogy 1: the Fragment Targum adds "between the parts" to the beginning of the second night passage. This serves to specify Genesis 15:17 as the relevant allusion. Of course, this is not as substantial an addition as Luke's, the purpose is to fix the second night exegetically, rather than geographically or chronologically, and it may be argued that Neophyti implies the allusion already. Nonetheless, the fact remains that, at the beginning of a passage, the Fragment Targum augments the narrative content relative to Neophyti.

Deviation 2 is also narrative, but its purpose is to explain the course of events more fully than Matthew's "afterward he hungered" does.

Analogy 2: where, in the first night passage, the Fragment Targum reads "the LORD's memra illuminated and enlightened," Neophyti has "the LORD's memra was light," thereby explicating the scene in terms of Genesis 1:3. (Alternatively, the Fragment Targum might be considered to fill out a bare scriptural reference in more narrative terms.) Again, the Targumic addddition is less fulsome than Luke's, and it explicates the Poem in respect of scripture, not event. But it must be borne in mind that the Meturgeman's text was the written word, while the Evangelist's "text" was Jesus, and that the Poem is less susceptible of narrative embellishment than is a haggadic story.

Deviation 3 is a simple case of preferred idioms used of the same referent.

Analogy 3: in each of the three cases (in the first, second and third night texts) where Neophyti speaks of the LORD being revealed, the Fragment Targum meticulously refers to the LORD's "memra." Similarly, in the prologue and epilogue to the Poem, Neophyti says the night is remembered "to the name of the LORD," while the Fragment Targum simply has "before the LORD."

Deviation 4 instances an abbreviated citation of a biblical passage, and it is interesting that Luke's comparative lacuna is filled in many manuscripts.[45]

Analogy 4: the Poem in Pseudo-Jonathan actually presents the nearest such instance, but it has already been pointed out that Neophyti omits the reference to Genesis 15:17 (see Analogy 1). Without "between the parts" the second night might be thought of as referring simply to Genesis 17 and 18. The sphere of ideas remains the same, but the precise allusions do vary somewhat between the Fragment Targum and Neophyti.

Deviation 5 is again essentially narrative, but it performs a dramatic function in emphasizing the devil's power.

Analogy 5: in the fourth night passage, the Fragment Targum explicitly refers to the messiah, but Neophyti does not. While Moses and messiah appear on clouds in the Fragment Targum, Moses and the (so far unidentified) figure in Neophyti lead the flock.[46] This complex of variants is more important than may at first appear, because Neophyti then has the second figure speak as "I", presumably an allusion to God himself. This adjustment in reference is a more extreme development than the change from Matthew to Luke, but the Fragment Targum does present a more balanced portrayal of the dramatis personae.

Deviation 6 is the sole alteration in Luke which constitutes a significant omission.

Analogy 6: as has already been mentioned (see Analogy 5), Neophyhti simply deletes "and the king messiah from above" from the fourth night text.

At several points we have already had to acknowledge that the analogies posited are defective. Where it is a question of narrative deviation (see 1, 2, 5), the Gospels appeared to embellish the Temptation, while the Targums in two out of three of those cases (1, 2) merely added a biblical reference or made the reference more explicit. The difference in procedure may tell us more about the distinction between Targum and Euanggelion in respect of purpose than about any qualitative difference in the manner in which they were transmitted. Analogies 1 and 2 are, it is true, rather more restrained than Deviations 1 and 2, but the evidence we have considered prevents us from saying that Targumic transmission was more conservative than Evangelical transmission. Deviation-Analogy 5 would overturn such a generalization: the Targumic variation in defining the second figure in the fourth night passage is more radical than the Evangelical shift in emphasis on the devil's power. The extent of the change in the Targumic text is further indicated by the fact that the same text presents the closest analogy to Deviation 6, where Luke drops an important element of the Temptation. Deviation-Analogy 4 is also not very exact, curiously because the Gospels of Matthew and Luke are more extensive and precise in their biblical citation than the Targums in question are at this particular point. Deviation-Analogy 3 is unquestionably the best of the lot, and it is surely of interest to the student of the Gospels that these Targums present a pattern of distinct but practically synonymous expression - the very linguistic relationship which lies at the heart of the Synoptic Problem.

When dictional agreements and disagreements among the Targumic Poems are considered in comparison with the Synoptic Temptation, and one bears in mind how similar the Poem appears to the Temptation in its structure and variations of order and size, the possibility does emerge that the Gospels may have taken shape according to a process cognate with that which produced the Targums. The exampled analysis suggests that the possibility might be used as a hypothesis for treating more material of different types. Both the Temptation and the Poem are basically sui generis within the documents within which they appear; a representative sampling from the major strata of the Gospels and the Targums would have to be dealt with in this way, and similar results to those achieved in the present study obtained, before the hypothesis here suggested could justifiably be callsed a thesis.[47] Nonetheless, we do have before us a possibility which might warrant such further research.

For those seeking the appropriate focus for future research, the analysis here conducted offers certain warnings. Quite obvi-

125

ously, nothing we have observed in the Temptation as compared to the Poem should incline us to describe the Gospels as a species of Targum.[48] On the contrary, our consideration of dictional disagreements which are narrative (Deviations 1, 2, 5) plainly showed that these embellishments on the story line, specifying Jesus' attitude and position in the proceedings and the power of the devil he faced, were of a different order from the exegetical notes and haggadic digressions added in the Fragment Targum and Neophyti. The goal of Targums is to provide an understanding of a written text, while Gospels are designed to explain the significance of a person. The "text" of the Evangelists was Jesus, and as soon as we have said that, we realize that it is meaningless to say the Gospels are Targumic in form, even though they occasionally cite Targumic renderings.[49] Nor is the distinction between Targum and Gospel merely formal: each form is congruent with the purpose of its genre, and the Targums interpret a text as consistently as the Gospels interpret a person. It follows that the processes which produced Targums and Gospels should not be confused, because the controlling influence on one process is textual while the controlling influence on the other is personal. For this reason, I speak of the two processes as being "cognate" rather than "identical," and of the similarities between the two as "analogies," not "parallels."

If these processes are cognate, then the Targums give us a handle for grasping the interplay between tradition and interpretation in the Gospels. When the meturgeman rose in the synagogue to translate, his duty was twofold: (1) he had to do justice to the biblical text in Hebrew which he was to render in Aramaic, but (2) he was also obliged to look away from any text, to face the congregation and in so doing to explain what had been read in terms the congregation could appropriate. At times these two ends could seem to be in tension, as for example in the case of the question of how Exodus 24:10 should be rendered. The Hebrew text is: "and they saw the God of Israel." This was impossible in the contemporary understanding, so perhaps one should say "and they saw the angel of the God of Israel." R. Judah condemned both renderings in his famous and paradoxical dictum (Kiddushin 49a):[50]

If one translates a verse literally, he is a liar; if he adds thereto, he is a blasphemer and a libeller.

In the same Talmudic passage, Onqelos ("our Targum") is authorised as normative: "Then what is meant by translation? Our translation." And Onqelos solves the problem:[51]

and they saw the glory of the God of Israel.

"Glory" is not an addition in the sense that "angel" is, because God is not replaced with another figure; at the same time, the lie that God is visible to men is not perpetrated. The authority of a

Targum resides in its care for tradition (sc. the text and the efforts of earlier translators), but not only in that; the other constituent of its authority is its adequacy as a statement about the God referred to in the text.

Such interplay between tradition and redaction is easily instanced in the Gospels. The portrayal of Jesus which we see in them is definitely conditioned by the traditions about him which were available, but these traditions are selected and shaped in the course of transmission (both at the traditional and the redactional levels).[52] A single example will perhaps suffice to illustrate. In the controversy centered on the man with a withered hand (Matthew 12:9-14; Mark 3:1-6; Luke 6:6-11), Jesus confronts his opponents with a saying (about doing good on the Sabbath; vv. 12, 4, 9 respectively) and an action (the healing; vv. 13, 5, 10). The attitude of the opponents is clear: they wish to find a reason to accuse Jesus (vv. 10, 2, 7). But what was the attitude of Jesus himself? In what seems an early characterization of his attitude,[53] Mark 3:5 presents Jesus "looking round at them with anger, grieved at their hardness of heart." Luke eschews this affective language: Jesus merely fixes them with a stare ("looking round at them all") and performs the healing which causes them to be "filled with fury" (6:10, 11). Matthew has no reference to emotion on either side in the two verses in question (12:13, 14), but pursues his characteristic tendency of letting dialogue alone tell the tale.[54] Slight changes of diction, such as we have seen in the Temptation passages and their Targumic analogies, manifest distinctive emphases in the portrayal of Jesus. The Markan Christ is consumed with the acute emotions which almost force him to behave as he does;[55] the Lukan Lord is the master of the situations that confront him;[56] the Matthean Son is best characterized by the words and deeds he himself provides as teaching.[57] The Church which authorized these portraits of Jesus, and many others, by including them in its canon attested not only to their value as tradition, but to their efficacy as interpretations which illuminated Jesus' person for believers.[58] The integrity of such tradition was not a strait jacket which forced Gospel tradents into merely mechanical transmission; the paramount concern was rather for the significance of tradition for faith, so that explication was as much a part of the authority of these books as their incorporation of previous data.

"Oral tradition" is widely posited as the medium of gospel transmission between the resurrection and our written Gospels, largely on the faute de mieux argument that something of the kind must have taken place during that period. The insecurity felt by many at the notion that the facts about Jesus should have been handed down in this fashion is inevitable, despite the familiarity we all have with the howlers to which the written word is liable, since "writing" and "accuracy" are so closely allied in our culture. Birger Gerhardsson's contribution has reminded us that this was not the case in the New Testament period, and unease has been somewhat allayed. By way of summary, we might contrast our findings with those of the Gerhardsson thesis. He has suggested that mishnaic transmission, in which the opinions of various rabbis were recorded with a view to their relevance in legal controversies, might be a model for understanding the pre-written history of our Gospels. As mentioned above, Morton Smith has reminded us that the Mishnah is simply too late (in comparison with the New Testament) to supply us with an immediate model for Jewish oral tradition in the first century. And we must stress again that the Mishnah is essentially a tool for rabbinic discussion, not a catechetical document for popular use. These objections vitiate Gerhardsson's thesis, and they must be answered before it is appealed to as a support for the authenticity of the Gospel tradition as a whole. Further, we might point out that Jesus' disciples obviously did not transmit his sayings as those of the rabbis in Mishnah. Mishnah presents a collection of sayings from various sages,[59] but the early Christians never handed on dominical logia as if their significance lay in their relationship to the assertions of others. From the collector who first brought together the sayings which we know from the Synoptic Gospels to the Coptic Gospel according to Thomas, what Jesus had to say was seen to have divine authorization. Indeed, Christians ultimately went so far as to take the audacious step (from a conservatively religious point of view) of adding something they called the New Testament to Tanach. They saw the words and deeds of Jesus as having a status equivalent to that of Moses and the prophets.

With this in mind, I see nothing inappropriate in the claim that the disciples might have used Targumic methods to transmit the words and deeds of Jesus. They were certainly important enough to them to merit such treatment, and our observation of synoptic analogies between the Palestinian Targums and the first three Gospels suggests that they may actually have received such treatment.[60] Of course (once again) we must always bear in mind that Targums are essentially Aramaic paraphrases of Hebrew texts, while the Gospels are expositions of Jesus' life, death and resurrection which only occasionally (and largely inferentially) translate Semitic locutions. The evidence permits of no confusion between Targums and Gospels, but it also intimates that the latter were handed down by the use of procedures which were developed in connection with the former. Our suggestion is not that the Gospels are Targums, but that the Gospels took shape in much the same way that Targums did. We have already seen that the extant Palestinian Targums may be quite late, but the process of Targum formation is agreed to be primitive in origin. Also, the linguistic and substantive continuity betwen the Palestinian Targums with which we have been concerned suggests that they stem from about the same period, so that the synoptic relationship between these texts need not have taken any longer to develop than the synoptic relationship between the first three Gospels. Just as the present suggestion is not as sensitive as Gerhardsson's when the question of dating is raised, so it fares better when we recall that, unlike Mishnah, the Targums belonged to the people in the synagogues as well as to the experts in the academy. The disciples of Jesus, as synogogue participants, would have had first hand knowledge of such sacred oral tradition: that knowledge, it seems, was an important resource to them as they tried to transmit the words and deeds of Jesus.

Their choice of a medium, no doubt more reflexive than deliberate, evidences their apparently immediate appreciation that the words and deeds of Jesus were of the order of the words and deeds of the God of Tanach, and were accordingly to be handed down by a method akin to that used by the meturgeman. Tradition and interpretation were the proper means of making what God had once done comprehensible, and were now embraced and developed to announce what it was that God had done in Jesus.

NOTES

Essay 10 first appeared in Gospel Perspectives I (ed. R.T. France and D. Wenham; Sheffield: JSOT 1980) 21-45.

1   "Our Rabbis taught: As regards the Torah, one reads and one translates, and in no case must one read and two translate. As regards the Prophets, one reads and two may translate. As regards the Hallel and the Megillah, even ten may read [and ten may translate]. What is the reason? Since the people like it, they pay attention and hear." The translation is that of M. Simon in the I. Epstein edition, The Babylonia Talmud, published by Soncino Press.

2   Gustav Dalman, Grammatik des jüdisch-palästinischen Aramämaisch (Leipzig: Hinrichs, 1905) 12 (citing Genesis Rabbah 79).

3   Kiddushin 49a, which is discussed below (cf. note 50).

4   Targum Onqelos on Genesis 49: Translation and Analytic Commentary: SBL Aramaic Studies 1 (Missoula: Scholars Press, 1976).

5   Cf. Martin McNamara, Targum and Testament. Aramaic Paraphrases of the Hebrew Bible: A Light on the New Testament (Shannon: Irish University Press, 1972) 12, on the Palestinian Targum, "Being a paraphrase rather than a translation proper, this targum...gives us a good idea of the religious concepts current when it was composed."

6   Cf. John Bowker, The Targums and Rabbinic Literature (Cambridge: CUP, 1969) and Roger Le Déaut, Introduction à la littérature targumique (Rome: Pontifical Biblical Institute, 1966).

7   In which endeavour there are two indispensable aids: the two volume contribution of Bernard Grossfeld, A Bibliography of Targum Literature: Bibliographica Judaica 3, 8 (New York: Ktav, 1972, 1977) and The Newsletter for Targumic and Cognate Studies (produced at the University of Toronto).

8   At Deuteronomy 33:11, Pseudo-Jonathan adds, "and let there not be for those that hate Johanan the high priest a foot to stand on;" cf. McNamara, The New Testament and the Palestinian Targum to the Pentateuch (Rome: Pontifical Biblical Institute, 1966) 114-117. As McNamara also mentions (p. 61), Genesis 21:21 in Pseudo-Jonathan refers to Ayisha and Fatima, the wife and daughter of Mohammed.

9   Megillah 3a: "The Targum of the Prophets was composed by Jonathan ben Uzziel under the guidance of Haggai, Zechariah and Malachi...." This passage is discussed in the introduction of The Glory of Israel, and collated with other evidence.

10   Joseph's translation of Isaiah 5:17 as reported in Pesaḥim 68a is strikingly similar to the Targumic rendering, but at times (e.g., in Sanhedrin 94b) Joseph refers to renderings of the Prophetic book in Aramaic as already extent. See the monograph cited in note 9 for further discussion and many more examples.

11   This procedure is instanced in the previous literature and refuted by A.D. York in "The Dating of Targumic Literature" Journal for the Study of Judaism 5 (1974) 49-62. York's position derives from the classic warning voiced in an article in Hebrew by Ch. Albeck entitled "The Apocryphal Halakhah in the Palestinian Targums and the Aggadah" in: J.L. Fishman (ed.), Jubilee Volume to Dr. Benjamin Menashe Lewin (Jerusalem: 1940) 93-104.

12   Pseudo-Jonathan at Leviticus 18:21 refers to intercourse with Gentiles, a reference censured in Mishnah Megillah 4:9; Mishnah Megillah 4:10 forbids the interpretation of Genesis 35:22, which is translated in all printed Targums. These examples are provided by McNamara, New Testament (cited in note 8) 46-51.

13   Zu dem Targum der Propheten: Jahresbericht des jüdisch-theologisches Seminars (Breslau: Schletter, 1872) 13-16 (place names are treated on 25-28).

14   Op. cit. (n. 2), 60, 61 and 10, 13, 40-42.

15   So M. Black, "Aramaic Studies and the Language of Jesus" in: M. Black and G. Fohrer (eds.), In Memoriam Paul Kahle: BZAW 103

(Berlin: Töpelmann, 1968) 17-28, 18. Within the Kahle school, the major works are Kahle's own The Cairo Geniza (Oxford: Blackwell, 1959²) and Black's An Aramaic Approach to The Gospels and Acts (Oxford: Clarendon, 1967³).

16   Cf. Étan Levine, "Some Characteristics of Pseudo-Jonathan to Genesis" Augustinianum 11 (1971) 89-103; M.C. Doubles, "Indications of Antiquity in the Orthography and Morphology of the Fragment Targum" in: Black and Fohrer (n. 15), 79-89; McNamara, Targum (n. 5) 183.

17   Op cit. (n. 15) 19.

18   He has recently produced a lucid résumé of his position in "Le Targum palestinien" in: J.É. Ménard (ed.), Exégèse Biblique et Judaïsme (Strasbourg: Faculté de Théologie catholique, 1973) 17-77, cf. 36, 38f. The article is also available in Recherches de science religieuse 47 (1973) 169-231.

19   Compare New Testament (n. 8) 62-63 and Targum (n. 5) 12, 186.

20   See G.J. Cowling, "New Light on the New Testament? The significance of the Palestinian Targum" Theological Students' Fellowship Bulletin 51 (1968) 6-14 and Klaus Koch, "Messias und Sündenvergebung in Jesaja 53 - Targum. Ein Beitrag zu der Praxis der aramäischen Bibelübersetzung" Journal of Semitic Studies 3 (1972) 117-148, 118, 119 (that is, n. 5).

21   Cf. The Genesis Apocryphon of Qumran Cave I: Biblica et Orientalia 18 (Rome: Pontifical Biblical Institute, 1966, 1971²) 17-34
Stephen A. Kaufman, "The Job Targum from Qumran" Journal of the American Oriental Society 93 (1973) 317-327; A. Tal, The Language of the Targum of the Former Prophets and Its Position within the Aramaic Dialects (Hebrew): Texts and Studies in the Hebrew Language and Related Subjects (Tel-Aviv: Tel-Aviv University, 1975).

22   Art. cit. (n. 18) 27.

23   Art. cit. (n. 18) 35.

24   The Teaching of Jesus. Studies of its Form and Content (Cambridge: CUP, 1931) 77-80.

25   New Testament (n. 8) 133-138 or Targum (n. 5) 118.

26   "Regnum Dei Deus Est" Scottish Journal of Theology 31 (1978) 261-270 (cf. Essay 8 in the present volume, pp. 99-107) and God in Strength. Jesus' announcement of the Kingdom: Studien zum Neuen Testament und seiner Umwelt (Monographien) 1 (Freistadt: Plöchl, 1979).

131

27   Cf. A Galilean Rabbi and His Bible. Jesus' Use of the
Interpreted Scripture of His Time: Good News Studies 8
(Wilmington: Glazier, 1984 and London: SPCK, 1984, with the subti-
tle, Jesus' own interpretation of Isaiah).

28   Cf. P.R. Davies and B.D. Chilton, "The Aqedah: a Revised
Tradition History" Catholic Biblical Quarterly 40 (1978) 514-546.

29   The History of the Jews in Babylonia I: Studia Post-Biblica
(Leiden: Brill, 1965) 67.

30   Cf. the works of Kaufman and Tal, cited in n. 21.

31   Megillah 32a.

32   As Koch, art. cit. (n. 20) has shown in particular.

33   See the introductory comments of J.F. Stenning in Targum to
Isaiah (Oxford: Clarendon, 1949).

34   Targum (n. 5) 168.

35   On the Independence of Matthew and Mark: SNTSMS 32
(Cambridge: CUP, 1978).

36   For a convenient summary of the views of K.L. Schmidt and
his successors, see W.G. Kümmel, The New Testament: The History of
the Investigation of Its Problems (London: SCM, 1973) 327-338.

37   Die Jesus-Überlieferung im Lichte der neuern Volkskunde
(Göttingen: Vandenhoeck and Ruprecht, 1967).

38   Gerhardsson, Memory and Manuscript. Oral Tradition and
Written Transmission in Rabbinic Judaism and Early Christianity:
Acta Seminarii Neotestamentici Upsaliensis (Lund: Gleerup, 1961);
Smith, "A Comparison of Early Christian and Early Rabbinic
Tradition" Journal of Biblical Literature 82 (1963) 169-176.

39   "Isaac and the Second Night: a Consideration" Biblica 61
(1980) 78-88 (cf. Essay 2 in the present volume, pp. 25-37).

40   Unfortunately, Moses Ginsburger does not offer this passage
in Das Fragmententhargum (Berlin: Calvary, 1899), but cf. Bishop
Walton's Polyglot (London: 1655- 1657), Le Déaut's La nuit pascale: Analecta Biblica 22 (Rome: Pontifical Biblical Institute,
1963, 1975) and J.W. Etheridge's translation (New York: Ktav,
1968) for the text here postulated. In the same year Essay 10 was
published, the edition by M.L. Klein, The Fragment Targums of the
Pentateuch according to their Extant Sources: Analecta Biblica 76
(Rome: Biblical Institute, 1980) appeared. Klein's edition of Ms

Vatican Ebr. 440 largely agrees with earlier work in respect of this passage, but there are certain important differences. Klein has the messiah come "from Rome," rather than "from above." His reading is the more plausible if, as in his ms, "flock" replaces "cloud" (cf. n. 46). Lastly, after "both," Klein reads, "and I and they lead together." Effectively, a text closer to Neophyti is what Klein presents, unlike the readings of other witnesses. The situation would seem to justify the propriety of a synoptic approach to the study of Targums.

In the case of Neophyhti I, we offer the following version on the basis of Díez Macho's editio princeps (Madrid: Consejo Superior de Investigaciones científicas, 1970):

It is a night to be observed and set aside for redemption to the name of the LORD in the time he brought forth those of the sons of Israel, freed from the land of Egypt. Indeed, these four nights are written in the book of memorials. The first night, when the LORD was revealed upon the world to create it, and the world was without form and void and darkness was spread on the face of the deep, and the LORD's memra was light and enl:ghtened; he called it the first night.

The second night, when the LORD was revealed upon Abraham, a hundred years old, and Sarah his wife, ninety years old, to establish what scripture says, will Abraham, a hundred years old, beget, and will Sarah his wife, ninety years old, bear? And Isaac was thirty-seven years old when he was offered on the altar. The heavens descended and came down and Isaac saw their perfections, and his eyes were darkened from their perfections, and he called it the second night.

The third night, when the Lord was revealed upon the Egyptians at the dividing of the night; his hand killed the firstborn of the Egyptians and his right hand shielded the firstborn of Israel, to establish what scripture says, Israel is my firstborn son, and he called it the third night.

The fourth night, when the end of the age is accomplished to be redeemed, the iron yokes broken and the generations of wickedness destroyed. Moses comes up from the desert. One leads in the head of the flock, and the other leads at the head of a flock, and his memra leads them both, and I and they lead together.

This is the night of passover to the name of the LORD, to be observed and set aside for redemption by all Israel in their generations.

133

The translations of the Fragment Targum and Neophyti here presented are designed to give the reader opportunity to compare more deviations than are discussed below. "The other" in Neophyti refers to a missing antecedent, such as the messiah (cf. Díez Macho, pp. 78, 79).

41   Le Déaut, La nuit (n. 40) 151 (n. 50).

42   See, e.g., the commentaries of Vincent Taylor (London: Macmillan, 1952) and C.E.B. Cranfield (Cambridge: CUP, 1959).

43   Cf. M. Ginsburger, Pseudo-Jonathan (Berlin: Calvary, 1903).

44   W.R. Farmer has been quick to call attention to the "Lachmann fallacy," which Lachmann himself did not perpetrate, but his logical acumen was not exercised by this more basic specimen of legerdemain. Cf. The Synoptic Problem. A Critical Analysis (London: Collier-Macmillan, 1964 and Dillsboro: Western North Carolina Press, 1976).

45   The text here used is Kurt Aland's eighth edition of Synopsis Quattuor Evangeliorum (Stuttgart: Württembergische Bibelanstalt, 1967).

46   The difference in Aramaic is between `anana and `ana, as Díez Macho points in the editio princeps (n. 40) 78 n. 10. What the editor and translators missed is that the "I" ('ana) reading of Neophyti represents a consistent application of the same basic word play. This suggests that the deletion of the clause about the messiah was not accidental. Cf. n. 40, and M.L. Klein, "The Messiah 'that Leadeth upon a Cloud,' in the Fragment Targum to the Pentateuch?" JTS 29 (1978) 137-139.

47   Moreover, a comparison with the (prima facie less similar) synoptic relationships in other rabbinic literature would be necessary. My preliminary conclusion is based on a reading of Jacob Neusner, Eliezer ben Hyrcanus: The Tradition and the Man: Studies in Judaism of Late Antiquity 3, 4 (Leiden: Brill, 1973). I am happy to report that Morton Smith was inclined to the same view, art. cit. (n. 38) 173 n. 9. Smith also agrees that the "Sitz im Leben" of the Gospels "seems to have been the synagogue, not the school," so he would logically find the present suggestion congenial.

48   Mutatis mutandis, on formal grounds doubt must also be cast on the attempt to understand the Gospels as a species of midrash, cf., for instance, Michael Goulder, Midrash and Lection in Matthew (London: SPCK, 1974).

49   This has been recognized by researchers from J.R. Harris ("Traces of Targumism in the New Testament" Expository Times 32

(1920-1921) 373-376) to Martin McNamara, who has wisely cautioned, "Pan-Targumism is no more a solution than Pan-Babylonianism, Pan-Hellenism or any of the other 'Pan's' which at one time or another have been put forward as explanations of the New Testament" (Targum [n. 5] 169).

50   See the text and notes provided by M. Freedman in the Epstein edition (n. 1), and McNamara's discussion in New Testament (n. 8) 41.

51   And, according to McNamara (loc. cit.), "all Tgs to Ex 24, 10."

52   The distinction between the two which I have attempted to explore elsewhere is not the focus of attention here. Cf. "An evangelical and critical approach to the sayings of Jesus" Themelios 3 (1978) 78-85; God in Strength (n. 26); "The Transfiguration: dominical assurance and apostolic vision" New Testament Studies 27 (1980) 115-124.

53   As Taylor (n. 42) observes, but Markan priority need not be assumed for the observation of divergence which is the present task.

54   Cf. H.J. Held, "Matthew as Interpreter of the Miracle Stories" in: G. Bornkamm, G. Barth, H.J. Held, Tradition and Interpretation in Matthew (London: SCM, 193) 165-299.

55   Taylor (n. 42) cites the evidence of other passages.

56   Cf. I.H. Marshall, Luke: Historian and Theologian (Devon: Paternoster, 1970).

57   Cf. J.D. Kingsbury, Matthew: Structure, Christology, Kingdom (London: SPCK, 1976).

58   Cf. R.M. Grant, A Short History of the Interpretation of the Bible (London: Collier-Macmillan, 1972).

59   Cf. B.T. Viviano, Study as Worship. Aboth and the New Testament: Studies in Judaism in Late Antiquity (Brill: Leiden, 1978).

60   But research into such analogies must obviously continue. Cf. F.G. Downing, "Redaction Criticism: Josephus' Antiquities and the Synoptic Gospels," JSNT 8, 9 (1980) 46-65, 29-48.

ESSAY 11 --
A Comparative Study of Synoptic Development:
The Dispute Between Cain and Abel in the Palestinian Targums and
the Beelzebul Controversy in the Gospels

The existence of a synoptic relationship among the Palestinian
Targums, comparable to the relations of Matthew, Mark, and Luke,
has been recognized at least since the publication of Martin
McNamara's second major discussion of the Targums and the NT.[1]
Moreover, studies have been available for some time which systematically explore the similarities between these Targums and the
idiosyncracies of each in respect of parallel passages,[2] but the
task of inquiring whether the Targumic synoptic relationship tells
us anything about the synoptic relationship between the gospels
has only recently been undertaken.[3] That study deals with the
"Poem of the Four Nights" (found at Exod 12:42 in the Palestinian
Targums) and the Temptation of Jesus in the first three gospels.
Analogies between the two were found:

> (1) the structural centrality of OT citations, carefully
> related to one another;

> (2) variations in order between one version of the pas-
> sage and another;

> (3) the radical brevity of one version as compared with
> the others;

> (4) six types of linguistic deviation among both the
> Targums and the gospels against a background of verbatim
> similarity.

From this evidence, the article proceeds to the conclusion, not
that there is a generic or literary similarity between Targums and
gospels, but that:

> When the dictional agreement and disagreement between
> the Targumic Poems are considered in comparison with the
> Synoptic Temptation, and one bears in mind how similar
> the Poem appears to the Temptation in its structure and
> variations of order and size, the possibility does
> emerge that the Gospels may have taken shape according
> to a process cognate with that which produced the
> Targums (35-36).

In order to pursue the possibility that the two synoptic relationships might be cognate, and might therefore reflect a common
medium of development, another test case is here offered. In the
instance of the Temptation, triple tradition is in question, and
the relationship between Mark and the so-called "Q" material is

problematic. A synoptic passage was therefore sought in which Marcan material is paralleled rather exactly in Matthew and Luke, and in which Matthew and Luke "add" tradition commonly designated as "Q." (In the study, we use such words as "add," "elaborate," "abbreviate," "alter," but in so doing we wish only to characterize one document in respect of others, not ab initio to posit literary dependence or precedence.) Accordingly, the Beelzebul controversy (Matt 12:22-30/Mark 3:22-27/Luke 11:14-23) was selected.[4] For several reasons, the debate between Cain and Abel, reported in the Palestinian Targums at Gen 4:8, seemed a good candidate for comparison with the Beelzebul pericope. Both complexes of passages are controversial dialogues, both involve substantive elaborations in some versions as contrasted to a single, briefer version, and both manifest the attempt to coordinate the material presented so as to achieve theological consistency.

Four versions of the Cain-Abel dispute appear in four Targums whose dates are uncertain; indeed the very method by which dates should be assigned to our documents is a matter for discussion. The Cairo Geniza fragments are commonly dated according to the period of their manuscripts, while the medieval attestation of Neophyti I has not prevented its ascription to a much earlier period on theological grounds; Pseudo-Jonathan is said to be post-Islamic on the basis of its latest identifiable historical allusion, but the Fragment Targum, as its designation suggests, is not extensive enough to be susceptible of such analysis and so escapes a late dating, despite the fact that its manuscript attestation is also medieval.[5] In the absence of a coherent method for establishing the dates and proveniences of these obviously related documents, the Palestinian Targums should be taken as evidencing -- in the main, given their clear affinity with Rabbinica -- interpretative activity in the Amoraic period.[6] Whatever the prehistory of each Targum, the linguistic similarity between them in forming a middle term between the Aramaic of Qumran, Onqelos and Jonathan on the one hand, and that of the Palestinian Talmud on the other would suggest that the Palestinian Targums achieved their recognizable form during a single period (that is, in the third and fourth centuries) and did not emerge sporadically.[7]

The substantive agreement between the Palestinian Targumim at Gen 4:8 suits the hypothesis sketched above. But neither our hypothesis, nor any comprehensive theory of how these Targums are related, permits us to say which of them, if any, is the "source" of another. To speak of "sources" may itself be misleading in any case given that -- as used in synagogue worship -- Targums were always oral in principle.[8] Yet we can proceed to characterize the Targums in terms of one another, once the texts themselves are set out,[9] bearing in mind that we are in no position to conclude that one is literarily prior to another.

138

THE TEXTS

CAIRO GENIZA

    I   Cain answered and said to Abel,
        I see that the world is created with mercies,
        and it is led with mercies:
        [-----------------] for what reason
        was your offering received from you with favor
        and it was not received from me with favor?

    II   Abel answered and said to Cain,
        what if the world is created with mercies
        and it is led with mercies? It is still led with
            fruits of good deeds:
        because my deeds were more correct than yours
        my offering was received from me with favor
        and from you it was not received with favor.

PSEUDO-JONATHAN

(A) I   Cain answered and said to Abel,
        I know that the world is created with mercies,
        but it is not led according to fruits of good
            deeds,
        and there is favoritism of persons in judgment:
            for what reason
        was your offering received
        and my offering not received from me with favor?

    II   Abel answered and said to Cain,
        the world is created with mercies,
        and it is led according to fruits of good deeds,
        and there is no favoritism of persons in judgment:
        and because the fruits of my deeds surpassed yours
               -- and were more timely than yours --
        my offering was received with favor.

(B) I   Cain answered and said to Abel,
        there is no judgment and there is no judge,
        and there is no other world,
        and there is no giving of good reward
            to the righteous
        and there is no repaying from the wicked.

    II   Abel answered and said to Cain,
        there is judgment and there is a judge,
        and there is another world,
        and there is giving good reward to the righteous
        and there is repaying from the wicked.

NEOPHYTI I

(A) I   Cain answered and said to Abel,
        I know the world is not created with mercies,
        and it is not led in respect of fruits of good
          deeds,
        and there is accepting of persons in judgment:
          for what reason
        was your offering received with favor
        and my offering was not received from me with favor?

  II   Abel answered and said to Cain,
        I know the world is created with mercies,
        and in respect of fruits of good deeds it is led:
        and because my good deeds surpassed yours
        my offering was received from me with favor
        while your offering was not received
          from you with favor.

(B) I   Cain answered and said to Abel,
        there is no judgment and there is no judge,
        and there is no other world,
        there is no giving good reward to the righteous
        and there is no repaying from the wicked.

  II   Abel answered and said to Cain,
        there is judgment and there is a judge,
        and there is another world,
        and there is giving good reward to the righteous
        and there is repaying from the wicked
          in the world to come.

FRAGMENT TARGUM

(B) I   Cain answered and said to Abel,
        there is no judgment and there is no judge,
        and there is no other world,
        and there is no giving good reward to the righteous
        and no repaying from the wicked:

(A) I   and the world is not created with mercies
        and it is not led with mercies:
                 for what reason
        was your offering received from you with favor
        and from me it was not received with favor?

(B) II Abel answered and said to Cain,
        there is judgment and there is a judge,
        and there is another world,
        and there is giving good reward to the righteous
              140

and repaying from the wicked;

(A) II   and the world is created with mercies
and it is led with mercies. It is still led
according to fruits of good deeds:
because the fruits of my deeds surpassed yours
my offering was received from me with favor
and from you it was not received with favor.

COMPARATIVE ANALYSIS

Cairo Geniza (hereafter: CG): This is the simplest version of the basically similar paraphrases of Gen 4:8 in the Palestinian Targumim. Cain charges that "mercies" determine God's behavior. The implicit accusation is that his justice is wanting: the entirely implicit nature of this complaint is a distinguishing feature of CG Gen 4:8 (which is why a lacuna is indicated after line 3). Abel agrees the world is created with mercies, but insists that "fruits of good deeds" are taken into account by God and that God's sensitivity to these was the basis on which his own offering was accepted in preference to Cain's.

Pseudo-Jonathan (hereafter: PJ): Relative to the simple version in CG, PJ presents an elaboration of the wording and structure of the debate between Cain and Abel. Cain's initial charge expressly doubts the divine justice: favoritism, not "fruits of good deeds" is said to occasion God's acceptance of Abel's sacrifice. Abel explicitly denies the accusation at each point, adding, in this version, that his own deeds were better and more punctual than Cain's. So far, we have described the elaboration found in PJ as compared to CG in that part of the Cain-Abel debate which is held in common by them. We designate this part of the structure of the passage in PJ Gen 4:8 as "A" to distinguish it from what follows. "B" in PJ is a substantive elaboration as compared to CG: the debate is extended to cover elements which are corollary to the denial or affirmation of divine justice. If God is not just, there is no theological basis on which to secure the hope of divine retribution in the next world, and Cain's next assault is in fact on such classical theodicies as we find in 4 Ezra.[10] Abel's reply is perfectly symmetrical to Cain's attack, and suggests that these specific affirmations are key tenets in the mind of the meturgeman.

Neophyti I (hereafter: N): The substantive structural agreement betwen N and PJ is obvious, and N can be characterized in respect of CG as much as PJ can be. The slight idiolectical variations between PJ and N (cf. I, lines 3, 4, 5; II, lines 2, 3-end) need not detain us, although N's omission of Abel's explicit denial of favoritism and of his insistence that his good deeds were timely is significant. The omission permits the meturgeman of N to devote more space, as compared to what we have in PJ, to the statements of Cain and Abel regarding the rejection or acceptance of their offerings: in this regard, N follows CG, not PJ. But N departs from both CG and PJ in having Cain deny the creation of the world "with mercies" (I,2), which is the very premise of his attack in CG and PJ. The structure of denial and affirmation has apparently influenced the way in which the theological argument is presented to the extent that this form determines content.

Fragment Targum (hereafter: FT): FT presents a most complex and unusual version of the dialogue, but it is nonetheless linguistically and substantively comparable with the other Palestinian Targumim. With N (and against CG and PJ), the creation "with mercies" is denied by Cain, but so is government "with mercies" (cf. CG): favoritism and fruits of good deeds are not mentioned by him. That is, Cain in FT simply negates what he says in CG. Moreover, the reply of Abel to this charge (i.e., not to Cain's doubts about theodicy) is also more similar to the CG version than to the others, although Abel's insistence that his deeds "surpassed" Cain's is more similar to PJ and N than to CG. The stress on the sentence regarding the respective offerings of Cain and Abel is more reminiscent of CG and N than of PJ. The argument about theodicy is presented in the terms of PJ and N, but its placement gives this version of the debate as a whole the most deviant structure among the Palestinian Targums. The denial/affirmation scheme of the theodicy debate has not only (as in N) contaminated the diction of the theological debate, but the order has been shuffled so as to give precedence to the dispute about the judgment, the judge, the other world and retribution. In the speeches of both Cain and Abel a statement on this subject is made first, and a theological assertion (regarding the divine disposition in creating and ordering the world) follows as subsidiary to it. The simpler structure of CG is approximated (in that there is only one denial and one response), but the substantive innovation of N is brought to a radical conclusion.

142

As in the case of the synoptic relationship between the first three gospels, we see here no simple progression from one Palestinian Targum to another. Each is distinctive in some way, and yet at the same time is related positively to the other three (collectively, and sometimes individually). Structurally, the phenomena to be accounted for can be imagined in a schematic way (cf. the sigla in the textual presentation and the discussion above):

```
CG:  AI AII
PJ:  AI AII BI BII
 N:  AI AII BI BII
FT:  BI AI BII AII
```

Basically, a theological debate (A) has been elaborated with an argument about theodicy (B). The latter material has influenced the presentation of the former (in N), even to the extent that it usurps pride of place (in FT). Our scheme is a responsible way in which to understand the lay of the evidence, so long as it is borne in mind that it implies nothing about the substantive priority of one Targum over another (in that CG, for example, might as well be an abbreviation of the others as their starting point), that it does not take account of the linguistic links noted above, which establish a mutual relationship of commonality and distinctiveness among the Targums, and that therefore simple literary dependence cannot be deduced from the susceptibility of the evidence to analysis along structural lines.

The sort of structural relationship described above can be instanced in the passage from the Synoptic Gospels chosen for analysis, i.e., at Matt 12:24-30; Mark 3:22-27; Luke 11:15-23. After the statement of the charge that Jesus is possessed (v 22), Mark has Jesus reply. This response, said to be parabolic (v 23a), presents a simple argument: the claim that Satan casts himself out is ludicrous (vv 23b-26), since only a power greater than Satan's could do that (v 27). We may designate this argument as "A," and we must distinguish it from the second line of argument ("B") presented only by Matthew and Luke. There we find elaborations: if I, Jesus asserts, exorcize by Beelzebul, so do your exorcists (Matt 12:27/Luke 11:18c-19), and in any case my exorcisms are a sign of the kingdom (Matt 12:28/Luke 11:20). Additionally, Matthew (12:30) and Luke (11:23) close the entire pericope with the saying, "Who is not with me is against me...." At one level, the procedures followed by Matthew and Luke in presenting their "B" material are identical. Each introduces the new argument after the question, "how will his (Satan's) kingdom stand?" (Matt 12:26c/Luke 11:18b), where Mark has the simple declaration (3:26c), "he is not able to stand, but has an end." The shift from an assertion to a question is rhetorically effective, since it smooths the entry of the question which opens the new material ("And if I by Beelzebul cast out demons, by whom do your sons cast them out?" [Matt 12:27a; Luke 11:19a]). That is, a change is made in "A" material in order to develop its relationship with "B" material, a technique we saw illustrated in Pseudo-Jonathan, Neophyti I and the Fragment Targum. After the kingdom saying (Matt 12:28; Luke 11:20), Matthew and Luke both return to the parable of binding the strong man (Matt 12:29; Luke 11:21-22), which is also found in Mark (3:27). Matthew more closely approximates the Marcan diction than does Luke (although even he deviates from Mark), but he maintains the rhetorical continuity between "A" and "B" material by introducing the image with another question beginning with pôs, and ê only serves to underline this continuity. Luke's diction, on the other hand, departs markedly from both Matthew's and Mark's in this section, and yet he is nearer than Matthew to Mark in the assertive form in which he presents the parable. We are reminded of the formal similarity in the context of marked deviation between the Cairo Geniza fragment and the Fragment Targum. Luke also deviates substantively from his colleagues in the addition of 11:16 ("And others, temptors, demanded a sign from him") which is paralleled elsewhere in Mark (8:11) and Matthew (16:1).

The tendency in Matthew and Luke, in contrast to Mark, is to focus on the christological dimension of Jesus' debate with his accusers. His exorcisms attest the kingdom; who is not with him is against him. Substantive linguistic adjustments in the material held in common with Mark sharpen the focus further. Jesus reads his opponents' minds (Matt 12:25a; Luke 11:17a), and the kingdom he opposes is not merely not able to stand (Mark 3:24), but laid waste (Matt 12:25b; Luke 11:17b). Such an emphasis might seem at odds with the saying which immediately follows the complex in Matthew, which exculpates blasphemy against the son of man in its insistence that blasphemy against the spirit is unforgivable (Matt 12:31-32). This tension does not occur in Luke, where the saying appears in a different context (12:10); but Matthew is not here following the Marcan tradition precisely (3:28-30), since no mention is found there of blasphemy against the son of man. Matthew is therefore closer to Luke in diction, and to Mark in order, and the impact of his presentation is to provide some balance to 12:30 ("Who is not with me is against me ..."). This saying is the reverse of Mark 9:40 ("Who is not against us is for us."). To some extent, Matthew has softened the contradiction by appending 12:31-32 to v 30. Luke does no such thing, but he presents a parallel to Mark 9:40 (at 9:50b), albeit not in proximity to the Beelzebul controversy, but in a context which accords with Mark's. But the remark in Luke concerns anyone who is against/for "you," so that a christological implication in possible conflict with 11:23 is avoided. A complex, three-handed interrelationship among the synoptics is evident. We can therefore see among the gospels the sort of non-linear connections which we discovered among the Palestinian Targums, cognate conflations of tradition resulting in tension between "A" and "B" material, and the attempt to resolve that tension.

144

In a recent treatment of the redactional procedure of Josephus, F. Gerald Downing remarks: "It is not the divergences among the synoptists (or even between them and John), in parallel contexts, that are remarkable: it is the extraordinary extent of verbal similarities.... The relationship may betoken a much greater respect, one for the other, even than Josephus' for Scripture."[11] He nonetheless concludes that "The example of Josephus' procedure reinforces the credibility of the four-document hypothesis" (47). Part of his argumentation is that the recent counter-proposal that the documents in question were formed by midrashic procedures fails to offer "any at all precise precedent or analogy for gospels so conceived" (46-47). Although the thesis of Goulder, Drury, and their predecessors has not yet been subject to full critical treatment, their resort to an ex hypothesi case is evident and -- on Drury's own admission -- can lead to a "certain totalitarianism, with resulting strain."[12] The present discussion, however, proceeds from the observation of the sort of "precedent or analogy for gospels" in their synoptic relations which Downing calls for.

If the synoptic gospels are analogous to the Palestinian Targums, what of that? The gospels are not Targums, not interpretative translations of scripture into Aramaic (or, for that matter, into Greek). Such analogy, then, can only suggest that the gospels were transmitted much as the Targums were, as essentially oral compositions ultimately fixed in written form.[13] A defined point of departure is also offered by the Targums for understanding the development of Jewish oral tradition for the benefit of the faithful, not only the learned, before, during, and after the period in which the NT took shape. In the present case, we have observed that analogous procedures to shaping, conflating, restructuring, and theologically synthesizing material seem to be operative in Matthew, Mark, and Luke on one hand, and the Cairo Geniza fragment, Pseudo-Jonathan, Neophyti I, and the Fragment Targum on the other. The kaleidoscopic relationship among the four Palestinian Targums, in which the evident, often verbatim contact between the Targums is combined with striking individuality, has not proved susceptible of an analysis under which one document fully explains another. The supposition of a literary hierarchy of influence might appear even less convincing in respect of the Synoptic Gospels[14] if we had recourse to as many witnesses to their traditions as we do in the case of the Palestinian Targums. But if there is anything in our proposed analogy, then perhaps it will lead us to dispense with the attempt to establish purely literary priority among our gospels.

Our model would then be that of a common tradition transmitted in a way which permitted of individual development and of mutual influence at every level in the course of its emergence. The interpretative process of transmission was, later in the day, probably more self-consciously literary than at the beginning (particularly in the case of Luke); this observation applies also to the Targums, in that the scribal and/or recensional activities involved in producing four separate versions did not likely occur in four culturally isolated centers.[15] But such written work was but one stage in a progressive continuum. To try to press all of the development of the synoptic tradition into this one stage when there are evident analogies in the Targumic tradition, which we can see to be the product of interrelation at more than one level of transmission, is illegitimately to force folk Jewish literature into the mold of Western literary activity. The objection commonly raised against a form critical approach to the NT -- that it presupposes centuries of development before oral tradition achieved written form -- is not altogether relevant here: the criterion of language puts the recension of the Palestinian Targums within a single epoch in the development of Aramaic, and their substantive reflection of Amoraic theology leads to the same conclusion. They appear to have emerged during this period, in oral or written form, with a basic exegetical framework in which earlier material was included and on which later views were hung.[16] That is, the period during which they achieved a recognizable form as Targums is more restricted than the period including all of the material they present. This should hardly surprise us, nor is the situation qualitatively different in the case of the gospels, in which pre-Christian material is evident to any tradition critic, and readings which supplement the work of the evangelists are obvious to any textual critic.

NOTES

Essay 11 first appeared in JBL 101 (1982) 553-562.

1   Targum and Testament. Aramaic Paraphrases of the Hebrew
Bible: A Light on the New Testament (Shannon: Irish University
Press, 1972) 168.

2   Cf.,   for   example,   P.   Grelot,   "Les   Targums   du
Pentateuque: Etude   comparative   d'après   Genèse,   IV,   3-16,"
Semitica 9 (1959) 59-88; G. Vermes, "The Targumic Versions of
Genesis IV 3-16," Annual of the Leeds University Oriental Society
3 (1960-61) 81-114; G. J. Kuiper, "Targum Pseudo-Jonathan: A Study
of Genesis 4:7-10,16," Augustinianum 10 (1970) 533-70, part of the
larger study, The Pseudo-Jonathan Targum and Its Relationship to
Targum Onkelos (Studia   Ephemerides   "Augustinianum,"   9;   Rome:
Institutum   Patristicum "Augustinianum," 1972).

3   Cf. B. D. Chilton, "Targumic Transmission and Dominical
Tradition," Gospel Perspectives: Studies of History and Tradition
in the Four Gospels (ed. R. T. France and D. Wenham; Sheffield:
JSOT, 1980) 31-45 (cf. Essay 10 in the present volume, pp.
113-136). In an introductory section, an orientation in Targumic
studies is offered.

4   The pericope is delimited according to the citation in
Aland's   Synopsis   Quattuor   Evangeliorum   (Stuttgart:
Württembergische Bibelanstalt, 1973). The introductory narrative
portions have been omitted from consideration, although it is
worth bearing in mind that the Targums and the gospels ground the
controversies they report circumstantially. As the inquiry proceeds, we will also find occasion to comment on the saying about
blasphemy, which follows the Beelzebul controversy.

5   For a discussion of these issues, cf. the introduction of The
Glory of Israel: The Theology and Provenience of the Isaiah Targum
(JSOTSup   23;   Sheffield: JSOT,   1982);   P.   Schäfer,
"Bibelübersetzungen II. Targumim," Theologische Realenzyklopädie
(VI.1,2; ed. G. Krause and G. Müller; Berlin: de Gruyter, 1980)
216-28.

6   So Grelot, "Les Targums," 86; cf. P. R. Davies and B. D.
Chilton, "The Aqedah: A Revised Tradition History," CBQ 40 (1978)
514-46; B. D. Chilton, "Isaac and the Second Night: A
Consideration" Biblica 61 (1980) 78-88 (cf. Essay 2 in the present
volume, pp. 25-37); Schäfer "Bibelübersetzungen II," 217-18, and
the monograph cited in n. 5.

7   Grelot, 86. He goes on to warn against the notion of fixed literary texts influencing each other on a purely literary level: "Peut-on parler vraiment de fixation? Plutôt qu'à un texte fixé ne varietur, ne doit-on pas songer à une tradition encore vivante, articulée sur des themes précis exprimés dans un vocabulaire toujours repris, mais encore souple et susceptible de développements ultériers? La seconde manière de voir est évidemment la plus vraisemblable." Further, he points out that the language of the Palestinian Targums does not provide a terminus post quem for all their traditions. The most succinct review of recent research into Aramaic dialects and their development, which I have cited with other work in the monograph cited in n. 5, is that of S. A. Kaufman ("The Job Targum from Qumran" JAOS 43 (1973) 317-27.

8   For a discussion of rabbinic notices regarding the use and formation of Targums, cf. Chilton, "Targumic Transmission" (cf. Essay 10) and The Glory of Israel.

9   For the texts here followed, cf. the articles cited in n. 2.

10   Cf. A. L. Thompson, Responsibility for Evil in the Theodicy of IV Ezra (SBLDS 29; Missoula: Scholars, 1977).

11   "Redaction Criticism: Josephus' Antiquities and the Synoptic Gospels (II)," JSNT 9 (1980) 29-48; part one of the study appeared in the previous issue. The quote is from p. 33.

12   "The Evangelists' Calendar by M. D. Goulder," JSNT 7 (1980) 71-73. The quote is from p. 73.

13   The analogy also provides a much clearer paradigm of oral literature, and one which is much better suited to the period, than we can discover among recent literature which supports an oral solution to the Synoptic Problem. Cf. J. M. Rist, On the Independence of Matthew and Mark (SNTSMS 32; Cambridge: Cambridge University, 1978); A. B. Lord, "The Gospels as Oral Literature," The Relationships Among the Gospels: An Interdisciplinary Dialogue (Trinity University Monograph Series in Religion 5; San Antonio: Trinity University, 1978) 33-91.

14   The recent breakdown of consensus among those who pursue a literary solution to the Synoptic Problem is too well known to require bibliographical elucidation here. Additionally, however, it might be noted that research into the sociology of early Christianity casts doubt on the assumption that Matthew, Mark, and Luke had the sort of resources available to them which a writer such as Josephus used. Cf. R. Scroggs, "The Sociological Interpretation of the New Testament: the Present State of Research," NTS 26 (1980) 164-79.

15   Cf. J. Neusner's five volume work, A History of the Jews in Babylonia (SPB 9,11-12,14-15; Leiden: Brill, 1965-70) for the excellent communications among learned Jewish communities in this period.

16   This view of the evolution of targums is worked out in respect of the Isaiah Targum in The Glory of Israel (cited in n. 5). Cf. A. Marmorstein, "Einige vorläufige Bermerkungen zu den neuentdeckten Fragmenten des jerusalemischen (palästinischen) Targums," ZAW 49 (1931) 225-37, 241-42.

APPENDICES

APPENDIX I --
Bibliographische Ergänzungen zu
Die Muttersprache Jesu
von Matthew Black

Bibliographien

B. Grossfeld, A Bibliography of Targum Literature I, II: Bibliographica Judaica 3, 8 (New York: 1972, 1977).

J.T. Forestell, Targumic Traditions and the New Testament. An Annotated Bibliography with a New Testament Index: SBL Aramaic Studies 4 (Chico: 1979).

P. Nickels, Targum and New Testament. A Bibliography together with a New Testament Index (Rome: 1967).

Einleitungen

J. Bowker, The Targums and Rabbinic Literature. An Introduction to Jewish Interpretations of Scripture (Cambridge: 1969).

G.J. Cowling, New Light on the New Testament? The Significance of the Palestinian Targum: Theological Students' Fellowship Bulletin 51 (1968), 6-14.

B.D. Chilton, The Glory of Israel: The Theology and Provenience of the Isaiah Targum: Journal for the Study of the Old Testament Supplements Series 23 (Sheffield: 1982).

A. Díez Macho, El Targum. Introducción a las traducciones aramaicas de la Biblia (Barcelona: 1972).

------, Le targum palestinien: Revue des Sciences religieuses 47 (1963), 169-231; auch erschienen in: J.-E. Ménard (Herausgeber), Exégèse Biblique et Judaïsme (Strasbourg: 1973) 15-77.

E.E. Ellis, Midrash, Targum and New Testament Quotations in Ellis und M. Wilcox (Herausgeber), Neotestamentica et Semitica (Festschrift M. Black) (Edinburgh: 1969), 61-69; vgl. Ellis, Prophecy and Hermeneutic in Early Christianity (Grand Rapids: 1978), 188-197.

J.A. Fitzmyer, Methodology in the Study of the Aramaic Substratum of Jesus' Sayings in the New Testament in J. Dupont (Herausgeber), Jésus aux Origines de la Christologie: BETL 40 (Gembloux: 1975), 73-102.

R. Le Déaut, The Current State of Targumic Studies: Biblical Theology Bulletin 4 (1974), 3-32.

------, Les études targumiques: Etat de la recherche et perspectives pour l'exégèse de l'Ancien Testament: Ephemerides Theologicae Lovanienses 44 (1968), 22-34.

------, Targumic Literature and New Testament Interpretation: Biblical Theology Bulletin 4 (1974), 243-289.

------, La tradition juive ancienne et l'exégèse chrétienne primitive: Revue d'Histoire et de Philosophie religieuses 51 (1971), 31-50.

M. McNamara, The New Testament and the Palestinian Targum to the Pentateuch: AB 27 (Rome: 1966).

------, Targum and Testament. Aramaic Paraphrases of the Hebrew Bible: A Light on the New Testament (Grand Rapids and Shannon: 1972).

M.P. Miller, Targum, Midrash and the Use of the Old Testament in the New Testament: JSJ 2 (1971), 29-82.

A.D. York, The Dating of Targumic Literature: JSJ 5 (1974), 49-62.

------, The Targum in the Synagogue and the School: JSJ 10 (1979), 74- 86.

F. Zimmermann, The Aramaic Origin of the Four Gospels (New York: 1979).

Literaturverzeichnis zu neutestamentlichen Stellen:

Matthäus 2:23

R.H. Gundry, The Use of the Old Testament in St. Matthew's Gospel. With Special Reference to the Messianic Hope: Supplements to Novum Testamentum 18 (Leiden: 1967), 104.

B.D. Chilton, God in Strength. Jesus' announcement of the kingdom: Studien zum Neuen Testament und seiner Umwelt (Monographien) 1 (Freistadt: 1979), 311-313.

Matthäus 3:7-10 und Parallelen

M. Delcor, La portée chronologique de quelques interprétations du Targoum Néophyti contenues dans le cycle d'Abraham: JSJ 1 (1970), 105-119.

A. Jaubert, Symboles et figures dans le judaïsme: RSR 47 (1973), 373-390, 374-376.

Matthäus 4:1-11 und Parallelen

B. Gerhardsson, The Testing of God's Son. Matthew 4:1-11 and Parallel: An Analysis of an Early Christian Midrash: Coniectanea Biblica New Testament Series 2.1 (Lund: 1966).

B.D. Chilton, Targumic Transmission and Dominical Tradition in R.T. France und D. Wenham (Herausgeber), Gospel Perspectives. Studies of History and Tradition in the Four Gospels I (Sheffield, 1980), 21-45 (cf. Essay 10 in the present volume, pp. 113-136).

Matthäus 5:12

McNamara, Targum and Testament, 131-132.

Matthäus 5:38

McNamara, The New Testament, 131.

Matthäus 5:48 und Parallelen

McNamara, The New Testament, 133-138.

Matthäus 6:11

R. Le Déaut, Le substrat araméen des évangiles: scolies en marge de l'Aramaic Approach de Matthew Black: Biblica 49 (1968), 388-399, 391-392.

Matthäus 6:12

A. Díez Macho, Le targum palestinien, 209.

Matthäus 6:19-20

F. Manns, "La vérité vous fera libres" Etude exégétique de Jean 8:31-59: Studium Biblicum Franciscanum Analecta 11 (Jerusalem: 1976), 129.

Matthäus 6:24

Fitzmyer, Methodology, 90.

Matthäus 7:6

Fitzmyer, Methodology, 95.

Matthäus 11:12 und Parallelen

B.D. Chilton, God in Strength, 203-230.

Matthäus 11:28-30

D. Muñoz León, Dios-Palabra. Memrá en los Targumim del Pentateuco: Institución San Jeronimo 4 (Granda: 1974), 494-495.

Matthäus 13:1-9 und Parallelen

B. Gerhardsson, The Parable of the Sower and its Interpretation: NTS 14 (1968), 165-193.

Matthäus 15:5 und Parallelen

Fitzmyer, Methodology, 89-90.

Matthäus 21:33-46 und Parallelen

M. Black, The Christological Use of the Old Testament in the New Testament NTS 18 (1972), 1-14, 11-14.

M. Wilcox, Peter and the Rock: A Fresh Look at Matthew XVI.17-19: NTS 22 (1976), 73-88.

Matthäus 22:1-14

J.D.M. Derrett, Law in the New Testament (London: 1970), 127-136.

Matthäus 27:46

Gundry, The Use, 63-66.

Markus 1:11

F. Lentzen-Deis, Die Taufe Jesu nach den Synoptikern: Literarkritische und gattungsgeschichtliche Untersuchungen: Frankfurter Theologische Studien 4 (Frankfurt: 1970), 195-248.

Markus 1:15 und Parallelen

Chilton, God in Strength, 27-95.

Markus 4:12

Gundry, The Use, 33-35.

Markus 4:24 und Parallelen

H. Rüger, "Mit welchem Mass ihr messt, wird euch gemessen werden" ZNW 60 (1969), 174-182.

Markus 7:34

M. Black, Ephphatha (Mk 7:34), Ta Pascha (Mt 26:18W), Ta Sabbata (passim), [Ta] Didrachma (Mt 17:24 bis) in: A. Descamps und A. de Halleux (Herausgeber), Mélanges bibliques en hommage au R.P. Béda Rigaux (Gembloux: 1970), 57-62.

I. Rabinowitz, Ephphatha (Mark VII.34): Certainly Hebrew, Not Aramaic: JSS 16 (1971), 151-156.

Markus 8:27

J. Bowker, The Son of Man: JTS 28 (1977), 19-48.

Markus 9:2-11b

B.C. Chilton, The Transfiguration: Dominical Assurance and Apostolic Vision NTS 27 (1980), 115-124.

J. Luzárraga, Las Tradiciones de la Nube en la Biblia y en el Judaismo primitivo: Analecta Biblica 54 (Rome: 1973).

Markus 11:10 und Parallelen

M. Aberbach und B. Grossfeld, Targum Onqelos on Genesis 49.
Translation and Analytical Commentary: SBL Aramaic Studies 1
(Missoula: 1976), 21.

Markus 14:36

B.D. Chilton "Not to taste death:" a Jewish, Christian and
Gnostic Usage in: E.A. Livingstone (Herausgeber), Studia Biblica
1978 II. Papers on The Gospels (Sheffield: 1980), 29-36.

Markus 15:34 und Parallelen

P. Lapide, Insights from Qumran into the Languages of Jesus: RQ
8 (1972-1973), 483-501, 496-497.

Lukas 1-2

C. Perrot, Les récits d'enfance dans la haggadah antérieure aux II
siècle de notre ère: RSR 55 (1967), 481-518.

Lukas 10:23

W. Grimm, Selige Augenzeugen, Luk. 10:23f. Alttestamentlicher
Hintergrund und ursprünglicher Sinn: Theologische Zeitschrift 26
(1970), 172-183.

Lukas 17:26-30

J. Schlosser, Les jour de Noé et de Lot. À propos de Luc, XVII,
26-30: RB 80 (1973), 13-36.

Lukas 18:20 und Parallelen

L. Díez Merino, El Decalogo en el Targum Palestinense. Origen, Estilo y Motivaciones: Estudios Bíblicos 34 (1975), 23-48.

Johannes 1:1-18

A. Feuillet, Le Prologue du Quatrième Evangile. Etude de théologie johannique (Paris: 1968).

M. McNamara, <u>Logos</u> of the Fourth Gospel and <u>Memra</u> of the Palestinian Targum (Ex 12:42): Expository Times 79 (1968), 115-117.

------, Targum and Testament, 101-106.

P. Borgen, Observations on the Targumic Character of the Prologue of John: NTS 16 (1970), 288-295.

------, Logos was the True Light: Contributions to the Interpretation of the Prologue of John: Novum Testamemtum 14 (1972), 115-130.

D. Muñoz León, Díos Palabra. Memrá en los Targumim del Pentateuco: Institución San Jeronimo 4 (Granada: 1974).

Johannes 3:14

M. Black, The "Son of Man" Passion Sayings in the Gospel Tradition: ZNW 60 (1969), 1-8.

Johannes 6

B. Malina, The Palestinian Manna Tradition. The Manna Tradition in the Palestinian Targums and its Relationship to the New Testament: Arbeiten zur Geschichte des späteren Judentums und des Urchristentums 7 (Leiden: 1968).

Johannes 8:44

A. Goldberg, Kain: Sohn des Menschen oder Sohn der Schlange?: Judaica 25 (1969), 203-221.

Johannes 12:34

B. McNeil, The Quotation at John XII 34: Novum Testamentum 19 (1977), 22-33.

B.D. Chilton, John XII 34 and Targum Isaiah LII 13: Novum Testamentum 22 (1980), 176-178 (cf. Essay 6 in the present volume, pp. 81-84).

Johannes 13-17

E. Cortès, Los discorsos de adiós de Gn 49 a Jn 13-17. Pistas para la historia de un género literario en la antigua literatura judía: Colectánea San Paciano 23 (Barcelona: 1976).

Johannes 19:6

L. Díez Merino, La crucifixión en la antigua literatura judía (Periodo intertestamental): Estudios Eclesiásticos 51 (1976), 5-27.

Apostelgeschichte 1:15-26

M. Wilcox, The Judas-Tradition in Acts I. 15-26: NTS 19 (1973), 438-452.

Apostelgeschichte 2

J. Potin, La fête juive de la Pentecôte: Lectio Divina 65 (Paris: 1971).

Apostelgeschichte 5:30

M. Wilcox, "Upon the Tree -- Deut 21:22-23 in the New Testament: JBL 96 (1977), 85-99.

1. Korintherbrief 15

C. Lehmann, Auferwecht am dritten Tag nach der Schrift. Exegetische und fundamentaltheologische Studien: Questiones Disputatae 38 (Freiburg: 1968).

Sennacherib: a Synoptic Relationship
among Targumim of Isaiah

Targums often appear to be a Cinderella, caught between her elder sisters, "the Old Testament," and the New Testament. Scholars of the former can still be heard to insist that "Targums are not in the mainstream of study;" armed with that slogan, one prominent publishing house, which prides itself on a fulsome list of biblical studies, refuses to countenance manuscripts which deal with Targumic subjects. Neutestamentler, on the other hand, commonly treat of the question of how the Hebrew scriptures were understood in the first century as a mere matter of background, the esoteric marginalia of a more obvious drama. In the passage now to be considered, it is not Cinderella, but Sennacherib, who is at issue, and the manner in which he features in Targumic representations is of evident significance to anyone who is concerned with how the Hebrew Bible was once understood, and with how traditions which were taken to be sacred were handed on. To ignore Cinderella is mean-spirited; to ignore Sennacherib is folly.

The invitation to discuss Targumic transformations of Isaiah 10:32, 33 within the on-going study of pronouncement stories, chreiai, and other rhetorical tactics, comes as a refreshing opportunity. Before the categories of Hellenistic rhetoric can be applied fruitfully to the Targumic treatments of Isaiah, however, some description of the texts in their own terms must be offered. That preliminary, heuristic task is the purpose of the present study. Our observations will develop in five stages, in order to include (1) a brief assessment of the passage in its literary context, which made the Targumic treatments possible, (2) the principal transformation of Targum Jonathan, (3) a sketch of textual deviations, and their usefulness in identifying alternative recensions of the Targum, (4) the fresh transformation(s) of Targum Jerushalmi, and (5) concluding remarks on the nature and interrelatedness of the Targumic transformations.

(1) Sennacherib and the Masoretic Text

Sennacherib makes his appearance through what is superficially a small chink in the Hebrew text of Isaiah 10:32, 33. In that passage, a nameless warrior climaxes a description of violence, and God is pictured as responding:

> When there is day enough to stop at Nob, he will shake
> his hand at the mount of the house (or: daughter) of
> Zion. Behold, the Lord, the LORD of hosts is cleaving
> boughs with an awesome shock, and those great in stature
> are cut down, and the lofty will be laid low.[1]

The association of this passage with Sennacherib, even in its Hebrew form, appears possible, because Assyrian power is contextually at issue (cf. v. 24, where Assyrian might is compared to the former power of Egypt). More importantly, from the point of view of the received shape of the book overall, the events concerning Sennacherib's miraculously abortive campaign constitute a pivotal part of Isaiah (chapters 36, 37). They are the chronicled emblem of Israel's redemption, which otherwise can only be prophesied, and Hezekiah's failure to see the significance of those events is what portends exile (chs 38, 39). Because the account of Sennacherib's divinely wrought failure is central within the book, to see 10:32, 33 as metaphorical allusions to a coming threat and vindication appears plausible, if (perhaps) unnecessary. Pierre Grelot represents a consensus when he takes the Masoretic Text as a reference to an unnamed invader.[2] The image expresses metaphorically in vv. 28-32, in the language of an invader's campaign, what the oppression of Assyria's rod (v. 24) amounts to. Similarly, the metaphor of God's deforestation in vv. 33, 34 vividly conveys the divine retribution referred to in vv. 25-27. Whether anyone familiar with the book of Isaiah would have failed to be reminded of Sennacherib's campaign, is a matter of speculation, but the matter would better be put that way 'round, in preference to asking whether such a reading would be in the least plausible.

The extant Targumic recensions of Isaiah manifest, as we will see, a rich degree of variety, but they agree in construing the passage in respect of Sennacherib. The means of that identification are not linguistic, nor are they (strictly speaking) based on a contextual reading; their laconic reference to Sennacherib reflects an awareness of what the passage, in their understanding, comes to represent. What we today might call an exegesis of the final form of the text, or canonical interpretation, could apparently be accomplished by the meturgeman within the activity of translation.

(2) Sennacherib in Targum Jonathan

The simplest version of the passage, within Targumic tradition, is presented by what I here regard as the primary text of Targum Jonathan.[3] Targum Jonathan presents an Aramaic paraphrase of both the Former and the Latter Prophets. The Targum is traditionally ascribed to Jonathan ben Uzziel, a disciple of Hillel, but critical investigation suggests it is composed of the aggregate work of interpreters during the Tannaitic and Amoraic periods.[4] The style of interpretation of Targum Jonathan varies somewhat. Generally speaking, the style within the Former Prophets is characterized by a fairly strict adherence to the Hebrew text, along the lines of the Pentateuchal Targum called Onqelos.[5] Even within that corpus, however, there are some remarkable departures from a policy of

164

what we would call formal correspondence (or even, perhaps, one of dynamic transference). The most obvious instances of such innovative departure concern the use of the term "messiah."[6] Nonetheless, the interlarding of extensive (and even narrative) additions, which is a feature of such Pentateuchal Targums as Neophyti I and Pseudo-Jonathan, is not a characteristic within Targum Jonathan. A greater freedom in paraphrase is certainly apparent when we come to the Latter Prophets, and several readings within that corpus are notably important for the study of the historical reception of scripture within Judaism and Christianity.[7] Even here, however, extensive intercalation is not normally associated with the exegetical profile of the work.

Against the background of the normal, exegetical pattern of the Isaiah Targum, the rendering of 10:32, 33 is unusual. In addition to identifying the nameless invader of the Hebrew text as Sennacherib, the king's specific threat is spelled out discursively, and with certain narrative elements:

> While the day was still young and he had much time to enter, behold Sennacherib the king of Assyria came and stood at Nob, the city of the priests, opposite the wall of Jerusalem. He answered and said to his forces, "Is not this Jerusalem, against which I stirred up all my armies? Behold, it is fainter than all the fortresses of the peoples which I have suppressed with the strength of my hands." He stood over it shaking his head, waving back and forth with his hand against the mount of the sanctuary which is in Zion, and against the courts which are in Jerusalem. Behold, the Lord of the world, the LORD of hosts casts slaughter among his armies as grapes trodden in the press and those great in stature will be cut down, and the strong will be humbled.[8]

The issue of the textual attestation of the passage will occupy us in due course; first, an appraisal of this transformation of the Hebrew text is in order.

That it is a transformation, rather than a straightforward translation, is apparent from the outset, in the quantity of innovative material which is conveyed. (The presentation adopted here sets out such additions in underlined text.) But the continuity of the Targum with the Masoretic Text can be traced in their shared diction (which is indicated by the printing of words from the Targum in ordinary, roman type).[9] The number of such instances would be increased, of course, were one to include terms which are closely related to one another, such as shpl in the MT, and m'k in the Tg (v. 33, end). The verbal continuity of the two versions, however, makes it all the more apparent that the one is a transformation of the other: the mere rendering of the MT into Aramaic, even within the controlling assumption that Is. 10:32, 33 referred to the failure of Sennacherib's campaign, cannot account for the extensive features, discursive and narrative, introduced by the meturgeman(in).

165

The most curious thing about this haggadic representation of Sennacherib is that it is not collated with the material in ch. 36, where Rabshakeh communicates Sennacherib's policy, in mocking terms, to the leaders of Jerusalem. Indeed, chs 36 and 37 of the Targum are far more formally correspondent in their interpretative profile than is our passage in ch. 10. The presentation of Sennacherib which is most strikingly similar to what we find in Targum Isaiah 10:32 appears, not in Targum Jonathan, but in Talmud (Sanhedrin 95a). There, an opinion is handed on in the name of the Babylonian Amora, Rabbi Ḥuna, in which the advance of Sennacherib is described:

> The way he required of the multitudes in ten days, he completed in that very day. When they reached Jerusalem, he threw together cushions for himself until he ascended and sat higher than the wall, and saw all Jerusalem. When he saw it, it was reduced to insignificance in his eyes. He said, "Is not this the city of Jerusalem, against which I stirred up all my armies, and against which I pressed all my provinces? Is it not smaller and fainter than all the fortresses of the peoples which I have suppressed with the strength of my hand? He stood over it shaking his head, waving back and forth with his hand against the mount of the sanctuary which is in Zion, and against the courts which are in Jerusalem.[10]

The close association between Targum Jonathan and the Talmud at this point is indicated by the scant number of deviations[11] of Sanhedrin 95a from the Targumic version (here marked out by underlining) once Sennacherib begins to speak. Even those deviations are present in the alternative transformations we shall consider below, for example in the margin of the Codex Reuchlinianus; that is, textual variants support, rather than refute, the observation of a relationship between Targum Isaiah 10:32 and Sanhedrin 95a.

The nature of that relationship must remain an open question for the moment. We may not assume a literary awareness of one text by the tradents of another. On the other hand, features of the presentation in Sanhedrin do serve to illuminate otherwise puzzling elements in the Targum. The first, and most striking, of these elements is the statement in the Targum that Sennacherib "had much time to enter." That is, a delay is signalled between Sennacherib's arrival, and the commencement of his campaign against the city. Some delay, of course, must be envisaged in any conflation of Is. 10:32, 33 with Isaiah 36, 37: time must be allowed for the negotiations which are related in the later chapters. But, at 10:32, 33 itself, the Targum does not execute that particular conflation. Rather, Sennacherib's delay is caused by his insistence on railing against the city. Is there some other reason for this delay, or at least, a narrative explanation which makes some sense of it? In Rabbi Ḥuna's haggadah, there is indeed. The entire point of the episode, signalled by openning and closing notices, is that Sennacherib is told by the "Chaldeans," "If you

166

go now, you will overcome him (sc. Hezekiah); if not, you will not overcome him." For that reason, the quick journey mentioned in Sanhedrin 95a, and the reference to his having time in hand in the Targum, has a dramatic import which only makes sense within the Talmudic context of the story (at least, among the extant versions of it). Although the conditions of the oracle seem to have been fulfilled in Talmud, Sennacherib goes on (after his bombastic mockery of Jerusalem) to give his troops a night of rest. He does so despite their express willingness to fight "now" (h'ydn'), precisely as the oracle stipulated. That night of intended rest, of course, proved final for 185,000 men, who died at the hands of an angel (cf. 2 Kings 19:35 and Isaiah 37:36). The haggadah closes with a remark of Rabbi Pappa, "It is as people say, A judgment deferred is a judgment denied."[12]

The next odd mention in the Targum is to Nob as "the city of the priests." Of course, Nob can be so identified by any interpreter, especially on the basis of 1 Samuel 21:2; 22:11, 18, 19. As a matter of fact, that last reference is apposite. It represents the slaughter of 85 priests, and innumerable inhabitants of this city of priests, by a Gentile, Doeg the Edomite, in a campaign against David, the messiah. In Talmud, the haggadah of Rabbi Ḥuna opens, "Until today, the sins of Nob remain." In the case of Sennacherib, arrogant delay meant that 185,000 of the invaders died. A numerological connection to the passage in 1 Samuel is not made in Talmud, but it may be a strand in the association of the texts. Talmud is also silent, at this point, in respect of the messianic analogy of David and his distant son, Hezekiah. Curiously, however, the Targum provides an innovative, messianic note in v. 27, immediately before the mention of the figure who is ultimately identified as Sennacherib:
    ...and the Gentiles will be shattered before the messiah.
Here, then, the usual relationship, in which Sanhedrin 95a provides a fuller reference to what is alluded to in Targum Isaiah 10, is reversed.[13] The texts seem to be mutually explicating, rather than to be explicable as the simple derivation of one from another. In other words, their relationship is such that each text becomes clearer, but only on the grounds of their shared understanding of Sennacherib, not on the grounds of a precise history (literary or otherwise) of the development of that tradition.

Two final elements in the Targum of Is. 10:32, 33 are evocative of its usual relationship to Sanhedrin 95a, in that the Talmud appears to provide a fuller account of what the Targum merely alludes to. The description of Sennacherib standing "over" (`l) Jerusalem, as if he were an overbearing presence, is spelled out in Talmud in some detail; after his arrival, and before his declamation, he is said to order himself cushions to sit on, until he is able to climb up to a point higher than the wall of the city. There is, of course, no way confidently to determine whether the

Targumic oddity generated, or rather reflects, the surreal image of the Talmud. (In any case, `l might be understood in the sense "against," or "opposite," in which case, the evocation of the image found in Talmud would not be an issue in a reading of the Targum.) It seems wiser merely to note the congruence, which may in any case be the result of independent transformations of an underlying theme, rather than attempt to write a genetic account of how the passages came to be. Lastly, the Targumic statement that the LORD "casts slaughter" among the armies of Sennacherib is somewhat out of the ordinary: 41:2 represents the most similar usage,[14] and even there, the image of casting slain people before a sword (cf. 10:34; 27:12; 34:3; 54:15; 56:9; 63:6) is of a different order. In the Talmudic passage, the notice of Sennacherib's delay is followed by that of the angel's coming forth and killing 185,000, so that at morning they are all dead (cf. 2 Kings 19:35; Isaiah 37:36). To describe the angel's coming as the casting of slaughter into the Assyrians' midst would be appropriate. (Indeed, it might be observed that the angel is said to kill (qtl) the troops in the Targumic version of Is. 37:36, rather than merely to strike them, as in the MT). The Aramaic verbal usage is cognate of the noun "slaughter" (qtwl) in 10:33. Here, too, Talmud permits us to see more plainly a motif which in Targum is, at most, allusive.

What joins Sanhedrin 95a and Tg Isaiah 10:32, 33 is an evidently similar interpretation, expressed in similar terms, of the significance and nature of Sennacherib's threat to Jerusalem. A genetic construal of their relationship, owing to a lack of firmly datable evidence (and of an agreed tradition history of Targumic and Talmudic development), is not attainable at the moment. In fact, it may prove to be unobtainable. Generally speaking, one can say that the Talmud spells out more discursively what is accomplished by allusion in the Targum, but that generalization is not accurate at every point (cf. above, on the reference to the messiah in the Targum). Even if it were, priority, indeed literary contact of any sort, could not be proven on the basis of the generalization. What can be stated with confidence, is that Sanhedrin 95a and Targum Isaiah 10:32, 33 represent substantially the same transformation of traditions concerning Sennacherib, a transformation which avails itself of biblical passages including 1 Samuel 22:18, 19; 2 Kings 18:13-19:35; Isaiah 10:32, 33; 36:1-37:36.[15] But the heart of the transformation, as represented both by Targum and Talmud, is a non-scriptural element, the derisory speech of Sennacherib. The narrative construals, which place that speech in contexts of events, circumstances, and scriptural allusions (or references), vary as one moves between Targum and Talmud. The former functions within the constraints of offering a defensible translation of Isaiah, and so operates by allusion. The latter functions within the constraints of collating haggadoth with scriptural discussion, and so conveys a more discursive version of the transformation.

(3) Textual Deviations

The Targumic text we have so far considered is that of the Antwerp Polyglot (cf. Sperber [1962] 24), the primary text of the Codex Reuchlinianus (cf. Grelot [1983] 206), and several other mss cited by Stenning ([1949] 38-41). Stenning himself, largely in dependence upon Lagarde,[16] accepted this, the shorter of the possible readings. Pauli made the same decision, based upon the reading "of the Royal Polyglot, which agrees with the Paris edition."[17] In arriving at that choice, Pauli overruled his stated policy (pp. vi, vii) of accepting the readings of the Rabbinic Bible. His reason for doing so here is that he finds a longer reading at this point, "a sadly fabulous interpolation" (p. 38). In so preferring the short reading, Pauli departs also, and consciously, from Walton's Polyglot (p. 38). Sperber, on the other hand, prints a longer version of the passage, of a sort we shall presently consider. He does so principally for the perfectly sound reason that the mss of the British Museum (as it then was, now the British Library), B. M. 2211, B. M. 1470, and B. M. 1474, support the reading (with some variations; cf. Sperber, pp. 23-25). The evidence of these mss, especially as supported by the Rabbinic Bibles, is certainly to be taken seriously, and preference for B. M. 2211 is generally assumed by students of the Targum today. There are, however, serious reasons for which the pedigree of the longer readings, as part of Targum Jonathan, might reasonably be questioned. As Sperber clearly indicates (p. 24), a marginal note in B. M. 1474 associates the reading with "Targum Jerushalmi." That is the normal heading, in the margins of the Codex Reuchlinianus (cf. Sperber, p. x), for readings of an alternative recension, not of Targum Jonathan itself. In fact, the margin of Reuchlinianus presents a longer reading under precisely that heading (cf. Grelot [1983] 203).

In my translation of the Targum (cf. n. 4), I have--on this question--sided with Stenning and Pauli, against Sperber and Walton. Two considerations prompted that decision. The first was the simple oddity of the longer reading, as compared to the normal, interpretative practice of the meturgeman(in) of the Isaiah Targum. Obviously, that consideration alone cannot be determinative of the outcome of one's decision, but the additions in the texts we are about to consider are of greater length than even the more extensive addenda in Targum Jonathan, and they are consistent with neither the Masoretic Text nor the conventional diction of Targum Jonathan. The second consideration is the presence of the reading in B. M. 1470 in particular. As is well known, that ms is a collection of haphtaroth, not a continuous Targum. That fact ordinarily is cause for no special comment, but there is some evidence to support the suggestion that what the scribe of Reuchlinianus calls "Targum Jerushalmi" is a collection of occasional readings. There is no doubt but that its variant construals of Isaiah only appear sporadically, and, at 33:7, the reference to the Aqedah in the margin is best explained on the grounds of a lectionary, in which that verse from Isaiah was associated with Genesis 22.[18] The late Alejandro Díez Macho, as well as Pierre Grelot, have argued that the longer Targumic readings of Is. 10:32 have affinities with the book of Exodus (as mentioned below), which may suggest that, here too, Targum Jerushalmi is to be seen as a sporadic series of readings occasioned by a lectionary, and therefore to be read in association with passages from the Pentateuch (cf. Grelot [1983] 226, 227). The alternative provenience of the longer passages, outside the mainstream of Targum Jonathan (although none the less interesting for that reason) seems a probable conclusion.

Sennacherib in the Targum Jerushalmi

However one assesses the provenience of the longer readings, they evidently present, not merely a relative extension of the short text, but an alternative transformation. It will be convenient to consider the fresh rendering in its form in the Codex Reuchlinianus, perhaps the purest form of the Targum Jerushalmi. In this case, underscoring will highlight the differences between this variant and the text of Targum Jonathan:

While the day was still young and he had much time to enter Jerusalem, behold Sennacherib the king of Assyria set out and made three bivouacs, and he took with him four thousand of the kings' sons, wreathed with crowns which rested upon them. And he took with him four thousand warriors wielding swords, and those who draw bows, and warriors as swift as the eagle, who ran before him, one hundred thousand. The number of his armies was two hundred and six myriads, less one, because his armies were about to lack at the hands of Gabriel, one of the commanders and ministers before the LORD. The length of his armies was four hundred parasangs, the neck of his horses, from end to end, forty parasangs. They were divided into four. The first army, when they crossed the Jordan, drank all the waters of the Jordan. The second army, when they crossed the Jordan, the hooves of their horses brought up water, and they drank water. The third army, when they crossed the Jordan, did not find water, and they dug wells and drank water. The fourth army, when they crossed the Jordan, there was in it Sennacherib, and Nebuchadnezzar his son in law, and Adrammelech and Sharezer and Esarhaddon his sons were crossing the Jordan, and the earth was sending up dust from the dry ground. He came and stood at Nob, the city of the priests, opposite the wall of Jerusalem. He answered and said to his forces, "Is not this the city

170

of Jerusalem, against which I stirred up all my armies, and against which I gathered all my provinces? Behold, it is smaller and fainter than all the fortresses of the peoples which I have suppressed with the strength of my hands." He despised it, he stood, spiteful, shaking his head, waving back and forth with his hand against the mount of the sanctuary which is in Zion, and against the courts which are in Jerusalem.

The extent of coherence with the primary text, Targum Jonathan, makes it impossible to conclude that the Targum Jerushalmi is an altogether independent version of Isaiah. Moreover, the departures of Targum Jerushalmi from Targum Jonathan within the speech of Sennacherib itself agree almost exactly with what Sennacherib has to say in Sanhedrin 95a. On the basis of that coherence, Pierre Grelot has come to the conclusion that the Talmudic passage is based upon a recension similar to the Targum Jerushalmi ([1983] 220). But the Targum Jerushalmi might also be described as conflating disparate elements in Talmud, since, under the name of Rab, Sanhedrin 95b conveys an extensive haggadah in respect of Sennacherib, in which the numbers and dimensions of his armies (set out in similar, but not identical, terms) figure prominently.

As in the case of Targum Jonathan, Talmud helps to explain the allusive imagery of the Targum Jerushalmi. It is stated, as a Baraita within Sanhedrin 95a, that the first of the armies, which together numbered two hundred sixty myriads of thousands less one (!), crossed into Judea by swimming, while the last stirred up dust. The biblical triggers of this thought are given as Is. 8:8 and Is. 37:25: an image which might be taken as purely fanciful receives its explanation as part of the exercise of midrashic logic, and the Targum would appear to imbue the image with a narrative logic all its own. (Structurally, the Baraita and the Targum are also similar, albeit distinctive, in their references to a number of crossings.) On the other hand, the reverse operation may also help to explain the Talmudic passage. For the two hundred six myriads of Sennacherib are said in Targum Jerushalmi to lack one "at the hands of Gabriel." The larger number given in Talmud perplexes even Abaye in Sanhedrin 95b; he asks, "Is the lack one myriad, one thousand, one hundred, or just one?" The sad answer comes back, "It is an open question." The meturgeman(in), however, thought he (or they) knew. Gabriel is said in the Targum of 2 Chronicles 32:21, as well as later in Sanhedrin 95b,[19] to be responsible for the annihilation of Sennacherib's troops, and the Targum Jerushalmi would seem to allude to the same idea.

The reference to Targum Chronicles takes us into a new and later sphere in the development of the Targumic tradition regarding Sennacherib. Earlier, Targum Jonathan itself (2 Kings 19:35) followed its Hebrew text in offering no identification of the exterminating angel, while an identification with Michael is made in the Codex Reuchlinianus. But Reuchlinianus does here give us a hint of the pedigree of its transformation in Is. 10:32 by dating the night as that of Passover (Grelot [1983] 216), and by placing Nebuchadnezzar, as Sennacherib's son in law, in the army with Adrammelech, Sharezer, and Esarhaddon. The last three could have been referred to by anyone with a knowledge of Is. 37:38, but the mention of Nebuchadnezzar appears to attest the continuity of thought within Reuchlinianus from 2 Kings to Isaiah. The Paschal connection also attests a certain continuity, but continuity with Targum Chronicles, as well (cf. 32:21, Grelot [1983] 218). The link between Is. 10:32 and Passover is provided by Megillah 31a, in which Is. 10:27-34 is set to be read as a haftarah on the day after the observation of the feast (Grelot [1983] 226, 227).

Grelot ([1983] 227 n. 64) observes that, via Exodus 14:31, a connection is made between Pharaoh and Sennacherib in Sanhedrin 95b, in the name of Eliezer ben Hyrcanos. The following chapter of Exodus, of course, celebrates the drowning of Egyptian horses and riders in the reed sea; Sennacherib and his forces are a mirror image of that triumph, in that they consume the very waters they cross. Such an inversion of Passover imagery may provide the key to the central, innovative transformation of Targum Jerushalmi. Sennacherib's horses and troops are not described in such detail merely to do justice to Is. 8:8; 37:25 (cf. Sanhedrin 95b). Rather, the meturgeman(in) is (are) describing the overwhelming forces faced by the Jewish people. The narrative transformation of the passage reflects social experience; at 33:7, the margin of Reuchlinianus refers to the departure of the righteous, and the desolation of Israel. There, reference is made to the Aqedah, by way of lamenting that Isaac was saved in a way Israel now is not. Here, the imagery of Israel's exodus is reversed to allude to the terrible strength of Arab horsemen.[20]

The continuing, intertextual relationship between Talmud and Targum in the instance of Sennacherib is indicated by another element. The statement is made in Sanhedrin 95b, after Sennacherib's entourage is numbered, "So did they come against Abraham, and so are they about to come with Gog and Magog." This mysterious statement does not appear in the Codex Reuchlinianus, but a fuller explanation appears in B. M. 2211, which appears to represent a form of the Targum Jerushalmi at this point:

So did they come against Abraham, our father, when they cast him into the midst of the burning furnace of fire, and so are they about to come with Gog and Magog when the world achieves its end, to be delivered.[21]

Such a legendary representation of Abraham can be found in the Targum Pseudo-Jonathan at Genesis 11:28f.; 15:7; 16:5; the eschatological material is redolent of the same Targum at Exodus 40:11; Leviticus 26:44; Numbers 11:26; 24:17; Deuteronomy 32:39; 34:3 (cf. Grelot [1983] 207, 208, nn. 25, 26),[22] but also of Sanhedrin 94a.

172

(5) Conclusion

The images of Sennacherib we have considered, presented in Targumim as actual representations of the figure mentioned in Is. 10:32, resolve themselves into two major transformations of scripture. The first transformation, represented by Targum Jonathan, portrays Sennacherib by means of his own speech as the epitome of arrogance against Jerusalem, the city of the sanctuary and of David. The second transformation, represented by the Targum Jerushalmi, portrays Sennacherib as a foe more terrible than Pharaoh, a surreally vital opponent, who anticipates eschatological catastrophe. But even Targum Jerushalmi has an equivalent of v. 33, and has Sennacherib punished for his boasting, and v. 32 itself mentions the very sons who will later kill him and replace him (cf. 37:38). Both of these transformations, and their variants, manifest an intertextual relationship with Talmud, such that Targum and Talmud are mutually illuminating.

As we pursued a nexus of mutual explication, however, we became involved with an increasing number of documents: Targum Jonathan, Targum Jerushalmi, the Masoretic Text, the Talmud, each with its own variants of textual attestation. A genetic explanation of one document in terms of another may appear a goal which common sense would commend, and if one's consideration could be limited to only a few shared elements among only two or three witnesses, the goal might indeed be achieveable. But the fact is that a genetic approach to the transformations we have considered only weakens the power of the documents to explain one another, which is their most obvious application.

By pursuing a comparative reading of these witnesses, on the other hand, Sennacherib emerges as having a distinctive profile, articulated by the two major transformations we have considered. Those profiles in themselves, of course, must have had their own historical matrices; the first transformation seems at home in the Amoraic framework of Targum Jonathan, the second in the post-Arabic world of the later Targumim. But whatever their periods, the transformations evince the understanding of Israel and of threats to Israel among those who promulgated the Targumim. Each in its own way demonstrates that midrashic logic was an instrument, a means to an end. Scripture was used to explicate scripture, but that was only the beginning. Sennacherib had his own, substantial meaning, which scripture was used to convey by embedding it in a discursive or narrative transformation.

The hybrid presentation of speech and action within the Targumic transformations of Isaiah 10:32, 33 perhaps qualifies them as instances of "mixed chreiai," if the categories of Hellenistic rhetoric may be invoked. Similarly, the structure of situation, followed by response (both verbal and active) may be

compared to the pattern laid out in such handbooks as the
Progymnasmata of Aelius Theon. Even the phenomenon of relative
expansion, as is evident in a comparative reading of Targum
Jonathan and Targum Jerushalmi, is reminiscent of Aelius Theon,
and (less theoretically) of Plutarch.[23] Before such observations
can be pursued, however, certain prior issues need to be
addressed. One would need, for example, to be clear on the extent
to which writers such as Aelius Theon were simply describing good
rhetorical practice, which might have been hit upon and exploited
by any competent speaker. In such instances, coincidence with a
Targumic transformation would not be remarkable. On the other
hand, the study of Hellenism as a Judaic phenomenon, whose foundations have been laid by Saul Lieberman and Martin Hengel, leaves
the possibility open that a specifically Hellenistic form of rhetoric might have left its trace within the Targums. Such
preliminary questions must be acknowledged, and--however they are
answered--light is likely to be shed on the rhetorical milieu of
the New Testament.

Those who produced these Targums knew that Sennacherib, however
arrogant or terrible, had to be faced. The LORD's promise could
only be realized after the enemy had been dealt with. In more
domestic terms, one might say that, her housework done, and her
scriptural furniture polished, Cinderella might at last be allowed
to attend the ball.

NOTES

Appendix II was first written for the purposes of discussion
within the "Pronouncement Story Group" of the Society of Biblical
Literature.

1   K. Elliger and W. Rudolf, Biblia Hebraica Stuttgartensia:
Jesaia (Stuttgart: Württembergische Bibelanstalt, 1968). The
interpretative line taken in the LXX is quite evidently of a different order, cf. J. Ziegler, Isaias: Septuaginta XIV (Göttingen:
Vandenhoeck and Ruprecht, 1967):
>   You hills in Jerusalem, exhort this day to remain in the
>   way; exhort with the hand the mountain, the daughter of
>   Zion. For behold, the master, the Lord Sabaoth, will
>   confound the glorious ones with strength, and the lofty
>   in pride will be crushed, and the lofty will be humbled.
The mutuality of translation and identification is nonetheless
manifest in this rendering, as well.

2   Pierre Grelot, "Le Targum d'Isaïe, x, 32-34 dans ses diverses
recensions," RB 90 (1983) 202-228, 204, 205.

3   For reasons which will become apparent, the textual construal
of Targum Jonathan at this point is problematic, and demands

treatment ad hoc. The mss followed for this passage (i.e., for the short recension of 10:32, 33) are not generally to be taken as reliable witnesses of Targum Jonathan.

4   The composition of the Targum of Isaiah in particular is described in The Glory of Israel, The Theology and Provenience of the Isaiah Targum: JSOTS 23 (Sheffield: JSOT, 1982). A more introductory work, including a fresh translation, an apparatus, and notes, is now in proof with Michael Glazier, Inc.

5   This impression, which even a superficial reading of Targum Jonathan bears out, is richly evidenced in the translation of Daniel Harrington and Anthony Saldarini, which is also in press with Glazier. I am grateful to Prof. Saldarini for making proofs of the work available to me.

6   Cf. Samson H. Levey, The Messiah. An Aramaic Interpretation. The Messianic Exegesis of the Targum: Monographs of the Hebrew Union College 2 (Cincinnati: Hebrew Union College, 1974).

7   Cf. A Galilean Rabbi and His Bible. Jesus' Use of the Interpreted Scripture of His Time: Good News Studies 8 (Wilmington: Glazier, 1984).

8   Cf. Alexander Sperber, The Bible in Aramaic based on Old Manuscripts and Printed Texts. III The Latter Prophets (Leiden: Brill, 1962). It must be noted, however, that Sperber's normally lucid edition becomes confusing at this point, owing to the complexity of the textual issues involved. A clearer presentation of the short recension is available in J. F. Stenning, The Targum of Isaiah (Oxford: Clarendon, 1949).

9   A consideration of the two documents, in Hebrew and Aramaic, will normally engender a clear impression of what is innovative, and what more strictly interpretative, in the Targum. Obviously, however, judgments regarding that question will vary from reader to reader.

10   Cf. J. Shachter and H. Freedman, Sanhedrin: Hebrew-English Edition of the Babylonian Talmud (London: Soncino, 1969) and Grelot (1983) 219. The point cannot divert us now, but it might be worthy of observation that the reference to the way ('wrh') may evince some relationship with the LXX (cf. n. 1). Rabbi Ḥuna is said to associate this passage as a whole with Sennacherib in Sanhedrin 94b.

11   The language of deviation is used in the present paper in a purely comparative manner. We shall programmatically avoid the unnecessary assumption of a fixed, literary relationship among the texts discussed.

12   In the present case, I have attempted a somewhat idiomatic translation, cf. Shachter and Freedman (1969) and Grelot (1983) 220.

13   An echo of such an understanding may also be heard in Sanhedrin 94b; after a citation of Is. 10:27, an opinion of Rabbi Isaac is cited, in which Sennacherib is to be destroyed in view of "the oil of Hezekiah."

14   Cf. J. B. van Zijl, A Concordance to the Targum of Isaiah: SBLAS 3 (Missoula: Scholars Press, 1979).

15   For the rabbinic procedure of concatenating analogous passages, cf. A. Finkel, The Pharisees and the Teacher of Nazareth. A study of their background, their halachic and midrashic teachings, the similarities and differences (Leiden: Brill, 1964) 126.

16   Paul de Lagarde, Prophetae Chaldaicae (Leipzig: 1872).

17   C. W. H. Pauli, The Chaldee Paraphrase on the Prophet Isaiah (London: London Society's House, 1871) 38, 39.

18   Cf. Essay 3, pp. 39-49, and Essay 2, pp. 25-37.

19   Cf. R. Le Déaut and J. Robert, Targum des Chronique (Cod. Vat. Urb. Ebr. 1) 1, 2: Analecta Biblica 51 (Rome: Biblical Institute, 1971).

20   Cf. A. Azzaroli, An Early History of Horsemanship (Leiden: Brill, 1985). The reference to the use of weapons, especially bows, on horseback, corresponds well to the development of military equestrianism under the Parthians and the Sassanids (cf. pp. 92, 93). The design of the Sassanid bit, which was particularly damaging to the mouth (p. 93) may figure in Targum Jonathan at 37:29. Certainly, the development of heavy calvary was a hallmark of Sassanid culture (Azzaroli [1985] 89-92). As Azzaroli discusses (pp. 93, 94), the stirrup only figured near the end of the Sassanian period, and was more characteristic of Arab equestrianism (p. 63). Stirrups are not mentioned in Reuchlinianus, but the tight organization of the phalanxes described might presuppose their usage. Arab breeding of horses was a medieval development (pp. 180, 181), but the usage of the horse made rapid advance possible during the eighth century (p. 41). Only the extent, discipline, and equipment of the calvary in Reuchlinianus may be held to be consistent with the late Sassanid and Arab period. The division of forces into four goes back to the battle of Kadesh in 1266 B.C. (pp. 40, 41). The numerical strength of the forces of Sennacherib also manifests a certain kinship with legends concerning the extent, and the relative sizes, of the hosts of Israel and Egypt at the time of the exodus (cf. L. Ginzberg [tr. H. Szold], The Legends of the Jews II [Philadelphia: Jewish Publication Society, 1913] 370-374 and [tr. P. Radin], III [1911] 5-31.)

21 Cf. Sperber (1962).

22 Cf. E. G. Clarke, Targum Pseudo-Jonathan of the Pentateuch. Text and Concordance (Hoboken: Ktav, 1984), for the references which supplement and correct Grelot's observations.

23 For these observations, I am in the debt of Professor Vernon Robbins. The hope is that the group will be able to expand on such observations, and evolve a perspective within which they might be discussed. Cf. R. C. Tannehill (ed.), Pronouncement Stories: Semeia 20 (SBL/Scholars Press: Chico, 1981); R. F. Hock and E. N. O'Neil, The Chreia in Ancient Rhetoric. I The Progymnasmata: Texts and Translations 27. Graeco-Roman Religion Series 9 (Atlanta: Scholars Press, 1986).

Index of Modern Authors

The format of this index is most easily described by means of an example:

Author, J., "Short Title": 8; 3) 45, 48n; 7) 95f n, 96n.

The hypothetical entry would mean that the article is cited in the Introduction (which is not assigned a number, as are the other essays) on p. 8, in Essay 3 on p. 45 and in some note or notes on p. 48, and in Essay 7 in some note or notes on p. 95, the last of which continues to p. 96, and some other note(s) on p. 96. An author's entries are ordered by publication date.

The central criterion for inclusion is some discussion of the work. Not indexed are: Appendix I; certain purely bibliographical notes [such as 2) 34 n.1; 3) 47 n.1; 4) 59 n.3; 11) 147 n.2]; nor editions of texts (e.g., BHS, Walton's Polyglot, Nestle-Aland[26]) unless the editor's opinion is discussed (e.g., Sperber, but only when under discussion). Reviews of certain books are noted at that book's entry. Appendix I is keyed to this index.

It is hoped this index itself provides an approach, one hermetic or virgilian, to these Targumic and Gospel studies and their "intertextuality."

Berger, K., Die Amen-Worte Jesu: 1) 15f, 17f, 21, 22n. Reviews: 1) 22n.

------, "Zur Geschichte...'Amen ich sage euch'": 1) 15, 16, 17f, 21, 22n.

Billerbeck, P., Kommentar zum N.T.: 8) 107n.

Black, M., An Aramaic Approach: 1, 16n; 10) 131n; Appendix I.

------, "Aramaic Studies": 10) 115, 131n.

------, "The Syriac Versional Tradition": 1) 17, 22f n.

Boman, T., Die Jesus-Überlieferung: 10) 119, 132n.

Bowker, J., The Targums...: 8) 105n; 10) 130n.

Brandon, S., Jesus and the Zealots: 9) 109, 111.

Brownlee, W., "The Wicked Priest...": 4) 58, 61n.

Bruce, F., New Testament History: 5) 73n.

Buchanan, G., Jesus, the King and His Kingdom: 9) 109-112.

Bultmann, R., Jesus and the Word: 8) 99, 105n.

Chilton, B., Targumic Approaches to the Gospels: Essay 1: 2, 10; 7) 96n. Essay 2: 4, 10; 3) 40, 42, 43; 10) 119, 132n; 11) 147n; Appendix II) 176n. Essay 3: 4, 10; Appendix II) 176n. Essay 4. Essays 5-7: 10. Essay 8: 10; 7) 96n; 10) 117, 131n. Essay 9: 10. Essay 10: 8f, 10; 11) 137, 147n, 148n. Essay 11: 10.

------, "The Aqedah", see Davies, P.

------, "An evangelical and critical approach to the sayings of Jesus": 8) 106n; 10) 135n.

------, God in Strength: 5) 80n; 7) 92f, 96n; 9) 111; 10) 117, 131n, 135n.

------, "The Transfiguration": 10) 135n.

------, The Glory of Israel: 4, 9, 12n, 13n; 3) 48n, 49n; 4) 59n, 60n; 5) 67-74, 75, 77n, 78n, 79n, 80n; 6) 84n; 9) 111; 10) 117, 130n; 11) 147n, 149n; Appendix II) 175n. Reviews: 4, 13 n.14; 5) 78 n.13, 79 n.16.

------, The Kingdom of God: 7) 93n.

------, Galilean Rabbi: 5ff, 13n;   5) 80n;   Appendix II) 175n.
Reviews: 5f, 13f n.

------, "Three Views of the Isaiah Targum":   5) 79n.

------, Beginning N.T. Study: 5) 78n.

------, The Isaiah Targum: 4) 59n;   5) 77n, 78n;   6) 84n;
Appendix II) 175n.

------, "The Temple in the Targum of Isaiah":   5) 77n.

------, in Gospel Perspectives 6:   5) 78n.

Churgin, P., Targum Jonathan: 4) 60n;   5) 74, 79n;   6) 83n;   8)
99f, 106n.

Clarke, E., Targum Ps.-Jonathan of the Pentateuch: Appendix II)
177n.

Cowling, G., "New Light on the N.T.?":   10) 131n.

Cranfield, C., Mark: 10) 134n.

Dalman, G., The Words of Jesus: 8) 106n.

------, Grammatik des...Aramäisch: 10) 115, 129n, 130n.

------, Aramäisch-neuhebräisches Handwörterbuch: 3) 48f n;   5)
78n, 80n.

Davies, P., & B. Chilton, "The Aqedah: a Revised Tradition
History":   2) 34n, 35n;   3) 39, 40, 41, 42, 47n, 48n;   10) 117,
132n;   11) 147n.

Davies, P., "Passover and the Dating of the Aqedah":   2) 32, 37n;
3) 47n.

Díez Macho, A., Neophyti I: 2) 36n;   3) 47n;   10) 115f, 133f n,
134n.

------, "Le Targum palestinien":   10) 115f, 116, 131n.

Dodd, C., The Parables of the Kingdom: 7) 85, 89f, 91, 92, 95n,
96n.

Doubles, M., "Indications of Antiquity...of the Fragment Targum":
10) 131n.

Downing, F., "Redaction Criticism: Josephus' Antiquities and the
Synoptic Gospels":   10) 136n;   11) 145.

------, review of McNamara, N.T. and Targum: 6) 84n.

------, Les poèmes du Serviteur: 5) 74, 79n.

------, "Le Targum d'Isaïe, x, 32-34": Appendix II) 164, 169, 171, 172, 174n.

Grossfeld, B., A Bibliography of Targum Literature: 10) 130n.

------, see also Aberbach, M.

Harris, J.R., "Traces of Targumism": 10) 135n.

Hasler, V., Amen: 1) 15, 21, 22n.

Hayman, A., SJT 38 (1985): 14n.

Hayward, C.T.R., "The Present State of Research into the Targumic Account of the Sacrifice of Isaac": 3) 39-44, 47n.

Held, H., "Matthew as Interpreter": 10) 135n.

Hill, D., Greek Words and Hebrew Meanings: 12n.

Hock, R., & E. O'Neil, The Chreia in Ancient Rhetoric. I: Appendix II) 177n.

Jeremias, J., Golgotha: 5) 76, 80n.

------, "Kennzeichen": 1) 21, 23n.

------, Neutestamentliche Theologie: 7) 92, 95n, 96n.

------, "Zum nicht-responsorischen Amen": 2; 1) 16, 22n.

------, Die Gleichnisse Jesu: 7) 85, 89, 90-92, 95n, 96n; Eng. Tr. 8) 106n.

Kahle, P., The Cairo Geniza: 10) 115, 131n.

Kaufman, "The Job Targum from Qumran": 10) 118, 131n, 132n; 11) 148n.

Kee, H., Miracle in the Early Christian World: 5) 78n.

Kingsbury, J., Matthew: Structure..." 10) 135n.

Klein, M., "The Messiah 'that Leadeth upon a Cloud'": 10) 134n.

------, The Fragment-Targums: 3) 47n; 10) 132f n.

Koch, K., "Messias und Sündenvergebung": 10) 131n, 132n.

Koester, H., see Robinson, J.

Knoch, O., "Die eschatologische Frage": 8) 106n.

Kümmel, W., Das Neue Testament: 7) 93n, 95n; Eng. Tr. 10) 132n.

Lagarde, P. de, Prophetae Chaldaicae: Appendix II) 169, 176n.

Lattke, M., "Zur jüdischen Vorgeschichte des synoptischen Begriffs der 'Königsherrschaft Gottes'": 7) 97n.

Lauterbach, J., Mekilta: 3) 47n.

Le Déaut, R., "La présentation targumique du sacrifice d'Isaac et la sotériologie paulinienne": 2) 28, 34n, 35n; 10) 117.

------, "Abraham et le sacrifice d'Isaac": 2) 25, 28f, 29, 30, 31, 32, 33, 34n, 36n, 37n; 10) 117, 132n (La nuit).

------, Introduction à la littérature targumique: 8) 105n; 10) 130n.

Le Déaut, R. & J. Robert, Targum des Chroniques: Appendix II) 171, 176n.

Levey, S., "The Date of Targum Jonathan": 6) 83n; 8) 106n.

------, The Messiah: 6) 82f, 84n; Appendix II) 175n.

Lévi, I., "Le sacrifice d'Isaac et la mort de Jésus": 2) 25f, 27, 28, 34n, 35n.

Levine, É., "Some Characteristics of Pseudo-Jonathan Targum to Genesis": 2) 32, 37n; 10) 131n.

------, "La evolucíon de la Biblia aramea": 3) 48n.

Levy, J., Chaldäisches Wörterbuch: 5) 78n.

Lohse, E., Märtyrer und Gottesknecht: 2) 26, 35n; 3) 48n.

Lord, A., "The Gospels as Oral Literature": 11) 148n.

Malherbe, A., Social Aspects of Early Christianity: 5) 78n.

Manson, T., The Teaching of Jesus: 8) 99, 105n; 10) 116, 131n.

Marmorstein, A., "Einige vorläufige Bermerkungen zu den...Fragmenten des...Targums": 11) 149n.

Marshall, I., <u>Luke: Historian</u> <u>and</u> <u>Theologian</u>: 10) 135n.

Martin, R., "Syntax Criticism of the Testament of Abraham": 1) 16, 22n.

McNamara, M., <u>The</u> <u>N.T.</u> <u>and</u> <u>the</u> <u>Palestinian</u> <u>Targum</u>: 2) 28, 35n; 6) 84n; 8) 106n; 10) 115f, 116, 130n, 131n, 135n.

------, <u>Targum</u> <u>and</u> <u>Testament</u>: 8) 106n; 10) 115f, 116, 118, 129n, 131n, 132n, 135n; 11) 137, 147n.

------, <u>Palestinian</u> <u>Judaism</u> <u>and</u> <u>the</u> <u>New</u> <u>Testament</u>: 3) 48n.

McNeil, B., "The Quotation at John XII 34": 6) 81, 82, 83, 83n.

Meeks, W., <u>The</u> <u>First</u> <u>Urban</u> <u>Christians</u>: 5) 78n.

Metzger, B., "A Comparison of the Palestinian Syriac Lectionary...": 1) 17, 23n.

------, <u>Early</u> <u>Versions</u>: 1) 17, 22f n.

Moore, G., <u>Judaism</u>: 8) 106n.

Moule, C., see Bammel, E.

Neugebauer, F., "Geistsprüche und Jesuslogien": 1) 15, 22n.

Neusner, J., <u>A</u> <u>Life</u> <u>of</u> <u>Rabban</u> <u>Yohanan</u> <u>ben</u> <u>Zakkai</u>: 8) 101, 106n.

------, <u>The</u> <u>History</u> <u>of</u> <u>the</u> <u>Jews</u> <u>in</u> <u>Babylonia</u>: 10) 118, 132n; 11) 149n.

------, <u>Eliezer</u> <u>ben</u> <u>Hyrcanus</u>: 10) 134f n.

------, "The Judaic Side of New Testament Studies": 5, 13n.

<u>Newsletter</u> <u>for</u> <u>Targumic</u> <u>and</u> <u>Cognate</u> <u>Studies</u>: 10) 130n.

Nichols, P., <u>CBQ</u> 47(1985): 5) 72ff, 78n.

O'Neil, E., see Hock, R.

Otto, R., "Die Kantisch-Fries'sche Religionsphilosophie": 7) 95f n.

------, <u>Reich</u> <u>Gottes</u> <u>und</u> <u>Menschensohn</u>: 7) 95f n.

Owen, W., "The Parable of the Old Man and the Young": 3; 2) 27.

Pauli, C., The Chaldee Paraphrase on the Prophet Isaiah: 6) 82f, 84n; Appendix II) 169, 176n.

Perrin, N., The Kingdom of God..." 7) 93n; 8) 99, 106n.

------, Rediscovering the Teaching of Jesus: 8) 105n.

------, Jesus and the Language of the Kingdom: 7) 94n; 8) 99, 105n, 106n.

Reimarus, H.: 7) 87; 9) 109.

Rieder, D., Pseudo-Jonathan: 3) 47n.

Rist, J., On the Independence of Matthew and Mark: 10) 118; 11) 148n.

Ritschl, A., Die christliche Lehre: 7) 85, 87, 93n.

Robbins, V., private correspondence: Appendix II) 174, 177n.

Robert, J., see Le Déaut, R.

Robinson, J., & H. Koester, Trajectories: 5) 74, 79n.

Schäfer, P., "Bibelübersetzungen II. Targumim": 11) 147n.

Schoeps, H., "The Sacrifice of Isaac in Paul's Theology": 2) 26, 35n.

------, Aus frühchristlicher Zeit: 2) 26.

------, Paulus: 2) 26.

Schwarz, G., BibNot 11-15, 20, 25; NTS 27; ZNW 70-73, 75: 12n.

Schweitzer, A., Geschichte der Leben-Jesu-Forschung: 7) 85, 86-89, 89, 90, 92, 94n, 95n, 96n; Eng. Tr., Quest..., 8) 99, 105n.

Scroggs, R., "The Sociological Interpretation of the N.T.": 11) 148f n.

Silva, M., Biblical Words and Their Meaning: 12n.

Slingerland, H., The Testaments of the Twelve Patriarchs: 2) 26, 35n.

Smallwood, E., The Jews under Roman Rule: 4) 60n.

Smith, M., "A Comparison of Early Christian and Early Rabbinic Tradition": 10) 119, 132n, 134f n.

Smith Lewis, A., The Old Syriac Gospels: 1) 18ff, 23n.

Smolar, L., & M. Aberbach, Studies in Targum Jonathan: 4) 60f n; 5) 64f, 74, 77n, 78n, 79n.

Sperber, A., The Bible in Aramaic, vol. III, IV B: 3) 48n; Appendix II) 169, 175n.

Spiegel, S. (Tr. J. Goldin), The Last Trial: 13n; 2) 26, 27f, 34n, 35n, 36n; 3) 48n, 49n.

Stegner W., "The Baptism of Jesus": 13n.

Stenning, J., The Targum of Isaiah: 5) 77n; 6) 82, 84n; 10) 132n; Appendix II) 169, 175n.

Strack, H., Introduction to Talmud and Midrash: 4) 60n.

Strugnell, J., "'Amen, I Say Unto You' in the Sayings of Jesus...": 1) 16f, 21, 22n.

Tal, A., The Language of the Targum (Heb.): 10) 118, 131n, 132n.

Tannehill, R., Pronouncement Stories: Appendix II) 177n.

Taylor, C., Sayings of the Jewish Fathers: 5) 80n.

Taylor, V., Mark: 10) 134n, 135n.

Thackeray, H., Josephus II: 5) 77n, 78n.

Thompson, A., Responsibility for Evil in the Theodicy of IV Ezra: 11) 148n.

van der Kooij, A., Die alten Textzeugen des Jesajabuches: 4) 57, 60f n; 5) 64, 65, 74f, 77n, 78n.

van Unnik, W., "The Quotation from the O.T. in John XII 34": 6) 82, 84n.

van Zijl, J., A Concordance to the Targum of Isaiah: 4) 59n; 6) 83, 84n; Appendix II) 176n.

Vermes, G., "Lebanon": 3) 49n.

------, "Redemption and Genesis XXII": 2) 28, 32, 35n, 37n; 3) 47n, 48n; 10) 117.

------, Jesus the Jew: 7) 96n.

------, _Jesus and the World of Judaism_: 4, 13n.

Viviano, B., _Study as Worship_: 10) 136n.

Volz, P., _Die Eschatologie der jüdischen Gemeinde_: 4) 54, 60n.

Weir, G., "Tatian's Diatessaron and the Old Syriac Gospels": 1) 18f, 23n.

Weiss, J., _Die Predigt Jesu_: 7) 85f, 87, 88, 89, 90, 91, 92, 93n, 94n, 95n, 97n; 8) 99, 103, 106n.

Wilcox, M., "The Judas-Tradition in Acts I": 3.

------, "Peter and the Rock": 5) 80n.

------, "Semitisms in the N.T.": 1, 2, 3, 12n, 13n.

York, A., "The Dating of Targumic Literature": 10) 130n.